ANGLO-NATIVE VIRGINIA

Early American Places is a collaborative project of the University of Georgia Press, New York University Press, Northern Illinois University Press, and the University of Nebraska Press. The series is supported by the Andrew W. Mellon Foundation. For more information, please visit www.earlyamericanplaces.org.

ADVISORY BOARD
Vincent Brown, *Duke University*
Andrew Cayton, *Miami University*
Cornelia Hughes Dayton, *University of Connecticut*
Nicole Eustace, *New York University*
Amy S. Greenberg, *Pennsylvania State University*
Ramón A. Gutiérrez, *University of Chicago*
Peter Charles Hoffer, *University of Georgia*
Karen Ordahl Kupperman, *New York University*
Joshua Piker, *College of William & Mary*
Mark M. Smith, *University of South Carolina*
Rosemarie Zagarri, *George Mason University*

Anglo-Native Virginia

Trade, Conversion, and Indian Slavery in the Old Dominion, 1646–1722

KRISTALYN MARIE SHEFVELAND

The University of Georgia Press
ATHENS

Paperback edition, 2018
© 2016 by the University of Georgia Press
Athens, Georgia 30602
www.ugapress.org
All rights reserved

Most University of Georgia Press titles are
available from popular e-book vendors.

Printed digitally

Library of Congress has cataloged the
hardcover edition of this book as follows:
Names: Shefveland, Kristalyn Marie, 1979–
Title: Anglo-Native Virginia : trade, conversion, and Indian slavery in the Old Dominion, 1646–1722 / Kristalyn Marie Shefveland.
Description: Athens : The University of Georgia Press, 2016. | Includes bibliographical references and index.
Identifiers: LCCN 2016006702| ISBN 9780820350257 (hardcover) | ISBN 9780820350240 (ebook)
Subjects: LCSH: Virginia—History—Colonial period, ca. 1600–1775. | Indians of North America—Virginia—History. | British Americans—Virginia—History. | Colonists—Virginia—History. | Indians of North America—Virginia—Treaties. | Indians of North America—Commerce—Virginia—History. | Indian slaves—Virginia—History. | Social change—Virginia—History. | Virginia—Ethnic relations—History—17th century. | Virginia—Ethnic relations—History—18th century.
Classification: LCC F229 .S533 2016 | DDC 975.5/02—dc23 LC record available at http://lccn.loc.gov/2016006702

Paperback ISBN 978-0-8203-5466-8

CONTENTS

	List of Figures	ix
	Acknowledgments	xi
	Introduction	1
1	Treaty of Peace: 1646	8
2	Indian Trade and Upheaval: The Rise of Abraham Wood	21
3	The Rise of Indian Slavery: William Byrd and Bacon's Rebellion	44
4	In the Wake of War: Tributary Obligations	61
5	The New Paradigm: Alexander Spotswood's Trade Policies	80
6	Peace at Albany: 1722	104
	Conclusion	125
	Notes	129
	Bibliography	153
	Index	165

Figures

1 "Mapp of Virginia discouered to ye falls
  and in it's latt: from 35 deg: & 1/2 neer
  Florida to 41 deg: bounds of new England"   24
2 Physical Movements of Indigenous Peoples,
  Colonial Trading Posts, and Locations of
  the Tributary Reservations, 1646–1722   29
3 Map of Virginia and Maryland by John Speed, 1676   60
4 Seal of Virginia, 1714 (Queen Anne)   94
5 Westover Plantation, James River, Charles City County 126

Acknowledgments

I would like to express my gratitude to the many people who saw me through the transformation of this book from dissertation to the present volume. To my editor at the University of Georgia Press, thank you, Walter Biggins, for championing this project. I am appreciative of the anonymous readers, who provided insightful criticism. The following individuals discussed this book with me at great lengths, offering constructive commentary and criticism in their assistance with the editing process. I would like to thank Robbie Ethridge, Charlie Hudson, Wes Durham, Greg O' Brien, Jamie Carson, Boyd Cothran, Jim Buss, John Neff, Sheila Skemp, Joe Ward, Maureen Meyers, Matt Jennings, Brad Wood, Lou Roper, Joe Genetin-Pilawa, Autumn Quezada-Tavarez, Rachel Smith Purvis, Billy Pritchard, Amy Montz, Sonya Sawyer Fritz, Miranda Green Barteet, Dana Eatman Lawrence, Gina Opdycke Terry, and Sara Klassen Day. Assistance and avenues for interaction and discussion came from the University of Southern Indiana Department of History and College of Liberal Arts, the staff of the Rice Library Interlibrary Loan, the Virginia Historical Society, the Library of Virginia, the British Group of Early American History, the Kentucky Early American Seminar, the Native American and Indigenous Studies Association, and the American Society for Ethnohistory. And finally to Steven Abbey and Edmund Danziger, endless gratitude for the classes you taught and the conversations we've had. This work is dedicated to Florence Katherine Gilbert, my maternal grandmother, writer and muse. For my Liesebelle, the Kaintuck, Thomas and Lynn Telenko: supporters of the path least traveled, all the roads of long ago, and exploring the dustiest corner of the library, you have my heart.

Portions of chapter 2 appeared as "The Many Faces of Native Bonded Labor in Colonial Virginia," *Native South* 7 (July 2014), reprinted with permission from University of Nebraska Press. Portions of chapters 3–6 appeared as "'Willingly complyed and removed to the Fort': The Secret History of Anglo-Indian Visions of Virginia's Southwest," in *Beyond Two Worlds: Thinking with Place, Space, and Landscape in Native North American History*, edited by C. Joseph Genetin-Pilawa and James Buss (Albany, NY: SUNY Press, 2014), reprinted with permission from SUNY Press; "'Sic jurat transcendere montes' (Thus he swears to cross the mountains): Alexander Spotswood, Colonial and Native Diplomacy in the 1722 Albany Peace," in *Order and Civility in the Early Modern Chesapeake*, edited by Debra Meyers and Melanie Perreault (New York: Lexington Books, 2014), reprinted with permission from Lexington Books; and "Cockacoeske and Sarah: Women and Anglo-Indian Interactions in Early Colonial Virginia," in *Virginia Women: Their Lives and Times*, edited by Cynthia A. Kierner and Sandy Treadway (Athens: University of Georgia Press, 2015), reprinted with permission from University of Georgia Press.

Anglo-Native Virginia

Introduction

A Saponi tracker named Bearskin worked for the English settler William Byrd II to determine the boundary line between the colonies of Virginia and North Carolina. One evening he spoke to his employer about the spirituality and cosmology of the Saponi, an exchange that Byrd included in his "History of the Dividing Line." Bearskin told Byrd that, in the beginning, one god assigned roles to the sun, moon, and stars and they, "with good looking-after, have faithfully performed [those roles] ever since."

In this secondhand, and largely erroneous, understanding of Saponi beliefs, Byrd depicts with perfect ease the Virginia narrative that would unfold in the colonial and settler colonial era. It is a fascinating exchange that informs this book, a story about expectations and realities among a colonial government and Anglo settlers who firmly expected that their Native tributaries, with "good looking-after," would faithfully perform their role. Bearskin told Byrd that although "God had formed many worlds before he formed this," those worlds either had become "ruinous" or were obliterated for the "dishonesty of the inhabitants." God, to Bearskin, was "very just and very good, ever well pleased with those men who possess those godlike qualities." Therefore, he protected the good by making them "very rich," providing bountiful amounts of food, and shielding them from illness and "from being surprised or overcome by their enemies." But he also punished "all such as tell lies and cheat," never failing to punish these wicked men with "sickness, poverty, and hunger and, after all that, suffers them to be knocked on the head and scalped by those that fight against them." Byrd's erroneous impression of the tale told by Bearskin was that the Saponi religion was a "natural" one that contained three traditional articles: "a belief in god, a moral distinction between good and evil, and the expectation of reward or punishment in the next world."[1] Later Byrd wrote *A Journey in the Land of Eden*, where he also spoke of his dialogue with Bearskin. Byrd asserted that the Indians had "no notion of the Sabbath, and will hunt for dinner for the English on this day," on occasion bringing a young doe back for dinner. According to Byrd, "They laughed at the English for losing one day in seven," but he placed his judgment on the Indians when he added, "The joke may be turned upon them for losing the whole seven, if idleness and doing nothing to the purpose may be called loss of time."

Byrd's understanding of his conversation with Bearskin explains Byrd more than the Native people with whom he interacted during this period, particularly the Saponi. Byrd was obsessed with his daily schedule and routine. Reading his diary, one can see that he feared being idle, yet he had his personal quirks regarding relaxation and enjoyment, never missing an opportunity to relish a rich meal or the company of women.[2] Byrd was also consumed with anxiety over his stature in the colonial Atlantic world, constantly seeking to bolster his position by building works of lavish architecture and through political wrangling. While his exchanges with Bearskin might have been part of everyday conversations between English traders and their Native counterparts, they do not hint at Byrd's active role in stirring up Native dissatisfaction with the English, the role he played in the demise of Indigenous trade, or Bearskin's motivation for telling this story.

To understand the path that led to Byrd surveying the colony's border with Bearskin, one must take a look back. Virginians were unique among English colonists in their interactions with Native peoples in part because of their tributary system, a practice that became codified with the 1646 treaty of peace with Necotowance of the Pamunkey. This treaty created a new relationship between Algonquians of the coastal plain and the English settlers of Virginia. This book traces English establishment of tributary status for their Native allies and the use of the term and concept of "foreign Indians" for nonallied Natives. This book is the story of the Indigenous allies of these English traders, English colonial administrators, tributary Indigenous peoples, and "foreign" Natives. It examines the establishment of the Indigenous tributary system by the colonial administration after the defeat of Opechancanough of the Powhatan in

1646 through the Albany Peace with the Haudenosaunee Iroquois in 1722. While the overall framing of this work is controlled by the chronologies of the Anglo administrations, I argue that these time periods bookend an important era for considering Anglo-Native intentions as well as Anglo-Native reactions.

Involvement in trade had a dramatic effect on Native populations and their movements throughout the Eastern Woodlands. Throughout the colonial period, trade was a center of both conflict and amity between colonists and Indians. This story is not new; a number of scholars have traced the long-distance migration, coalescence of disparate groups, role of disease, emerging slave trade, and hostility and violence that shattered the Native Southeast. This book argues that Indigenous connections, particularly through trade into the piedmont, played a central role in the development of Virginia. In that vein, this work adds to a wealth of scholarship on the emerging plantation economy and the Indian experience in the Southeast.

The transformation of Virginia from a fledgling colony on the outpost of empire to a plantation model of English society did not occur without significant interactions between the colonizers and Indigenous peoples. By most accounts, the second half of the seventeenth century witnessed a transformation in Virginia, setting forth political, economic, racial, and class distinctions that typified Virginia for the next three centuries. Power became consolidated in the hands of a few wealthy landowners who looked to slave labor to run their plantation economy. Social stratification increased, and the planters eventually became the political and cultural authorities in the colony. An examination of the contemporary record indicates that English colonists had great concerns about how to interact with their Native neighbors. Anglo-Native interaction determined English settlement patterns, trade, and diplomacy. Debates over the rights of tributaries eventually set the stage for Indian relocation, displacement, and removal. Many of the powerful families that emerged to dominate Virginia's history gained their start through Native trade and diplomacy in this transformative period, and that is a central focus of this work. Of particular interest is the Stegg/Byrd family, who emerged as key figures in trade, slavery, diplomacy, and conversion.

While the Virginia Company first envisioned it, it was Governor Sir William Berkeley who established the Virginia Native tributary system, which was later expanded by Lieutenant Governor Alexander Spotswood. Three successive armed conflicts between settlers and the Powhatan eventually ended with the murder of the *weroance* Opechancanough and the tributary agreement forced on his successor, Necotowance. After the last of the conflicts, Virginia began shifting from an economy based on frontier exchange to one dependent on agriculture. At the same time, leaders of the colony were in the midst of determining how best to manage relations with Native peoples in the colony. They devised a tributary system for the coastal plain Algonquian speakers, whereby the remaining members of the former Powhatan confederacy and others of the coastal plain paid tribute to the English government in exchange for protection, land, and trade. Later this tributary arrangement expanded with the 1677 Treaty of Middle Plantation, and it reached its height with Spotswood's plan to incorporate Siouan- and Iroquoian-speaking groups of the coastal plain and piedmont as well. Virginians referred to all nonlocal Indians as "foreign" because they misunderstood Indigenous migration patterns and the role of trade in movement; for the purpose of this study, I will refer to these groups as nontributary Indians. Some of these nontributaries were displaced groups that had moved south for the advantages of trade, while others had long-established settlements in the piedmont.

A full understanding of the important role that Virginia tributary and nontributary Natives played in the trade in skins and slaves as it relates to the Atlantic economy and mercantilism has been the subject of important recent scholarship. Native peoples of Virginia have often been in the background of important studies that have focused on the Atlantic slave trade, mercantilism, and the plantation economy. With the work of April Hatfield, James Rice, Robbie Ethridge, Cynthia Van Zandt, C. S. Everett, Paul Kelton, Christina Snyder, Maureen Meyers, Ed Ragan, and a few others, this book contributes to an emerging field on Anglo-Native interaction that vastly expands our understanding of Virginia history. Virginia Natives took an active role in their engagement with the frontier exchange economy and the developing markets for skins and slaves, and this book sheds light on the mutual obligations and expectations present in the era of the tributaries. As a social and policy history, this book examines the realities of the tributary agreements and considers from an ethnohistorical perspective the imagery and meaning of Anglo texts in relation to their Native tributaries. The tributary system in its many forms represented an attempt and failure by the English to set the stage for all future relationships between the English and Native Americans throughout Virginia. This book argues that Indigenous interactions with the southwestern and piedmont settlements of the Virginia colony played a central role in the larger narrative of the colonial plantation south.

A Note on the Source Material and Phrasing

Naturally, a study of Indigenous and colonial interaction is limited by the historical record and the lack of funding for archaeological research. While European texts are problematic and provide only a partial and skewed view of the Native world, they are among the few views we have available. Where possible, I examine intentions and expectations on both sides of the exchange, noting the biases of English resources. Records from the very early period remain rather scarce, and locating documents related to a narrow focus is often a fruitless endeavor. Several Virginia counties, especially those in the eastern portion of the state, suffered devastating losses of their early records in the American Revolution, the Civil War, and various floods and fires during the last four centuries. The Library of Virginia categorizes the "burned record counties" as "hopeless" and their remaining records as "almost hopeless and difficult to read." Unfortunately, these include two of the counties where English settlement and Indian movement played a major role in southwestern Virginia: Henrico and Charles City.

But that is not to say that the area is truly without hope. Several key sources focusing on the exploration of southwestern Virginia are published and widely available: Edward Bland's "Discovery of New Brittaine" (1650), John Lederer's *Discoveries of John Lederer* (1671), the 1671 diary of Robert Fallam, and the letters of Abraham Wood and William Byrd I. There are also a number of unpublished sources to consider, most importantly a trade account by Richard Traunter held at the Virginia Historical Society and abstracts of colonial records and microfilmed sources of the counties readily available through the Library of Virginia. In this study I utilize the existing published journals of Virginia's Executive Council and House of Burgesses and the various laws of Virginia set forth by the General Assembly.[3] Records on Williamsburg, Virginia, at the Rockefeller Library and the Swem Library proved of great importance to the study of conversion and education. Additionally, materials at the American Philosophical Society and the British National Archives provided much-needed insight into diplomacy and trade. Of great interest were the letters of Lieutenant Governor Alexander Spotswood, letters and trade notes of William Byrd I and II, and the diaries of William Byrd II and John Fontaine. This work would not have been complete without the archaeological and anthropological data of scholars working in Virginia and in the piedmont, and there remains much to be done. Scholars believe that a recent archaeological project in the Richmond area might have brought forth material evidence from the 1656 Battle of Bloody Run.

Tributaries and the Shatter Zone

The present work begins with the closing peace agreement with the Pamunkey *weroance* Necotowance after the murder of *weroance* Opechancanough in 1646. This agreement for Native tributaries was an outgrowth of medieval treatment of subject nations and an Anglo attempt to re-create the Spanish *encomienda* and *repartimiento* system. Coupled with an understanding of the English perspective is a retrospective on the Powhatan chiefdom and expectations of tribute in the paramountcy. The 1646 treaty of peace set forth a series of mutual obligations and expectations, some of which were honored and some broken. The treaty determined that lasting peace required the subjugation of Indians; it created boundary lines between white and Native settlements; it required Europeans to hold a license and Natives to wear a badge in order to travel through the outer territories; it required tributaries to provide children as hostages to ensure the compliance of the adults; and, by sanctioning trade only at forts along the fall line, it sought to organize, control, and limit access to trade in the interior. This book argues that one of the most important outcomes of the treaty was the opening of the interior to trade with the assistance of coastal plain tributaries, who acted as guides to the English traders as they progressed south of the James River and into the piedmont.

Subsequent chapters then explore the emergent frontier exchange economy and the rise of Indian trade in the piedmont and areas south of Anglo settlements on the James River and tributary settlements of the coastal plain. The interior skins and slave trade was a fundamental part of the Virginia economy, utilizing Native tributaries as scouts, traders, and allies. These chapters introduce the major English traders Abraham Wood and Thomas Stegg, along with Stegg's successors William Byrd I and II. Another area of focus is the nontributary Natives, particularly the Westo, the Occaneechee, the Susquehannock, and the Haudenosaunee Iroquois.

Robbie Ethridge developed the theory of the shatter zone, and it is through this lens that later chapters explore and analyze the wars of trade, 1676–1715. Rumor and the use of violence as it relates to the rearrangement of Native power, particularly among the tributaries and nontributary Natives, is a focal point of this section. A new era in the tributary system arrived with Lieutenant Governor Alexander Spotswood's attempts to restructure the tributary system and expand governmental control of the trade through the establishment of the Virginia Indian Company. Although ultimately he failed, Spotswood's imperial ambitions provide an intriguing focal point through which to view expectation and reality in Anglo-Native interactions.

1 / Treaty of Peace: 1646

In October 1646 the English colonists of Virginia murdered Opechancanough in captivity. They dictated terms of peace with his successor, Necotowance, ending the last of the Tidewater Wars. The terms enforced English domination and undercut Necotowance's power as *weroance*. This agreement opened the interior to Anglo-Indian trade and ultimately placed all members of the Powhatan paramount chiefdom in the Tidewater under tributary status to the Virginia government. A lack of permanent and protected sovereign territory increasingly led to dispossession of Native land and rights, as the peace marked a boundary line between English and Indian settlements that "implied a recognition of the Indian's right of occupation although not his sovereign title to land."[1] To ensure the compliance of the adults, English officials required hostage children from the tributaries for placement in colonial homes. To boost the economy, the English hoped to regulate trade by licensing European traders, requiring a badge for tributaries for safe travel through the outer territories, and sanctioning Indian trade only at fall line forts. Fort Henry was one of only two places south of the James River at which colonists permitted tributary Indians to trade.[2]

The treaty itself is symptomatic of larger changes emerging in the Eastern Woodlands, including the arrival of militarized Native slaving forces resulting as a byproduct of the shatter zone of the Eastern Woodlands.[3] As the colonial government and settlers sought to organize trade in the interior, they also struggled with the place of tributaries and nontributary Indians within the colony. As trade expanded, a number of Native groups moved through Virginia regularly to hunt and trade. While the colonial government sought to control the tributaries by placing them on reserves of land, it also co-opted their government affairs. This included assuming the right to decide who would serve as primary leader, or *weroance*. Their tribute payment was largely symbolic, "annually twenty beaver skins 'att the goeing away of Geese." However, a more important part of the treaty emerged in the expectations that Natives would provide military assistance and act as trade envoys, key components of settler expansion into the piedmont.[4]

English colonists sought to create Native tributaries from their first interactions with the Virginia Company and the Powhatan chiefdom. In early modern Europe, tribute as a form of taxation was often accompanied by an assumption of submission and inferior status. For settlers, however, the concept of the tributary in North America had deeper meaning. For the English, assigning tributary status was one of several attempts to justify and conceptualize Native peoples as their subordinates. Historical precedents for tributaries existed in both Europe and Native North America. The Powhatan chiefdom expected tribute from the towns loosely held in alliance in the coastal plain. They also hoped to incorporate the English as tributaries through fictive kinship ties to the colonists.[5] English perceptions of the tribute system varied, but evidence suggests that the English in Virginia hoped to employ the power of the chiefdom to ensure success of the English colony. Colonist William Strachey spoke derisively of Wahunsonacock, the paramount chief (known to the colonists as Powhatan), as a tyrant who demanded "all the Commodityes growing in the [land], or of what ells his shiere brings forth apperteyning to the Land or Rivers, Corne, beasts, Pearle, Fowle, Fish, Hides, Furrs, Copper, beades, by what meanes soever obteyned" and spoke to ways the English would be better to their tributaries. Another list of tribute, obtained by John Smith, mentions "skinnes, beades, copper, pearle, deare, turkies, wild beasts, and corn." Smith's list came directly from *weroances*, while the Strachey list came from Natives living in Jamestown, and it is probable that the Smith list is more accurate.[6] Tribute expectations likely focused on luxury or prestige items, as each town could produce its own daily products, such as food, building materials, and simple utensils. Inedible luxury goods such as copper, iron, puccoon, shell beads, and pearls were among the most collected items. These luxuries "took up a limited amount of storage space," and there remains no "record of foodstuffs being stored by weroances for the benefit of common folk during the lean times of the year or of specialized foods being gathered centrally for dispersal later."[7] This is not to imply that the territories were under Wahunsonacock's political control. The territories paid some form of tribute to Wahunsonacock, but the Chickahominy, for example, governed themselves under their own council of elders and not by a *weroance* placed by Wahunsonacock.[8]

The historical record affords some insight into the nature of the polities that became the Powhatan chiefdom. Throughout the Late Woodland period, the numerous people along the coast consolidated into towns, and by the sixteenth century simple and complex chiefdoms developed.[9] The consolidation of settlements saw its greatest height in the coastal plain of present-day Virginia under the leadership of Wahunsonacock.[10] The Jamestown settlement in 1607 landed almost in the center of Powhatan's chiefdom. The Powhatan called their region Tsenacommacah, which translates as "densely inhabited land." Scholars have estimated the population of Powhatan at the time of contact at about fourteen thousand people.[11] In the last decades of the sixteenth and the early years of the seventeenth century, Wahunsonacock had varying control over about thirty-two simple chiefdoms encompassing 150 towns in the region. The paramount chiefdom ran from the fall line to the coast, based on the system of tribute, primarily in luxury goods. Wahunsonacock's influence was strongest over six town groups: Powhatan, the Arrohattoc, Appomattox, Pamunkey, Mattaponi, and Chiskiack. Other Algonquian-speaking groups that loosely affiliated themselves with the Powhatan paramountcy were the Kicoughtan, Youghtanund, Rappahannock, Moraughtacund, Weyanoke, Paspahegh, Quiyoughcohannock, Warraskoyak, and Nansemond.[12]

Although nearby and closely related in language and custom, the Chickahominy maintained their autonomy from the Powhatan. Also distinct from the Powhatan chiefdom were the Nottoway and Meherrin in the southern half of the coastal plain. These groups spoke an Iroquoian language and had an economy similar to the Powhatan's, fishing and hunting while supplementing their diet with crops such as beans, maize, and gourds. The major difference between the Powhatan and the Nottoway and Meherrin was that the latter two were not organized into chiefdoms but rather lived in autonomous towns without the influence of a powerful chief.

The coastal plain held the largest population and exhibited the most social stratification, but there were numerous settlements scattered throughout the piedmont as well. Indians in the piedmont did not come under Wahunsonacock's authority. The Monacan and Mannahoac confederations in the piedmont and mountainous regions of the Virginia colony were Siouan and Iroquoian speakers.[13] To the north of Wahunsonacock's paramount chiefdom lay Algonquian-speaking groups such as the paramountcy of the Piscataway.[14] Another Iroquoian group lived to the north of Chesapeake Bay, the Susquehannock.[15] Living along the northern Chesapeake Bay, by 1620 they had easy access to trading routes to Dutch, Swedish, English, and French settlers on the coast.[16] Their Native allies included the Erie, Neutral, and Huron, and they included among their enemies the Haudenosaunee Iroquois, Mahicans, and the Powhatan chiefdom.

When Englishmen of the Virginia Company made landfall in 1607, they entered into this territory of these powerful Native polities. By and large, despite brief expeditions into the interior, the English settlers remained tied to the territory of the Powhatan, in part because they hoped to appropriate Tsenacommacah's political and economic structure to benefit the fledgling colony.[17] The Powhatan did not initially view the English newcomers as a threat, and it took several years for Wahunsonacock to realize that the English did not view the land and its peoples on his terms. Scholars have described the English as "blustering foreigners who could not even feed themselves" and the Powhatan as "incredulous" that the English "actually intended to make Virginia into an outpost of English culture."[18] While the English depended on the Powhatan for food, they also thought of the Indians as inferior. Colonial leader John Smith harbored hopes that the Indians would eventually provide a source of riches and labor for the English, following a Spanish model of tributaries akin to the *encomienda*. Preconceived notions of Native polities, influenced by Spanish encounters in the Caribbean, Mesoamerica, and South America, played a major role in definitions of tribute by the English.

Through an analysis of colonist William Strachey's propagandist materials about the opportunities in Virginia, one can see that the English colonists of Virginia sought to model themselves after Spanish *encomienda* grants. These grants grew out of the *repartimiento* system of encounter that allowed grants of land and labor for one *encomendero* from Native caciques in the Caribbean, Mesoamerica, and South America. These systems often sought to build on existing precontact tribute structures of goods and labor in Mesoamerica, the Caribbean, and South America. It is important to consider Virginia not in a vacuum but as part of a wider Eastern Woodland zone of influence and of larger colonial efforts by not only the English but the Spanish. The English studied the

Spanish experience and sought to find ways to bring the "appropriation and transformation of Indigenous political and economic structures to serve the process of colonization."[19] Because of their reliance on Spanish histories and a desire to re-create lucrative alliances with Indigenous polities, there is some argument that English observers overestimated Wahunsonacock's influence and the potential for the territory to benefit English trade. Strachey's discussion of tribute (and the collection practiced by the *weroances* of the paramountcy) played an important role in English understanding of the territory. Early in the history of the colony, the English hoped to tap into the tribute system to "provide the English garrisons with corn and their storehouses with merchandise."[20]

Some form of tribute took place in the precontact Chesapeake, but it did not approximate the scale or the complexity of systems present in the Native Caribbean, Mesoamerica, and South America. Chiefdoms of varying levels of influence emerged throughout the Chesapeake by the end of the sixteenth century, yet independent polities continued, such as the Chickahominy, the piedmont confederations of the Monacan and Mannahoac, and the Piscataway of the northern Chesapeake. These groups were "anxious to retain their sovereignty."[21]

It was not only the Spanish influence that led to desires for tributaries. The whole European feudal system was based on fairly similar practices and premises, and Virginia Company officials used examples from their expeditions to Ireland, travels through Turkey, and "classical (particularly Roman) precedents to predict their own opportunities and evaluate what they found."[22]

Wahunsonacock hoped the English would serve as his tributary, providing metal tools and prestige items to his polity in exchange for food and access to limited areas of settlement. He fully intended to limit English expansion outside of Jamestown. This can be seen in the oft-described (but highly improbable) capture of John Smith by the Powhatan and his dramatic salvation by Metoaka (known to the English as Pocahontas). The event likely represented a diplomatic strategy employed by Wahunsonacock to incorporate the English into his paramountcy and force the English to cooperate with his plans for the region. Upon his release, John Smith agreed to shift the Jamestown settlement to Capahosick, the area in which Wahunsonacock wanted the English to live. Misunderstandings eventually led to open conflict. Despite stopping their expansion briefly, the English kept pushing, increasingly becoming more demanding on the resources of the Powhatan and encroaching on Powhatan lands. Soon the policy of accommodation of the English among the Powhatan chiefdom changed, and violence erupted.[23] In the first two conflicts, the colonists pushed further onto Powhatan land, culminating in 1634 with the establishment of the Chiskiack-Jamestown line, approximately three hundred thousand acres of land cleared of Native inhabitants and awaiting English settlement.[24]

It took thirty-seven years and three major conflicts to create an English tribute system in Virginia, one that April Hatfield argues was not an economic "means to wealth" but a "political symbol" highlighting the replacement of the polity of Tsenacommacah by Virginia.[25] The First Anglo-Powhatan War, between the Powhatan and the English colonists, lasted from 1610 to 1614. The English first attacked the Paspahegh, killing between sixty-five and seventy-five people and capturing the children and wife of the *weroance*, Wowinchopunk. The colonists threw the captured children overboard, making a game of shooting them in the head. Once in Jamestown, they publicly executed Wowinchopunk's wife. The killing of Wowinchopunk's wife and children required retaliation against the English by the Paspahegh, according to customs of blood revenge. As a result, retributive Indian raids began in earnest.[26] In the melee that ensued, the English continued their assaults and the Indians reacted in variety of ways. The Paspahegh never recovered from the initial English assault and abandoned their town. The Warraskoyak, fearing a similar fate, fled before the English arrived at their town. The Appomattox chose to ambush a small party of Englishmen in the fall of 1610, and skirmishes continued throughout the winter.[27]

The spring of 1611 saw the new English governor, Sir Thomas Dale, looking for places to establish new settlements outside the bounds set by Wahunsonacock. The Powhatan paramountcy began to fracture, with the Patawomeck breaking from Wahunsonacock and negotiating their own cease-fire with the English. The Patawomeck then captured Wahunsonacock's daughter, Metoaka, and handed her over to the English colonists, leading to an immediate lull in fighting and forcing Wahunsonacock to negotiate a peace settlement. Negotiations lasted over a year, until the peace concluded with the forced marriage of Metoaka to the English colonist John Rolfe. By late 1611, effective control of the Powhatan chiefdom shifted from Wahunsonacock to his younger brother, Opechancanough. The colonists then concluded a separate peace with the Chickahominy, assigning them tributary status to the English.

From the English vantage point, the years between 1611 and 1618 represented a period of peace and good relations with the Powhatan. This was not the case for the chiefdom. Settlers spent this time expanding farther inland, taking over a large amount of Powhatan territory along the James River. The Kicoughtan, Quiockohannock, and Paspahegh effectively lost everything, and the colonists continued to move into the Weyanoke, Appomattox, and Arrohattoc towns. By 1616 the Chickahominy had a change of heart and chose to become part of the Powhatan chiefdom rather than continuing to pay tribute to the English. It might be implied here that being a tributary was not irrevocable.[28] Although effective control of the chiefdom shifted to Opechancanough in 1611, it was not until Wahunsonacock died in 1618 that Opechancanough grew impatient with the English and their inability to act as proper allies and sought to teach them a lesson.[29]

The second major violent engagement began when Opechancanough determined that diplomacy and peace with the English had failed, and in 1622 he led attempts to force the English to stay within their bounds or abandon the colony, resulting in the death of 350 settlers in two attacks. The Powhatan targeted specific outlying settlements, and this "may provide the 'text' of the lesson—that the English should remain within their proper area." The initial attack was intended as a coup de main, but the Powhatan did not follow up after the initial attack, likely expecting English "retaliation, even as they would from another Native society.... They prepared for a war of raid and counter raid, but presumed that their initial successful attack would give them the advantage in the long run."[30] The colonists chose not to submit to Opechancanough and instead attacked, causing widespread destruction of Indian towns, crops, and buildings. The English also assaulted the Chickahominy, Appomattox, Nansemond, and Weyanoke. Violent skirmishes continued throughout the next ten years, until a final peace settlement was reached in September 1632. Settlers continued to move into Powhatan territory, claiming settlements on the Eastern Shore of Chesapeake Bay and along both sides of the James River as well as moving to the south side of the York River by 1633, and in 1640 they occupied the north side of the York.[31] A détente lasted for about twelve years before Opechancanough again attempted to teach the English a lesson about where their place was in Tsenacommacah. Even after the end of Opechancanough's allied attacks in 1632, colonists continued to harass the neighboring Indians, destroying their crops and food stores.

In April 1644, led again by Opechancanough, Powhatan warriors comprising Weyanoke, Pamunkey, Nansemond, and Chickahominy killed four hundred colonists in an initial surprise attack on Jamestown. Again, as in 1622, Opechancanough did not follow up with another attack.³² The colony of Virginia declared war against nearly the entire Powhatan chiefdom: the Pamunkey, Chickahominy, Appomattox, Weyanoke, Warraskoyak, and Nansemond, along with two groups not in the paramountcy, the Chowanoke and Secotan.³³ In the late summer of 1644 the English went forth on their "Pomunkye and Cheychohominy march" into the Chickahominy town of Oraniock, forcing the Chickahominy to abandon the town entirely.³⁴

The Virginia House of Burgesses, the lower house of the Virginia Assembly, ordered all inhabitants on the south side of the James River to make constant marches against the Indians. The colonial assembly took a further step toward infiltrating the interior with the construction of three forts: Fort Charles at the falls of James River, Fort James on the Chickahominy River, and Fort Royal at the falls of York River. The selection of these locations by the English suggests their knowledge of the importance of the fall line to trade and diplomacy; the Powhatan, Monacan, and other Virginia groups already utilized this region as a zone for trade, and infiltration of the region would prove paramount to the success of the English colony in the long term. The Powhatan fought for two years against these and other encroachments, until the capture of Opechancanough by Governor Sir William Berkeley's forces in 1646. Proceedings of the March 1646 meeting of the Virginia Assembly in James City record the progress of the war, relating that the Algonquian forces were "dispersed and driven from their townes and habitations, lurking up and downe the woods in small numbers." The assembly sought a peace, "if honourably obtained"; however, it also called for "three-score men" to gather and patrol for Opechancanough on the north shore of the James River equipped with guns, shot, and swords. If it came to it, Captain Henry Fleet had permission to erect a fort on the Rappahannock River in the case "that a peace may not or cannot be concluded."³⁵

Robert Beverley's *History and Present State of Virginia* (1705) provides interesting insights from a planter and member of the Virginia government about colonial perception and memory after the death of Opechancanough. To Beverley, Opechancanough was a man of "large stature, noble presence, and extraordinary parts," and the Powhatan formerly under his rule were aggrieved by encroachments onto their land by colonists encouraged by Governor Sir John Harvey.³⁶ Beverley described Opechancanough as infirm in his old age and fatigued by war, "in which Sir William Berkeley followed him close," and as a man who could no longer walk on his own but had his men carry him, with his flesh "all macerated, his sinews slackened," his eyelids so heavy that he could barely see without the assistance of a man to lift the lids. Because of these infirmities, Beverley felt it would be easy for Berkeley's forces to catch Opechancanough, and Berkeley had a mind to send the captive to England. Beverley alleged that Opechancanough still had the power to "call into the field ten times more Indians, than Sir William Berkeley had English in his whole government." For this reason alone, one must consider the power of perception and reality in the creation of the tributaries and the death of Opechancanough, who barely survived a fortnight in custody. A colonial guard shot the Powhatan *weroance* in the back while he was in custody, and he eventually died from the wound. At one point Beverley alleged that even while gravely ill, Opechancanough was defiant of Berkeley when English colonists crowded in to see him. The injured *weroance* opined that he would not have exposed Berkeley as a spectacle if the tables were turned.[37] The new leader, Necotowance, agreed to a peace agreement that the English intended to use to fundamentally change the nature of the Indians' relationship with the colony.[38] Unfortunately, Beverley left little interpretation of the treaty itself, opining only that "all thoughts of future injury from them were laid aside."[39] Neither the original, signed treaty nor any records of the negotiations or motivations of the parties survive.[40] One can surmise, however, that the treaty was a culmination of expectations that the English had long desired of their colony. The treaty of peace in 1646 set forth a series of mutual obligations and expectations, some honored and some broken. The record privileges the English perspective of events, yet the intended clear demarcation of bounds, rights, and regulations did not always reflect the reality of interactions between the colonists and their Native tributaries.

Tsenacommacah was no longer the paramountcy of the Native chiefdom with the signing of the 1646 treaty of peace with Necotowance. Over the next thirty-seven years, the settlers increasingly penetrated the coastal plain with repeated settlement. Prior to Opechancanough's defeat, the fall line of the major artery rivers to the coastal plain served as a boundary blocking colonial expansion into the interior. With the creation of fall line forts, Governor Berkeley sponsored trade explorations to populate the interior with Indian trackers and traders (some former Powhatan) as well as English colonists. The creation of boundaries and reservations along the coastal plain served to create boundaries of Native settlement (in the towns of Patawomeck, Pissaseck, Nandtaughtacund, Onawmanient, Sekakwin, Wicomico, Rappahannock, Mattaponi, Moraughtacund, Cuttawomen, Chiskiack, Chickahominy, Pamunkey,

Powhatan, Appomattox, Weyanoke, Nansemond, Occohannock, and Accomack/Gingaskin) that the English colonists hoped would act as a buffer between the interior (nontributary) Indians and the English settlements along the rivers.[41] This would become a recurrent mode of the tributary system, tributaries and settlements serving both as forms of control over Indigenous peoples and, for English settlers, as a buffer between interior Indians and their own settlements.

From the English vantage point, the treaty allowed Necotowance, *weroance* of only the Pamunkey but signing on behalf of the coastal plain Algonquians of the former Powhatan chiefdom, to hold certain land protected from English settlement on the north side of the York River. The English designated Fort Royal, also known as Ricahock Fort, under the command of Captain Roger Marshall, as a point for trade, where tributaries would receive their striped coats as badges for movement to trade or relay messages through English territories. The English placed limitations on travel and movements to the settlements of the Native Nansemond and Meherrin south of the James River between the Blackwater River and the English settlements. The area south of the James, beyond the Blackwater, soon became an area of trade and progressive English settlement, as Fort Henry on the Appomattox, home of Abraham Wood, became a starting point for trade in the interior and an official place of trade for tributaries. Captain John Flood's home was also a place designated for trade and to receive badges (striped coats).[42] Necotowance was also to return all English prisoners, African slaves, and runaway Indian servants to the English, surrendering any Natives who were under the age of twelve when they ran away. This provision and later discussions about Native children became important elements of the tributary era, a time when the English expected the surrender of Native children under the age of twelve with the promise that they be educated in Christianity and useful trades.

English officials' selection of Necotowance as the sole signatory for the treaty reveals a discord between English perceptions of local tribal governance and the realities of life in the Tidewater region. The English saw Necotowance as the responsible party for the entire Algonquian population of the coastal plain in the Tidewater Wars; however, looking at the conflict itself, one can see that that there was no cohesive Powhatan chiefdom at this time and that the record references only the Nansemond and Algonquian peoples of the counties of Isle of Wight and Upper and Lower Norfolk specifically.[43] Later discussions by colonists allude to the war as mainly the antagonisms of Opechancanough, and it appears that the Accomack and Rappahannock were "treated with and entertained for the further discovery of the enemy."[44] An important feature of the treaty was the manner in which the colonists used the generic term "the Indians" rather than referring to specific groups. However, tributary Indians after 1646 included more than thirty groups of Algonquian speakers who once made up the Powhatan chiefdom along the coastal plain, including the Wicomico of Northumberland County, the Mattaponi, the Rappahannock, the Nansiatico, Nansemond, and the Pamunkey.[45] They also included largely independent groups like the Eastern Shore Accomack and the Chickahominy of the southern coastal plain. The most populous group was the Anancock, an Eastern Shore Indian group, part of the Accomack whom colonists later referred to as simply the Eastern Shore Indians of Accomack and Northampton Counties. By having Necotowance, a Pamunkey, as spokesperson for all of the coastal plain, the English made the point that they believed Necotowance could be responsible for all Native peoples as tributaries but also that he was subject to the English by right of conquest.[46]

After 1646, encroachment of English settlers on Indian land led to disputes, many of which ended in violence. Ignoring the plans for buffer zones set by colonial officials, settlers chose instead to move onto Indian lands. The record includes both nonviolent acts by Indians in reaction to economic conditions predicated by loss of land and violent acts by Indians, such as killings and assault brought about because of their close proximity to settler encroachment. These settlers determined boundaries of property and settlement and thus frequently made allegations that tributary Natives trespassed by hunting, trading, or simply traveling through the area. Frequently these areas were supposed to be tributary lands and were lands that had been part of Native settlements for generations. The treaty stipulated that tributary Indians could not be killed by English settlers simply for trespassing, but they could be killed for acts that would be considered a felony for Englishmen. Nontributary Indians could be killed for any reason at all. When an Indian trespassed on or damaged an Englishman's property, regardless of whether that property was in tributary territory, the law required the Englishman to attempt to recover his losses by seeking satisfaction with the local *weroance*; yet most colonists ignored these laws. Instead they frequently chose to attack the nearest Indian settlement. To simplify matters for the courts, in October 1649 the Virginia Assembly decided that in the case of trespassing, a colonist could kill the offending Indian, even one who was a tributary, stipulating that evidence brought by the party discovering the trespassing Indian would be sufficient.⁴⁷ That same month, colonial officials sought to protect the tributaries by providing more badges for tributaries who were traveling through English settlements as messengers.⁴⁸ Seven years later, on March 31, 1656, colonial officials revised the 1649 law and declared it illegal for settlers to kill Indians believed to be trespassing on English land unless the Indians committed mischief—that is, had an intent to harm.⁴⁹

To further clarify its position on the killing of Indians and to protect the tributaries, in December 1656 the assembly added some qualifications to the 1646 peace. It proclaimed that no Indian could trespass on English land without a badge and that Indians possessing badges could pass through English lands to fish and gather fruits.⁵⁰ Yet settlers continued to move onto or near tributary land. Four years later, the House of Burgesses passed a law stating that English harassment of Indians trying to hunt or trade was punishable, that no trade with Indians would be allowed without special license from the governor, and that there would be no imprisonment of an Indian leader without a special warrant from the governor.⁵¹

The English gained power in the coastal plain as the geopolitical landscape of Virginia shifted with the demise of the Powhatan paramountcy. The Virginians increasingly pressured Necotowance to cede more Powhatan land to the colonists. Shortly after the 1646 agreement, the Powhatan ceded all territory between the York and Blackwater Rivers. In part, English patenting or licensing of deeds to Indian land represented the first codification of a legal process that protected colonial interests by moving the tributaries onto restricted reserves of land, an outgrowth of the bounds of the treaty.⁵² The Powhatan paramountcy physically dissolved as the Appomattoc, Nansemond, and Weyanoke moved south while the Pamunkey, Chickahominy, Rappahannock, and other smaller groups continued to live north of the York River. The Nansemond settled near the Nansemond River in central Virginia, the Mattaponi settled on the Mattaponi River in the Chesapeake Bay watershed along with the Rappahannock on the Rappahannock River, and the Chickahominy settled on the Chickahominy River near modern-day Richmond.

The piedmont, however, experienced its own shift in power as new Indian groups moved in and colonial efforts to trade in the area faced strong Indian polities. After Opechancanough's defeat, it is likely that the Monacan resettled south and west of the James River to participate in the burgeoning interior trade, where they became part of the groups later known as the Saponi and the Tutelo.[53] Settlements increasingly shifted into the Roanoke and Shenandoah Valleys in the post-1650 era as that region became an overwhelmingly important "exchange sphere."[54]

It was not until the establishment of Fort Henry and the defeat of the Powhatan in 1646 that English settlers began developing direct relationships with the piedmont Siouan speakers, although there is evidence that an indirect trade with Europeans existed much earlier. These relationships were purely commercial in nature, and although the records of the traders' journeys are fragmented, proceedings of the Executive Council to the Virginia governor records efforts to explore the Southwest.[55] It is probable that trade goods made their way into the piedmont through Native trade networks with early contact, but, beginning in the 1650s and rising to a climax by the 1670s, Virginia traders regularly made trips to the Southwest, intensifying their contacts with Siouan speakers and developing a trade in skins and in Native slaves.[56] This was one of the most important outcomes of the treaty. The English movement into the Southwest included a constant influx of new traders, both European and Native. Involvement in trade had a dramatic effect on the Native population and their movements throughout the Eastern Woodlands. Trading increased long-distance Native migration, forced the coalescence of disparate groups, heightened contact with disease, inspired hostilities, and most importantly, introduced the Natives to firearms, which led directly to their involvement in slave trading as well as the skins trade.[57] Trade would provide Natives a reason to go to war, the loss of trade would force the Indians to give up the fight, and the promise of trade's return would help to restore amicable relations with the colonists.[58] With the assistance of tributaries acting as guides, the English traders progressed south of the James River and into the piedmont. While the 1646 peace opened the interior to trade, it also led to a flood of new issues regarding the role of Indians in the colony. On occasion, the English colonial government actively sought to protect the interests of tributary Natives as part of the treaty agreement. Desperate at times, the colonial assembly tried to control the trade and the traders, but oftentimes colonial officials were unable to manipulate and codify the relationships traders made with the interior Native and even the trade itself. In the last half of the seventeenth century, Native partnerships with English traders were based on the needs of the colonists to utilize tributaries' knowledge of trading routes and the peripheral interior near Jamestown and later Williamsburg. Exploration and trade would not have been successful in Virginia without the consent and cooperation of Native partnerships, particularly their tributary traders.

2 / Indian Trade and Upheaval: The Rise of Abraham Wood

Indian trade was central to the vitality of the settlements in Virginia as the colony moved from a frontier exchange economy to an emerging plantation economy and slave society. Trade expanded into the piedmont and areas south of the Anglo settlements of the James River and the tributary settlements of the coastal plain. This economy quickly became a vital part of the colony as Virginians utilized Native tributaries as scouts, traders, and allies. Trade in the upper Chesapeake was an important part of the nascent English colony, but the development of the piedmont led to lasting changes for both the English settlers and the Native inhabitants of the region with the introduction of the commercialized slave economy. A focus on trade reveals the entangled political and socioeconomic worlds of the hide and slave trade. Virginia's history of successful plantation slavery (and thus its founding families like the Byrds) had origins in the wealth of the Indian trade. Indian trade shaped Virginia's colonial legislation and Anglo-Indian interaction by determining settlement patterns, diplomacy, and social connections between colonists and Indians. While Virginia's role in Indian trading networks declined significantly by the mid-eighteenth century, it fundamentally set the stage for future Anglo-colonial control of Indian trade and interaction in the colonies of Carolina and Georgia. The drive to control the Indian trade was at the epicenter of this period. Traders ignored laws and governmental regulations and believed themselves to be nearly untouchable. Indians did not blindly follow their European allies. On the contrary, alliances in the South were quite fluid, but Indian military power was too strong to ignore, so each European group that settled in the South sought Indian allies to help them get a share of the market in the Indian trade (both skins and slaves).[1]

Exploration and trade would not have been successful in Virginia without the consent and cooperation of Native partnerships. Until the mid-seventeenth century, the rapids at the fall line and the hostilities between the Powhatan and piedmont Siouan-speakers prevented direct English trade in the interior, but the 1646 peace opened up new possibilities. After 1646, colonial traders began to access interior Iroquoian- and Siouan-speaking peoples with the aid of their tributary allies and new allies they cultivated among nontributary Indians of the interior.

These entanglements were part of a larger arena of engagement, and thus it is important to note both the Virginian and the Atlantic context. The dismantling of the Powhatan chiefdom in 1646 opened an extensive interior trade. Although trade with neighboring Indians had played a role in Anglo-Indian interaction since the inception of the Virginia colony, the shifting of the Powhatan from independent entities to tributaries of the Virginia government set the stage for major English trading efforts in the interior. The English expansion into Albemarle Sound shifted trade away from the Powhatan by allowing a trade at garrisons that would include not only all tributary Indians but also new nontributary Indians whom the settlers encountered in the peripheral regions of the Southwest.[2] Events in England also affected the expansion, participation, and regulation of trade for the colony of Virginia. With the execution of Charles I in 1649 and the Puritan protectorate that followed, Parliament set forth to regulate the colonies, particularly by requiring all trade items to be carried on ships licensed by the admiralty in London. The execution of this policy was notoriously ill-managed, as the Virginians continued to ship on foreign vessels, particularly Dutch, with little concern for the law. While there were discussions in Parliament about enforcement of the law and Berkeley even went so far as to muster the local militia, the Virginians enjoyed a period of expansive and relatively free trade.[3]

Expansion focused on the Southwest and included a constant influx of new traders, both European and Indigenous. In October 1646 the Virginia Assembly determined that fall-line forts were no longer essential for defense and transferred their maintenance to private entrepreneurs. Abraham Wood held Fort Henry, a garrison located near modern-day Petersburg that served as the chief trading post of the southwestern territory, as it was one of only two places south of the James River where the assembly allowed colonists to trade with tributary and nontributary

Natives. It was also a demarcation line, as it was the legal crossing point for any Natives wishing to go east and any colonists wishing to trade west.[4] Thomas Rolfe, the only son of John Rolfe and Metoaka, had faithfully served the English in the late war and for his efforts gained Fort James on the Chickahominy River. Captain Roger Marshall was responsible for Fort Royal on the Ricahock River. Fort Royal and Fort James were primarily centers for local trade with the tributary Indians on the north side of established settlements on the James River. These forts were the first step toward English attempts at controlling Indian commerce and trade, but with Thomas Rolfe involved, they also showed Rolfe's personal choice to profit from the defeat of the tributaries and the trade.[5]

The explorations financed and supported by Abraham Wood and the caravans taken by Thomas Stegg and William Byrd I introduced the European market structure of goods to interior Indians. The records of these traders provide insight into the importance of the Indian trade in Virginia. Their reasons for exploration and trade varied, but the main motive was almost purely economic: traders were searching for gold, searching for products they could derive from plants and animals, and of course seeking access to skins and Indian slaves. The Virginians funded a number of expeditions that set the stage for trading in the interior piedmont of the lower Southeast.

Fort Henry's Abraham Wood started out in Virginia as an indentured servant in 1620.[6] At the age of ten, under the employment of Captain Samuel Mathews, who acted as a mentor and "taught him the intricacies of commerce with the Natives," Wood got an early lesson in the Chesapeake Bay trade.[7] With his earnings he purchased lands near the tributary Appomattoc and initiated a trade in skins. With the support of the Virginia Assembly, Wood quickly became one of the colony's foremost authorities on Indian trade and the interior, and his explorations paved the road for Indian traders moving Southwest through Virginia into the Carolinas, as far as the Tennessee River.[8]

One of the first expeditions to highlight the interest of both settled colonists and Atlantic merchants took place in 1650. In his first major expedition, Wood traveled with the English merchant Edward Bland south into the piedmont.[9] This was an important expansion of the Bland family's mercantile efforts in the Atlantic world. Edward was the brother of John Bland, a former member of the Virginia Company who sent his brothers Edward and Theodorick and his son Giles to Virginia to handle his estates and oversee trade. Edward Bland proved to be an advantageous partner for Wood, as Bland's merchant activities spanned the whole of the James

Figure 1. "Mapp of Virginia discouered to ye falls and in it's latt: from 35 deg: & 1/2 neer Florida to 41 deg: bounds of new England," by John Farrer, 1650. The University of Virginia Library, Special Collections, Tracy W. McGregor Library, American History Collection.

Scala Miliarum

A mapp of Virginia discouered to y Hills, and in its Latt: From 35. deg: & ½ neer Florida, to 41. deg: bounds of new England.

Noua Francia

James River, ouer these hills wily must run into y peace full English.

I Mighty great

Lake Brouxx lie

Canada flu

Fort granted Sweedland

A, & new

Massomericke

MARY LAND
the Lord Baltimores Plantation
begun 1635.

Eldort
Sweeds Holland
Plant at Plant
at Axion
Noua Albion

Anandale C

Erieworu

Checepiacke   200 miles land

Mont Players

Elk river

Raritãs

Rich nek woods

Nantcok

This River the Dutch haue in Plantatyon and

A great trade of Furrs

Cape Iames

Lord Delawares Bay and

Cape May

C V M

Egg bay

Hudsons

Long Iland

Cape Codd

1651

River. He likely sought to expand Wood's trading enterprise in addition to his own. The settling of Maryland stymied the Chesapeake fur trade and Bland and Wood sought to expand south and west to the settlements of the Nottoway (Rowantee, Tonnatorah, and Cohanahanhaka) and Meherrin (Meherrin Town and Cowinchcahawkon) along the main trading path, called Weecacana.[10] The group included Sackford Brewster, Elias Pennant, Robert Farmer, and Henry Newcombe, along with an Appomattox Indian guide, Pyancha. Shortly after they started the expedition, Oyeocker, a Nottoway *weroance*, joined the group.[11] Traders relied heavily on Native men such as Pyancha and Oyeocker to act as liaisons between interior Indians and the English. Bland's journal descriptions of the region in terms of trade were significant, and he provided key details of the Indian trading paths as the group moved one hundred miles Southwest of Fort Henry near the Occaneechee trading paths.[12]

On August 27, 1650, on their first day of traveling, the Wood and Bland expedition crossed Nottoway Creek and arrived upon an Indian settlement so suddenly that the Nottoway took their women and children into the woods to get away from the English. Only after an Indian man found them to be "peaceable," wrote Bland, did the inhabitants return.[13] It was there that Oyeocker joined the expedition to Nottoway Town. Oyeocker was a brother of Chounterounte, a headman of the Nottoway described as a "King" by the English. He was an important ally to have, someone to protect English interests but also a man who had the authority to accept and encourage trade. Bland noted that the town seemed to be a convenient site for settlement, with abundant timber, water, and land suitable for livestock.[14]

One must consider perspectives of legitimacy when reading about an act of violence or subterfuge. It can be an act of settler violence intended in and of itself to discredit and delegitimize the actions of the Indigenous peoples in their description in the colonial record. From Bland's record, it is pretty clear that he did not recognize the importance of Oyeocker and Chounterounte.[15] When Bland met with Chounterounte at Nottoway Town, Chounterounte tried to offer some advice about the interior. Bland wrote that he told Chounterounte that his men intended to go to the Tuscarora because they "envited us to trade." He also said that Governor Berkeley had ordered the expedition to find some missing English among the Tuscarora. Chounterounte adamantly insisted that they should not go, warning that the trip would be hard on the English because of swamps and rotten marshes. Nonetheless, the English pushed on. Bland believed that the warnings were a product of Chounterounte's own worries that he would be blamed if anything happened to the Englishmen. This would not be the last time that Bland would discredit the perspectives of his Native allies.[16] Chounterounte, for his part, likely wanted to protect the English as trade allies but also to maintain some degree of control over access to the interior.

Arriving at Meherrin Town on August 29, Bland indicated to the Meherrin that an extensive trade relationship with Jamestown was possible.[17] What Bland and the others took away from the encounter, however, was a lesson in competition among Native nations for control over movement in the interior. Bland learned that both the Tuscarora and a *weroance* of a Meherrin settlement on the Hocomawnanck River were excited by the possibility of English trade. Tempering their interest, however, were warnings from the Weyanoke about the English that had "disheartten[ed] them from having any trade with the English." It appears that the Tuscarora wanted to trade with the English, according to the Meherrin, but the Weyanoke discouraged the prospect by saying the English would demand high tributes of roanoke and/or kill the Tuscarora traders. Bland informed the Meherrin that the Weyanoke had "likewise spoken much against" the Tuscarora and that he (Bland) believed this sort of discussion and "treachery" to be common, alleging that Indians "tell nothing but lies to the English."[18] He took his leave of the Meherrin, and the expedition continued Southwest, where Bland, always appraising the landscape, marveled at the abundant prospects for timber harvest.[19] Always looking for gain, as they continued to another settlement, they witnessed Indians with copper and heard that "they tip their pipes with silver," which caused Bland to opine, "'tis very probable that they [sic] may be Gold, and other Mettals amongst the hills."[20]

Throughout his narrative, Bland repeatedly denigrates his Indigenous allies and their motivations. Describing what he saw as yet another example of Indian "treachery," Bland learned that the Indian runner he employed to send messages to the Tuscarora ran instead to the Weyanoke and that an Indian introduced as *weroance* of the "Blandina" was instead a "Woodford." These names are strange, and they likely are not Native names but a misunderstanding on the part of Bland and his interpreters of the Indian allies' calling themselves after rivers named by Bland and other English travelers. Bland believed it was a trick to gain an upper hand over the English or to gain more goods. He noted that Pyancha, the Appomattox guide, felt that Weyanoke spies were at work throughout the entire expedition to prevent English "journyings."[21] One must remember that the Weyanoke only loosely affiliated themselves with the

Powhatan paramountcy and had a greater degree of autonomy from the coastal plain. They likely sought to discourage further settlement into the interior to protect their own interests. Shortly thereafter, Bland and Wood returned to Fort Henry.

Bland's discussion of his efforts to trade with the Meherrin and Tuscarora as well as his description of material goods to be found in the interior make clear that the primary motive for his expedition was trade. They also make clear how dependent Bland was, despite his misgivings, on his tributary allies. Wood would not have financed the journey without considering trade opportunities, since his primary occupation at Fort Henry was Indian trade. Bland seemed pleased with what he found and petitioned the Virginia Assembly to allow further expeditions and to settle men in the region. He returned to England to publish an account of his adventures and to seek support for his plans.[22] After the Bland expedition, trade increased. By 1659 several Englishmen, such as James Thweatt, Robert Boling, Benjamin Harrison, and Henry Briggs, all claimed to be trading heavily with the Nottoway and Meherrin in southwestern Virginia, and there is some evidence of trade to the upper Tuscarora towns as well.[23]

As Wood developed a robust trade in deerskins from Fort Henry, another English settler and group of Indigenous people moved into the region near the falls of the James River in Henrico County. All of these newcomers would greatly affect the trade by capitalizing on the commodity of human labor. Thomas Stegg was a merchant and ship captain whose activities spanned trading on both sides of the Atlantic in the early settlement of Virginia. By midcentury his son, also named Thomas, had inherited his father's substantial property and trading company and set forth to engage in the skins trade. His enterprise set the stage for his nephew, William Byrd I, to inherit the trading company and emerge as the chief competitor of Wood in the 1670s.

Around the same time that Stegg was building his trade in Charles City and Henrico Counties, the Eries, called the Ricahecrian by the Virginians and later the Westo, abandoned their territory near Lake Erie and arrived at the James River falls with beaver pelts, seeking trade with the colonists.[24] The development of Virginia's involvement in the Indian slave trade began with the rise of the Iroquois in the Northeast and Great Lakes regions. The Haudenosaunee Iroquois acted as powerful intermediaries between smaller Indian groups and the European settlers, trading skins for weapons. One outcome of their dominance in the trade was the loss of tribal members. To compensate for their losses and to establish further dominance over the region, the Haudenosaunee undertook decades of mourning wars, capturing

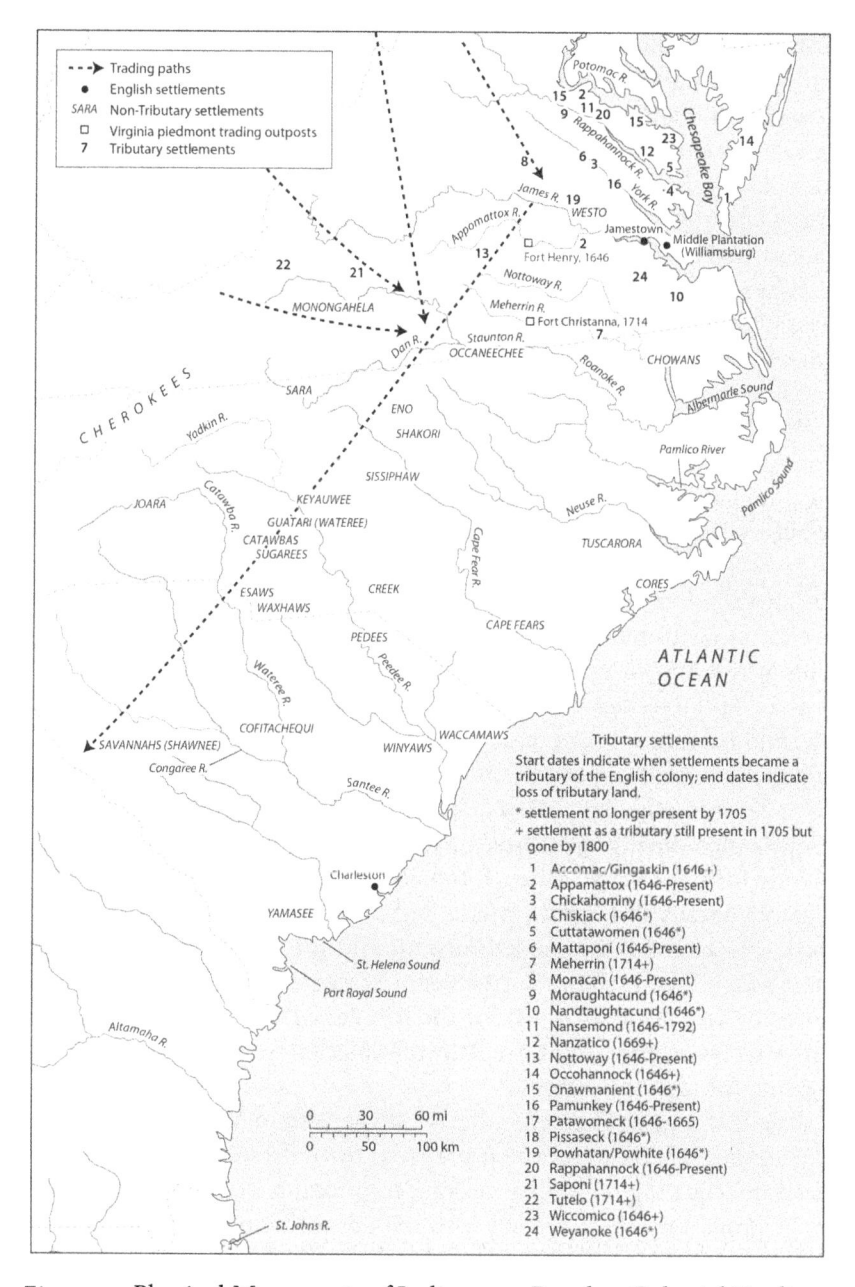

Figure 2. Physical Movements of Indigenous Peoples, Colonial Trading Posts, and Locations of the Tributary Reservations, 1646–1722. Based on maps by Robbie Ethridge, Charles Hudson, and Helen C. Rountree.

Indigenous people of the Great Lakes to adopt or sacrifice as needed. They eventually dominated the entire region, forcing the Westo to move south during the mourning wars in 1656. The Westo moved to Virginia and began to work with the Susquehannock, who received guns from their trade partners, the Swedes and the Dutch.[25] Factors surrounding the Westo move south to Virginia suggest their previous connections to the region, as the Westo knew that the falls were the center of trade with the Monacan, Mannahoac, and Powhatan.

When news of the arrival of northern Indians reached the Virginia Assembly, instead of encouraging trade with the Westo, it chose to remove them by mustering a colonial militia led by Colonel Edward Hill and assisted by Pamunkey and Chickahominy tributaries. The English motivation to do so likely reflected their desire to prevent incursions of nontributary Indians and possible threats to existing trade relationships, but they might also have been motivated by their tributary allies. The tributary Pamunkey, led by Totopotomoy, who had succeeded Necotowance as *weroance*, likely aligned with Hill to increase their control of the area south of the James. There were also other factors at work, as the Westo, as an Iroquoian group, had previously allied with the Susquehannock, a known enemy of the Pamunkey.[26] Although the assembly ordered Hill to remove the Westo without resorting to war, Hill's colonial and tributary militia attacked the Westo almost immediately.[27] The engagement itself was chaotic and violent, as the Westo quickly took the field, defeating the Pamunkey and English militants. Despite losing five of their men during the course of what became known as the Battle of Bloody Run, the Westo killed Totopotomoy.[28] In the end, it was a Westo victory; dozens of English militia and a hundred Pamunkey bowmen died. The assembly suspended Edward Hill for improper conduct and charged him with paying for the peace agreement.[29] The death of Totopotomoy was not only a loss for the tributary Pamunkey, but it would prove to be an important event in the interior for Indigenous traders moving through the region.

Scholars suggest that when the Westo arrived in Virginia, they were heavily armed. They were also prepared to trade and especially interested in acquiring more direct access to firearms. Prior to their arrival in Virginia, the Westo traded with the Susquehannock for guns from Dutch and Swedish suppliers. Once they moved into Virginia, they were able to cut out the middleman. After defeating the Pamunkey and Hill's militia, the Westo likely secured an agreement with Virginia traders, particularly Abraham Wood and Thomas Stegg, to procure Native slaves from the interior in exchange for guns. Although he is not mentioned in the records of the assembly, it was likely Wood who brokered the peace agreement with the Westo.[30]

In order to be a slaving militaristic group, the Westo (and others like them) needed to have direct access to guns, and many colonists were willing to trade guns and ammunition for slaves. The trade in slaves was directly related to the gun trade, which contributed to the development of what Robbie Ethridge calls the "shatter zone," an area of destabilization that came with the introduction of the colonial commodities trade and settler pressures. Indians affected by the shatter zone responded in a variety of ways. Migrations toward trade or away from settler antagonisms were common. The most common response was dependency on the trade, which led to militarization and, at times, a coalescence of similar polities to protect access to trade or to prevent extinction. All Indigenous polities became enmeshed in the trade arena, and thus their relationships to one another "became predicated on their positions within and responses to living in the shatter zone." Militarization was one way of coping with contact. The Westo were responding to the threat of Haudenosaunee mourning wars but also to the allure of the trade in slaves. Acquiring European weapons and using those weapons to achieve dominance in the region allowed Native groups to control European traders' access to the interior.[31] From there, the emerging plantation economy and a need for cheap labor spread throughout the upper and lower South as well as the West Indies, thus creating a market for Indian slaves and Indian slavers. Eager traders frequently ignored the legalities of trading in Indian slaves by selling Indians who were not captured in war but were part of a new slaving market created by militarized polities.[32]

With Edward Hill out of the picture, the Westo went from enemies to allies for Abraham Wood's nascent slave trade. Once in Virginia, the Westo were able to act as one of the dominant Indian traders and take advantage of the colonists' inexperience and lack of knowledge about the interior geography and Native groups. The Westo traded not only with Wood but also with the young English trader William Byrd I.[33] Their move south was a calculated emigration to a more advantageous region. Because the Westo wanted direct access to European trading partners, they deliberately broke ties with the Susquehannock and became directly involved in the lucrative skins and slave trade. Within a few short decades, the Westo were "market predators, controlling the [slave] trade and conducting destructive raids throughout much of the South."[34]

In late 1656 the Westo moved from the piedmont of Virginia to the Savannah River in order to facilitate a trade in slaves from Spanish mission towns. By 1659 the Spanish reported roving raiders on Indian settlements along the coast of Florida. The Spanish called the raiding Westo *chichimeco*, meaning "hostile northern enemies."[35] Their trading route took them near the towns of the Occaneechee, another polity who militarized and sought to control access to the interior, leading Wood to utilize his traders and the Westo to circumvent Occaneechee power. By 1662 Governor Berkeley placed Wood in charge of trading with all non-tributary Indians, including the Westo and Occaneechee. In an effort to break Westo power and send a message to Wood, the Occaneechee targeted and killed Westo raiders working for Wood.[36] A robust trade with the Westo is evident in South Carolina colonist Henry Woodward's account of his 1674 visit to a Westo town, where he found the Westo "well provided with arms, ammunition, tradeing cloath and other trade from the northward [Virginia] for which at set times of the year they truck drest deare skins furrs and young Indian slaves."[37]

As the Occaneechee sought to gain access to the slave trade, another piedmont Indigenous group, the Tomahitan, began working with Wood. Gabriel Arthur returned to Fort Henry in 1673 and met with the chief man of the Tomahitan, a piedmont group. At this meeting, the Tomahitan leader presented Wood with a Spanish Indian boy captured during raids into La Florida looting for children to sell.[38] The Tomahitan raided not only Florida but also north into the Ohio Valley, attacking and looting for slaves among towns that did not have access to guns.[39]

The government of Virginia was conflicted over the role of Indian laborers and thus passed a wide variety of laws alternately legalizing and banning Indian slavery.[40] It is important to recognize the role of Indian slavery in Virginia and the lower Southeast, especially considering that there was a precipitous rise in Indian slavery after the opening of southwestern Virginia in 1646. The Virginia record shows a practice of Indian slavery hidden in plain sight, as numerous court and probate lists of the era show a robust trade in selling Indian laborers. Most historians agree that until the end of the seventeenth century, Virginia was not a slave society, dependent upon and defined by slavery. By the mid-seventeenth century, however, the Virginia elite began to purchase African and Indian slaves for long-term labor, although they did not know quite how to regulate the lives of the men and women whose labor and bodies they purchased. Until 1705, with the passing of Virginia's first slave code, there existed rather loose and frequently changing legal conceptions of slavery applied to both African and Indian bondsmen. In their efforts to develop legal slave codes, the Virginians borrowed heavily from the Barbadian experience with African and Indian slavery while grappling for a defining status for Indians.[41]

The first mention of an Indian slave in Virginia occurs in George Percy's manuscript "A Trewe Relacyon," written between 1609 and 1612, which mentions an Indian slave named Kempes whom the colonists utilized as a guide.[42] In 1622 an Indian servant or slave named Chawco warned Captain William Perry of an impending attack by Natives aligned with Opechancanough of the Powhatan.[43] While these notable examples of Indian slavery exist prior to the mid-seventeenth century, they were rare. The most striking and obvious cases of Indian slavery came around midcentury. The 1646 accounts of the estate of Thomas Smallcomb at Fort Royal indicate that he sold two Indians to Governor Berkeley for six hundred pounds of tobacco, two Indians to John Hammon for five hundred pounds of tobacco, and one Indian to Captain Thomas Petters for six hundred pounds of tobacco.[44] Governor Berkeley included provisions for enslavement of nontributary and hostile Indians in a military expedition north. In a letter from Governor Berkeley to Major General Robert Smith in 1668, Berkeley said that proceeds from the sale of Indian slaves, particularly women and children, could be used to defray the costs of excursions against the northern Indians.[45]

Trade in guns, although at times prohibited by the Virginia government, played a crucial role in the emergence of the trading caravans bartering for skins and slaves. Native dependency on guns grew as they faced attacks from gun-wielding predators.[46] The Virginia Assembly actively encouraged the gun trade during the 1650s. In 1658 the assembly specifically allowed every man to trade with the Indians using guns, powder, and shot. They did this in direct response to the Dutch traders in the northern Chesapeake who provided the Indians with arms and ammunition.[47] The effects of the trade can be seen in a House of Burgesses discussion on the debts of the *weroance* of the Weyanoke, the same group that tried to prevent the Bland excursion earlier. At some point they became deeply involved in trade and the *weroance*, who "by reason of many disadvantageous bargains, made with the English," had debts that he could not repay and was imprisoned by the English, "whereby much detriment hath accruwed to the public," and so he was released with an order of protection.[48] Interestingly, one of the reasons he was in debt was that he was seeking to "maintain his reputation for chiefly generosity in the face of growing demands on the part of his people for European goods."[49]

The Virginians seemed unable to come to a consensus on how to regulate the trade or whether there should be a trade at all. The debate itself highlights the problems between the colonial government, at both the assembly and the county levels, and the settlers themselves. At times it was illegal to employ tributaries as traders; at times it was legal and encouraged. At other times it was perfectly legal to sell powder and shot, and yet frequently this was a fineable offense, as was the case in 1655.[50] But in 1659 the assembly permitted trade with all tributary Indians for guns, powder, and shot.[51] In a reversal of opinion, by late 1661, likely in response to rumors of and concerns about Native violence, the assembly made it a crime to supply the Natives with guns, and persons selling guns risked two years' imprisonment.[52] Although colonists found it was very difficult to acquire more than a handful of guns for illegal sale in the English colonies, scholars speculate that the traders continued to supply guns to the Indians. The majority of guns, however, came from European sources such as the Swedes and the Dutch.[53] This was problematic for Virginians, as other traders gained easy access to guns for trade, and in 1665 the assembly again attempted to prohibit the trade in guns. Traders openly defied the laws, and numerous regulations put into effect brought little change.[54] Virginia regulations could do little to stop the trade in weapons, particularly weapons obtained from other European traders, as the market for slaves through weapons provided the most immediate material advantage to Native militarized polities like the Westo and Occaneechee.

The taking of war captives or obtaining of captives through militarized polities were not the only ways Indians might have been enslaved, as the colonists likely used the threat of enslavement to keep disobedient tributaries and hostile nontributary Indians at bay. In Charles City County in October 1660, John Powell registered a complaint about property damage with the county court and alleged that Indians committed the crime. The court issued a judgment that if the Indians did not pay for the property damages, Powell could secure reparations by selling the Indians "into a fforaigne countrey to satisfie the award."[55] In October 1666 the assembly passed a law regarding refractory Indians, stating that such persons could be "reduced to obedience" if they disobeyed English law.[56] Considering that the Powell incident may have resulted in the sale of Indians to pay the debt owed to Powell, it is possible that the 1666 law could be interpreted as a license to sell so-called refractory Indians into an indenture or slavery.[57]

Another avenue for Native enslavement and trade in peoples was the hostage children component of tributary agreements. Hostage children and captive taking were a part of Anglo-Indian relationships from the onset of English settlement. After the 1646 peace agreement, however, the Virginians codified their requirement that tributaries provide children in order to ensure the compliance of adult Natives. By law, the English allowed settlers to keep tributary children to convert to Christianity and as apprentices for useful trades. Settlers utilized the children as servants and at times sold them to other colonists or out of the country as slaves.[58] Colonial households found children to be the best option for servitude, evidently feeling that their youth made them more "tractable and useful," while adults were "in most cases unmanageable, and hardly worth the constant attention required to control them."[59]

Recognizing the trade in kidnapping Native children, the Virginia Assembly responded in 1649 by enacting two laws to prevent the sale of Indian children. The first act stipulated that no child of a tributary taken into a household for education could be sold as a slave. The first and second laws both pointed out that tributary children should be freed at the age of twenty-five.[60] Another portion of the second law dealt with the taking of children as slaves. Some colonists "violentlye, or fradulentlye" took children by force, the assembly wrote, and allegedly this caused the Indians to view Christianity and the colony as "odious to them." Should this abomination continue, the assembly added, it "may be a verye Dangerous, and important Consequence to the Collonye if not timelye Prevented."[61] The assembly passed similar laws again in 1655 and 1656.[62]

Time and again the assembly passed laws banning the practice of enslavement of Native children. In 1657, the assembly again ruled against the stealing of and selling of Indian children and held that "noe person or persons whatsoever shall dare or presume to buy any Indian or Indians from or of the English." The assembly further stipulated that if a complaint regarding stealing Indians proved true, "such person shall return such Indian or Indians, within ten days to the place from whence he was taken."[63] Interestingly, however, no evidence remains that the assembly ever enforced this stipulation or sought to prevent the sale of Native children beyond the passing of a law. In March 1658 the assembly yet again reaffirmed the 1649 law, making it illegal to steal Indian children to be sold as slaves. The 1658 laws virtually replicate the earlier 1649 laws, but the assembly also expressed its great concern about Indian children whom the assembly had assigned to families, who then transferred or more likely sold the children to other families for labor. Once more, despite this statement, the assembly did not stipulate a fine or punishment for the offense.[64] While the laws banned the practice, there is no proposal within them that indicates how the assembly intended to eliminate the problem. It is logical to question the purpose of the laws to begin with.

One thing is certain: despite the laws, the sale of Indian children continued. Indian slaveholding even went to the highest levels of Virginia society. In 1655 Governor Berkeley wrote to Indian trader Thomas Stegg regarding a known Indian slave owner, Thomas Ligon. The letter refers to a payment of tobacco to satisfy a debt incurred by Ligon to Stegg, a debt for the procurement of Indian children.[65] Thomas Ligon was married to Mary Harris, the sister of Major William Robert Harris of the Henrico County and Charles City County militia, who had participated in the 1669–70 John Lederer expedition, and of Thomas Harris, another known Indian slave owner. Tacit consent to the taking of Indian children is evident in a March 1660 Charles City County Court ruling granting John Beauchamp permission to take his Indian boy to England. While it stipulates that he should have parental permission, the ruling provides no advice on how Beauchamp should obtain the parents' permission or who the boy's parents were, nor does it stipulate how long the boy could be in England.[66]

While taking a Native child to England was rare, in most cases Natives sold into forced labor moved quite far away from their families. On September 5, 1660, Major George Colclough, from Northumberland, received 1,050 acres of land for the importation of twenty-one servants to Virginia, including Francisco, an Indian. Colclough also received 150 pounds of tobacco for selling an Indian to James City County for the public use.[67] In March 1662 Thomas Busby of Surry County sold William Rollinson an Indian boy, aged five. In a quick turnaround, Rollinson sold the boy to Francis Radford of Charles City County.[68]

Little regulation over the use of Native laborers is evident in the haphazard record keeping of the period. In at least one case, the House of Burgesses chose to cancel the sale of an Indian because the child in question was a member of a tributary group. On July 3, 1659, the king of the Weyanoke, a tributary, sold an Indian boy to Elizabeth Short of Surry County. Upon reviewing the terms of the sale, the burgesses chose to nullify the transaction because the colonists discovered that the boy, Metappin, was a Powhatan tributary, spoke English, and desired baptism.[69] This is likely the only case of its kind, but a growing number of records on the issue of how to regulate Indian labor indicate a desire on the part of the colonists to codify their actions and to consider the tributaries' concerns. In at least one case, the petition of a parent of a captive child forced the court to break his indenture. In May 1697 a Northampton County Court granted the petition of Toganaquato regarding her son Assabe and made the indenture of Assabe invalid.[70]

The General Assembly and county courts also sought to control the use of Indian labor by requiring indentures and licenses to employ Indian servants. Various licenses to employ an Indian remained on the record, with varying and sometimes unknown terms for indentures. These records show attempts by particular counties to regulate the trade in Indians and, at times, to protect some tributary interests. On August 13, 1658, John Pratt received an order from Charles City County allowing him to employ an Indian "under the hands," or under the supervision of, his presumably English servants, Mr. Drewe and Mr. Wyatt. The following year the county permitted John Howell, John Drayton, and John Holmwood to employ Indians "according to law." Yet on September 14, 1661, for reasons unknown, the county revoked all previous licenses to keep Indians, permitting only John Drayton and Jason Crewes to keep their servants.[71] At the same time, other counties began issuing more licenses as the demand for Indian servants rose. While the record indicates a growing number of licenses received, it also highlights concerns over English settlers using Indian labor without a license.

Overall, indentured children had contracts that lasted until they were anywhere from twenty-four to thirty years of age, despite rules stating that the age limit was twenty-five. The length of indenture typically obligated the adult Native for five or six years, but the Anglo master could legally lengthen the indenture to anywhere from twelve years to life. Ways of legally lengthening an indenture included punishments for running away, insolence, laziness, and moral delinquency. In complaints, the county courts generally sided with the English owner. In fact, Virginians often ignored the indentures of their Indian servants and refused to set them free after their period of servitude ended.

The English utilized Indian laborers, whether indentured or enslaved, frequently, and the interactions between the master and servant sometimes left a court record, through which one gains some understanding of Native people's reactions to servitude and slavery. In at least some situations, violent, desperate acts of defiance occurred. In February 1663 Captain John Wall brought Elizabeth, an Indian servant of unknown origin, to court at Westover in Charles City County because of her repeated attacks. The court heard the deposition of settler John Monke, who swore that while out in the country at the home of Captain Wall, he witnessed Elizabeth repeatedly striking Mrs. Wall. Then another witness, Henry Tame, testified that a year before he had witnessed an altercation between the two women in which Elizabeth acted so violently that she bit Mrs. Wall on the chest and, in yet another incident, she had tried to shove Mrs. Wall's head into an oven "then red hott and ready for bread." There is no mention of the cause of the altercation, nor of how Mrs. Wall responded or if she fought back. Unknown is Elizabeth's motivation for at least two separate physical altercations against her mistress. As punishment, the court extended Elizabeth's indenture for "insolent resistance and opposicon."[72] A surreptitious trade in humans existed in Virginia despite legal and political restrictions, and Indigenous reactions to their forced labor are relevant to a better understanding of the emerging settler economy. While Elizabeth reacted violently to her servitude, other Indian servants chose other routes of expression. Many of the tributary servants worked peacefully and disappeared from the record after their initial date of indenture as their names changed to English. Some even went on to become overseers or petitioned to remain in English towns after their indenture ended.[73]

As illustrated by the legal cases above, there was a demand for Indian labor and English traders sought to fulfill that void. While illicit trade in forced laborers began to grow, Abraham Wood continued to capitalize on his advantageous position, exploiting alliances and fueling conflict among enemies, particularly to further English trade in the piedmont as well as to gather more slaves. To that end, he sponsored further expeditions into the piedmont. In March 1669, with the permission of William Berkeley, the German immigrant John Lederer made his first foray into the interior, leaving the York River settlement of Shickehamany and heading for the Appalachian Mountains with three Indigenous guides, Magtakunh, Hopottoguoh, and Naunnugh. For the most part, his descriptions of the expedition focused on the region and its inhabitants, as well as his perceptions of Native religions and history. Of note, he passed the site of the Battle of Bloody Run and the site of Totopotomoy's death, a site he deemed important to the Indigenous trackers with him. He also surveyed the region for trade, as when he described a wildcat, whose fur was very warm "though not very fine." Lederer thought that this cat pelt might be of use for local trade.[74] At various intervals he also described deer, bears, small wildcats, beaver, gray foxes, and otters.[75]

In May 1670 John Lederer received authorization from Governor Berkeley for a second trip to search for a passage across the Appalachians.[76] Lederer set out from the falls of the James River on May 22, 1670, with Major William Robert Harris, twenty horses, and five Indians.[77] After a few days, all of the party returned except Lederer and a

Susquehannock man named Jackzetavon.[78] In his journey south, Lederer met with six Westo men working for Abraham Wood at Ackenatzy. The Westo men told him about an event in which the Occaneechee "darkened" a room in which a group of Indians were dancing and killed the Westo who were there, in order to send a message of their dominance to both the Westo and Wood.[79] Lederer reported to Berkeley and Wood the existence of a large Occaneechee Indian town and two Saponi towns. Lederer's descriptions warranted further trading ventures by Wood into the region and provided Wood with information regarding the piedmont Tuscarora at the town of Katearas. Lederer called Katearas a "place of great Indian trade and commerce," where some of the women had "bedecked themselves" with copper, leading Lederer to suppose that the area might have copper mines. Katearas likely was a focal point for Native interaction and trade that was yet untapped by European markets.[80]

Lederer arrived at Wood's Appomattox settlement after being in the interior for seventeen days. He traveled to the interior for a third time in August, leaving the falls of the Rappahannock River and heading west. On this journey he again noted the large number of red deer in the region.[81] He also gave instructions to anyone wanting to travel through the interior. According to Lederer, expeditions should provision themselves with parched corn instead of biscuits. Guns were essential because the woods were full of game.[82] Regarding Indian trackers and the danger of the interior, he wrote that it was important to have one tracker "as far before the rest of the party as they can in sight" and to have another Indian on both the left- and right-hand sides of the party. He continued by explaining that when approaching an Indian settlement, an Englishman should consult with his Indian guide on the best way to proceed. Lederer believed that if the Indians in the settlement were related to the Susquehannock, the trader should first fire his gun to announce his arrival, but he should not do so for other groups, as it might frighten them. Lederer also noted that an Englishman should never enter a house without an invitation, should accept invitations from the elders before those from young men, and should refuse nothing when it was offered.[83]

Two distinct types of trade existed after the opening of the interior in 1646: trade with local tributary Indians and trade with nonlocal Indian populations. As the trade increasingly shifted to nontributary Indians by the late seventeenth century, the types of trade goods also changed. Neighbor Indians (tributaries) provided the skins of deer, beaver, otter, wildcat, fox, and raccoon. To purchase these items, traders offered trading cloth for matchcoats, axes, hoes, knives, scissors, or other iron tools.

The Indians also desired guns, powder, and shot, but Lederer warned that "to supply the Indians with Arms and Ammunition, is prohibited in all English Governments."[84] Trading with nontributary Indians was a different affair. Lederer opined that to trade with nontributary Indians in the interior, the trader might bring with him "small Looking glasses, Pictures, Beads and Bracelets of glass, Knives, Sizars, and all manner of gaudy toys and knacks for children" and trade for skins with roanoke or "perhaps with Pearl, Vermillion, pieces of Christal." Although Lederer did not mention trading guns to the nontributary Indians, they too desired access to firearms.[85]

He finished his narrative with advice about the advantages "to be made by a trade with those remote Indians," although he admitted that he might have gone better supplied. Still, he observed that it would have been dangerous to travel through so many different communities with trade goods and suggested that any future traders should go well armed and in numerous company.[86] The dangers of travel in the interior were obvious as competing Indigenous militarized polities fought for control of the trade.

After hearing Lederer's positive report, Wood sought to find a way to circumvent the Occaneechee.[87] He began dispatching representatives, such as Thomas Batts, to open trade with the Saponi.[88] In 1671 he sent Batts and Robert Fallam (whose real surname was Hallom; his name was misspelled in published accounts of the journey) to find another route through the mountains that would bypass the Occaneechee towns.[89] Fallam's journal of the trip was a meticulous record, recording the details he would need for the return trip. Upon their arrival at Saponi Town, Batts and Fallam hired a Saponi to guide them to Tutelo. Wood sent along seven tributary Appomattox from Fort Henry to help them on their journey.[90] Arriving at Tutelo, they hired another Indian to replace an Appomattox who was ill. From there they traveled to the mountains, where the ascent was "steep" and they had a difficult time finding food.[91] The journal also likely provided other explorers and traders with information regarding the climate, terrain, and plants and animals Fallam encountered. Such knowledge would be useful as the trade expanded throughout Virginia. While in Tutelo, Batts and Fallam also learned of the "great" companies sent out by William Byrd that had been in the area previously.[92]

Although Thomas Stegg traded for years with the Indians in the piedmont in competition with Wood, the entry of his nephew, Byrd, shaped the trade into a stronger market economy that connected with transatlantic commerce. Stegg settled at the James River falls, where he had a packhorse trade to the Indians from about 1656 on.[93] In 1671 Stegg died and bequeathed to Byrd his stone house and land near the falls on the south side of the James River, along with his trade with the Indians, particularly in "guns, rum, hardware, and woolen yardage."[94] Stegg included in his will an Indian slave girl named Sarah and instructions to his wife to help Byrd for a year or two because his nephew was still too young to understand the types of transaction necessary in his trade.[95] Stegg's primary business was the Indian trade, and the young Byrd followed in his footsteps.

Wood became determined to send out further expeditions, especially into the piedmont, as he continued to seek ways around the Occaneechee dominance and to try to circumvent the Stegg-Byrd trade. In 1672 Wood sent out Gabriel Arthur and James Needham.[96] Arthur was likely Wood's indentured servant, while Needham was a Carolinian trader.[97] Needham was associated with the famed Carolinian trader Henry Woodward. The extent of the relationship between Abraham Wood and Henry Woodward remains to be determined; however, C. S. Everett claims that Woodward was in Virginia at one point to investigate the Indian trade. In 1671 the Carolinian trader and Westo ally Dr. Henry Woodward traveled the same routes as Wood's associates Needham and Arthur. Woodward was a *truchement*, or cultural broker, who had lived among the Indians of the Southeast, including the St. Helenas, a Cusabo group near Port Royal. The English-run Indian slave trade in Virginia grew in size by the time of the inception of the Carolina colony. Thus when settlers founded the Carolina colony in 1670, the trade in Indian slaves was already there and may have been "just expanding" due to the massive need for slaves in the West Indies during the Sugar Revolution and the fact that Virginian tobacco plantations were beginning to bear fruit. By the time the Lords Proprietors founded the colony of Carolina, a broad array of Indians already were engaged in trading with the English of Virginia and more than likely were aware that the English were planning to settle in Carolina and were interested in the possibilities of new trade ventures.[98]

The Virginia Assembly paid traders for the importation of English servants and African and Indian slaves into the colony. Captain John Custis and Thomas Fowkes received land in return for their importation of Indian slaves and English servants into the colony in 1671. Captain John Custis received six hundred acres in January for transporting ten persons, including Jefferey, an Indian, and Pongohomeny, an Indian, to Virginia. Thomas Fowkes received six hundred fifty acres in November for transporting thirteen persons, including Peter, an Indian.[99] The means by which these men brought the Indians into the country is unknown. However, the General Assembly stated in 1670 that Indians brought by ship should be considered slaves, while those captured by land in war should be servants, an act that revised the previous justification for selling Indians captured in war as slaves.[100] While the distinction was seemingly important, in reality the trade in Indigenous peoples was gaining momentum in the southwest piedmont and the enslavement of peoples captured "by land" in allegedly just wars was still an accepted mode of acquisition of slaves.

Needham and Arthur, on behalf of Abraham Wood, were searching for a trading path through the Occaneechee villages into piedmont Carolina in order to keep the Indian trade in Virginia's control. Accompanied by eight Indians, Needham and Arthur left Fort Henry on April 10, 1673, in search of trading opportunities in fur and slaves.[101] They hoped to reach the mountains and open up a productive trade into the interior. However, the Occaneechee were too powerful for Wood's traders to circumvent and continued their control over the trade arena of the South. The Occaneechee held their position on an island below the Dan and Staunton Rivers from which they controlled access to the interior.

Trading was a dangerous and costly enterprise, but it could also be quite lucrative. Traders such as Wood and Byrd, utilizing existing trading paths created by the Native inhabitants of the piedmont and coastal plain, found access to skins and slaves in abundance, especially when they supplied their Native allies with European guns and other weapons that tied the Natives to European trade and thus to the colony itself. The chief items of the trade (skins, guns, and slaves) helped solidify Anglo-Indian interaction in a commodities market that led to further English entrenchment in the interior and changed the ways in which the English and the Indians viewed the Native role in the colony. In May 1673 Wood sent Gabriel Arthur and James Needham to try and circumvent the Occaneechee again. The two men fell in with a party of Tomahitan Indians, passed through an Occaneechee town, and traveled an additional nine days into the interior. Traveling west by south, past nine rivers and creeks, Needham and Arthur came within two days' journey of present-day northwest Georgia and a major town of the Tomahitan. Needham left Arthur among the Tomahitan and journeyed back to Fort Henry, where Abraham Wood appeared overjoyed by their successful trading contacts and immediately sent Needham out again.

In January 1674 Wood heard that an Occaneechee guide from the former expedition, Indian John, had killed Needham near the trading ford at Yadkin River. Wood learned that after shooting Needham, Indian

John had stepped across his body and proceeded to rip out Needham's heart. He "held the heart up in his hand" while making a statement to the English observers that he "valued not all the English."[102] Indian John then challenged the Tomahitan to follow his lead and kill Arthur, but they had plans of their own: to gain a foothold in the slave trade.[103] Arthur promised to help the Tomahitan raid against the Spanish and their Indian allies for slaves. According to Wood's account, the *weroance* of the Tomahitan commanded Arthur to go with a raiding party to the Spanish settlements and promised Arthur he would be returned to Wood the following spring. Inserting his opinion on the events, Wood wrote, "In the deplorable condition he [Arthur] was put in arms, gun, tomahawk, and target, and so marched away with the company."[104]

Arthur would end up spending nearly a year with the Tomahitan, participating in at least six raids, including one in South Carolina that was "a very great slaughterhouse upon the Indians."[105] Near a town Arthur thought was Moneton, he was separated from the Tomahitan and shot with two arrows by a group that was likely Shawnee.[106] Arthur became a prisoner once again, this time of the Shawnee, who took his weapons away from him. Thinking on his feet, Arthur audaciously took advantage of this opportunity to make trade agreements. Upon seeing a beaver the Shawnee had recently killed, Arthur indicated that the English to the east would buy those skins and would barter a hatchet for eight skins. Arthur negotiated with the Shawnee, saying that if they let him return to the English settlement, he would "bring many things amongst them." The Shawnee agreed, took him to a path that would lead him back to the Tomahitan, and gave him "rockahomony for his journey."[107]

Eventually Arthur made his way to near an Occaneechee settlement where he encountered another of Wood's agents, sent to find him. He arrived back at Fort Henry by June 18, told Wood about his new trade agreement with the Moneton, and reunited with the *weroance* of the Tomahitan, who happened to be at Fort Henry at the time.[108] Wood saw opportunities for profit in this encounter, as Arthur let him know that the Indians "made very much of him," particularly his knife, gun, and hatchet. This engagement with the Shawnee opened an opportunity for both the English and Native groups of the interior to expand access to guns and the European trade, an opportunity that small groups like the Shawnee and Tomahitan could use against their enemies.[109] Despite this perceived success, after these series of expeditions Wood's trade in the region began to be eclipsed by that of William Byrd I and the rising mercantile plantation economy of the James River settlements.

3 / The Rise of Indian Slavery:
William Byrd and Bacon's Rebellion

The introduction of the slave market, in addition to the competition that emerged from the skins trade, led to destabilization throughout the Eastern Woodlands of North America. With the creation of English settler colonies, the Native peoples of the Chesapeake experienced a changing economy. European traders and merchants introduced a market economy of finished goods in exchange for deerskins, beaver furs, and Native slaves throughout the Southeast. The Indian slave trade spread rapidly and had a profound and lasting effect on Native peoples of the lower woodlands and in the colonies of Virginia, North and South Carolina, and Georgia. Virginia settlers and traders engaged in the enslavement of Native peoples throughout the seventeenth and eighteenth centuries to provide a workforce for English plantations and households. English traders frequently utilized Native allies to provide the slaves by targeting Indian groups on the periphery of English settlement; however, they also enslaved Native children from tributary Natives under the guise of servitude.

While there are examples of continued enslavement of Native peoples throughout the early settlement of the colony, mass slavery typically coincided with the upheaval of war. Enslavement reached its height during the mid- to late seventeenth century as the Virginia colony shifted to a plantation economy based on agricultural labor demands. Native slaves provided a plentiful and cost-effective solution to the labor needs of the colony. Native slaves could be procured easily through a trade in guns and ammunition with Native enslavers. Racial and class-based antagonisms fueled debate within the colony over the enslavement of Native peoples, alongside the shifting labor relations of English indentured servitude and the shift to chattel African slavery. English, Dutch, French, Spanish, and Swedish traders worked alongside Doeg, Occaneechee, Iroquois, Westo, Pamunkey, and Susquehannock traders in an attempt to gain dominance over the skins and slave trade. The upheaval and anxiety brought on by the competing polities and rising antagonisms over power in the Virginia colony led to Bacon's Rebellion. This event has proven to be quite a topic for colonial historians in the study of political change and in the history of slavery in the lower South. This was an Indian war involving the trade in Indian slaves, with far-reaching effects whose themes include, but are not limited to, social change and race, changing attitudes toward the Native American population, and the divide between rhetoric and reality. Most important to this study is the contentious debate over the role of tributaries within the colony. Within the chaos of the war, a number of important voices emerged, particularly those of the tributary *weronsqua* of the Pamunkey, Cockacoeske, and the Byrd/Stegg family of English traders. In their involvement in the devastating trade war, one can see the diverging interests of English settlers, traders like Byrd and Wood, tributary allies, and nontributary Indians (allies and foes).

In June 1666 Virginia colonists accused the upper Chesapeake Bay Doeg, who lived along the Maryland border, of various crimes, including murder. According to English reports, the Doeg killed settlers along the northern border with alarming frequency and were present daily in increasing numbers. Governor Berkeley commissioned a militia to destroy the Indians, defraying the cost of the endeavor by selling Doeg women and children into slavery.[1] On July 10, 1666, the General Court proposed to force the northern towns of Monzation, Nansemond, and Port Tobacco as well as all Doeg and Potomac into submission by threatening war "to their utter destruction" and removing their women and children: all in response to the alleged killings committed by Indians.[2] Details of what transpired are not available. It is likely that the campaign against the Doeg was handled quickly by the militia of Rappahannock County, as there is no mention of the disturbance in the records of the October meeting of the Virginia Assembly. Additionally, a reference in a letter by the Virginian secretary Thomas Ludwell on February 1667 that Virginia was "very peaceable and undisturbed by any enimy except some few Indians from whom we cannot feare any great misfortune" diminished any public proclamations of the upheaval and violence of the period.[3]

An integral moment that highlights the struggles present for Native peoples at this time is the death of Totopotomoy in 1656 and the rise of Indian slavery with the power of the Westo-English alliance. The structure of Pamunkey society prior to and in the early years of English contact was a paramount chiefdom—that is, a political organization that had three tiers of authority: paramount *weroance*, district *weroance*, and town *weroance*. Totopotomoy, *weroance* of the Pamunkey, died during the battle, near the falls of the James River. Cockacoeske, the wife of Totopotomoy and a descendant of Opechancanough and relative to Powhatan, then rose to power, and the colonists came to call her "Queen of the Pamunkey."[4] There is evidence that Totopotomoy's widow, Cockacoeske, desired a return to the paramount chiefdom.[5] As mentioned in the previous chapter, the Battle of Bloody Run took place at the falls of the James River in Henrico County near what is now Richmond, Virginia, close to the growing settlements of Indian traders and hopeful planters.

Colonel Thomas Stegg developed Falls Plantation with his entry into the Indian trade after the 1646 peace.[6] Because of its proximity to the battlefield, ownership of Falls Plantation likely placed Stegg at a slight advantage in the peace process with the Westo and made him a natural competitor with Abraham Wood in the Indian trade.[7] It is highly probable that Stegg, with his wife, Sarah Harris Stegg, and later his nephew, William Byrd I, was involved in trade with the Westo, who were known for trading Indian captives for English guns.

Indian slavery emerged as an easy and highly profitable enterprise for traders such as Thomas Stegg and his wife, Sarah, who lived in the southwestern periphery of Virginia. Their involvement directly contributed to Bacon's Rebellion, as the English and their Indian allies used slave raids to create fear and establish military superiority over their enemies. It was a general period of anxiety, as demand for laborers led not only to violent raids on nontributary Natives but also to the theft of children from local tributaries. By coercing tributaries into handing over their children, ostensibly for education and apprenticeships, the English stole children for servitude. The tributaries were not fooled by this ruse. By the late seventeenth century they refused to provide children to the English, remarking on "the breach of a former contract made long ago," when their children were sent to "other Countrys" as slaves.[8] The tributary Pamunkey complained on October 26, 1708, of "diverse of their nation" being taken away. Although the council repeatedly passed resolutions that the Indians should be returned, in reality, the colonists probably sold these Indians into slavery and never returned them.[9]

Thomas Stegg died in 1670 and passed on his trade enterprise to his nephew and widow. Stegg's will, dated March 31, 1670, and proved on May 15, 1671, included a number of provisions for Sarah. Naturally, he left her "ornaments for her person" and a young Indian slave girl as a reminder of his "loving remembrance." He provided instructions for his wife's accommodations and items necessary in case she desired to return to England. Additionally, he left it to Mr. Thomas Grendon of London to pay his wife the remainder of her inheritance after all accounts were settled. Regarding his landholdings, he left all of his property to his nephew, William Byrd. In his instructions, however, he revealed some interesting detail about Sarah's role in his life and just how important she was to the trade: "But because my cousin [his nephew, Byrd] is yet young and not so well experienced in the transactions of the world I desire my loving wife, for a year or two that she continues in the country, to continue the managing of the estate, etc. charging my cousin not to be led away by the evil instructions he shall receive from others but to be governed by the prudent and provident advice of his aunt."[10] By 1673 William Byrd, with the help of his aunt Sarah at Falls Plantation, held and sold Indian slaves. Byrd quickly became a competitive trader and planter with interests throughout the Atlantic world, importing white indentured servants, trading African and West Indian slaves, and trading into the Virginia piedmont. Byrd sent trade groups of up to fifteen men and one hundred packhorses into the interior, and such caravans became common sights at Falls Plantation.[11] He quickly expanded his uncle's trade into Carolina and, playing the roles of both merchant and planter, developed a trade in skins and slaves.[12] In 1673 Henrico County records mention William Byrd selling a young Indian boy named Taythee to Thomas Harris, most likely brought from an expedition into the interior.[13]

William Byrd I was a worthy competitor to Wood and his consorts throughout the latter half of the seventeenth century. In a letter to the Royal Society in 1688, Reverend John Clayton characterized Byrd as the man who knew more about Indian affairs than any other colonist.[14] Byrd's traders eventually moved south to the Occaneechee and to the lower piedmont groups that would eventually form the Catawba, west to the Monacan, and north to the Pamunkey and Susquehannock. Byrd also acted as patron and business manager to the naturalist John Banister, who traveled along with Byrd's traders, describing his findings in detail along the way.[15] Byrd soon became one of Virginia's foremost

Indian traders, as well as an African slave trader, tobacco planter, and eventually one of the colony's political leaders. However, he was more than the colonial gentleman and the builder of a magnificent plantation near the James River falls. Neither he nor his son made a fortune on the fur trade and tobacco exportation alone. Westover Plantation, built by his son, William Byrd II, was a spectacular example of wealth and prestige in the eighteenth century; however, it was built at least in part on the proceeds of sustained commercial slaving of Indian people. During his first decade in the colony, Byrd I focused on the Indian trade and expansion into the interior.[16]

In response to the competitive rise in the Indian trade, the General Assembly sought to protect their tributary allies and to regulate who could trade with nontributary and tributary Natives in order to prevent war within the colony. Between 1646 and 1660, colonists engaged in Indian trade were required to have a commission from the governor. The General Assembly set the fine for trading with the Indians without a commission at five hundred pounds tobacco for the first offense, one thousand for the second, and fifteen hundred for the third, along with a forfeiture of all trading goods.[17] Illicit trade with nontributary Indians, enslavement of Indians, and unpaid debts to Native allies quickly began to mount up, particularly for the Doeg, Piscataway, Susquehannock, and Occaneechee, who began to lash out at interior English settlements near the Maryland border to the north and in Charles City and Henrico Counties to the south. English efforts at regulation were likely observed in name only, and by the 1670s the mistreatment of Indian traders and the enslavement of Natives by English traders became serious problems in Virginia.

Governor Berkeley sought to prevent hostilities along the fall line by arming garrisons in the frontier counties. Not surprisingly, however, the men and families involved in the slave and skins trades, who most likely were the cause of the problem, were members of the new militia. This group included Sarah Harris Stegg, now remarried to Thomas Grendon, through her nephew, William Byrd. In 1674 Byrd became captain of the Henrico County militia and headed a garrison of fifty-five men near the falls of the James River.[18] That same year Nathaniel Bacon, Governor Berkeley's cousin by marriage, immigrated to the colony with the intent to involve himself in the lucrative Indian trade. He quickly associated himself with Byrd and the interior trade. The Virginia House of Burgesses sought to prevent war with the Indians by banning the sale of arms or ammunition to any Indians—to do so was a capital crime.

The burgesses also sought to exclude previously licensed traders from trading, in the hopes of regulating and protecting tributary interests.[19] Nathaniel Bacon and William Byrd were among those banned. Bacon angrily accused the governor of monopolizing the trade by giving rights to his favorites, who lived near Jamestown, and ignoring the interests of traders in the interior counties.[20]

The way to understand and explain the attempts to regulate the trade is to apprehend the larger politics at play with tributaries and nontributary Indians. Many settlers had no desire to protect tributaries' interests and violently disavowed the 1646 treaty. By the late seventeenth century, records show increasing numbers of court cases about white encroachment on tributary lands and into the interior. Expansion was reckless and haphazard, and the government was virtually powerless to stop the colonists, who increasingly expressed contempt for the protected tributaries.[21] Most of the major histories of colonial Virginia focus on the arrival of African slavery and the question of race. The focus on Nathaniel Bacon's rebellion in terms of its role in the development of African slavery obfuscates the importance of Indigenous slavery and of the debate over tributaries in the development of the rebellion.

By all accounts, Bacon harbored a great deal of animosity for both tributary and nontributary Natives, with whom he intended to trade. In September 1675, in response to an alleged theft of corn, Bacon imprisoned a number of tributary Appomattox. This was neither Bacon's loss nor his neighbors'. Why Bacon took this path is not certain, but Berkeley's reaction was firm. He reminded Bacon that an attack on tributaries would create a war, "a General Combination of all the Indians against us."[22]

It is likely that Nathaniel Bacon and William Byrd sought Indian slaves and that a Susquehannock attack targeted Bacon and Byrd because of their activities as Indian traders. While Byrd explored the southwest piedmont, his activities likely also included supporting slave raids against the Susquehannock to the north. In 1675 Susquehannock warriors killed Bacon's overseer. Bacon was a partner with Byrd and had settled at Curles Plantation near Westover. In the aftermath of the rebellion and Bacon's death, the royal commission reported that Bacon had one African woman, one cook, a housekeeper, two white indentured servants, and seven Indian slaves ranging in age from one to forty years old. Scholars believe the overseer managed Bacon's Indian slave inventory and trade items, and they argue that the Susquehannock deliberately attacked and killed the overseer because of Bacon's trade of Indian slaves. There is evidence that the entire war was based on Bacon's desire to access more Indian slaves, including enslaving friendly tributaries whom Berkeley and Abraham Wood (allegedly) protected.[23] What eventually turned into armed rebellion against the governor of Virginia began as a series of small raids by discontented Indian partners angered by trade grievances and attacks by English colonists.[24]

After the passage of the 1676 act barring English trading privileges, Bacon sat down to drinks with his neighbors James Crews, Henry Isham, and William Byrd. Following a loss of three servants, Byrd was in favor of his neighbors' plan to wage war. All of the men present were angered by the assembly's decisions in March and expressed a sense of unease about Susquehannock movements around the James River falls. Additionally, there were rumors that local tributary Indian groups were planning for war. Bacon believed that it was time for action and that they should act "against all Indians in generall for that they were all Enemies," a sentiment that he later told Berkeley "I have always said and doe maintaine."[25] Bacon asked the governor for a commission to lead an expedition against the Indians in response to the concerns of the southwestern settlers. Governor Berkeley denied the request.[26] After Berkeley denied his request, Bacon led a group on an unauthorized attack against the Occaneechee, still an autonomous group labeled as nontributary by colonists. According to some of Bacon's men, the "great designe" of the expedition was to take from the Occaneechee a one-thousand-pound store of beaver skins.[27]

Attacking the Occaneechee was a strategic move for Bacon. The Occaneechee had a virtual stranglehold on the trade in the region, as indicated by the host of European tools, such as guns, iron tools, and hatchets, that archaeologists have discovered in Occaneechee Town. Their role as middlemen allowed them to control access to trade with the Europeans. Abraham Wood referred to the Occaneechee as the suppliers of guns and ammunition for "all the Indians for at least 500 miles."[28] In the attack Bacon and his men took several women prisoners, while the surviving members escaped to the Eno River in Carolina.[29] Bacon's Rebellion would eventually break the Occaneechee's dominance, opening the trade to other interior groups. Bacon then attacked the tributaries, including settlements of Pamunkey, Nansiatico, and Rappahannock.

On May 10, 1676, Berkeley denounced Bacon as a traitor.[30] On May 18 Bacon's forces stormed into Fort Henry on the Appomattox River and demanded that Abraham Wood hand over Jack Nessom, an Indian prisoner held by Wood. When Wood refused, the forces stormed into Wood's

The Rise of Indian Slavery / 51

home, broke Nessom's irons themselves, and took him to Charles City County.[31] By the end of May Bacon had garnered support in these settlements near the James River falls, and Henrico County voters elected him to represent them in the assembly. English settler women of the interior enthusiastically supported Bacon's plans alongside their husbands. Berkeley complained of Byrd's aunt, Mrs. Sarah Grendon's, support of Bacon and his plans. She was an agitator who, he proclaimed, claimed with inflamed rhetoric that Berkeley was "a greater friend to the Indians than to the English." This sentiment "spread through the whole country and in every part the Rabble so threatened the better sort of people that they durst not sterr out of their houses."[32] Another reflection of the sentiment of the time is present in a comment from William Byrd's wife, Mary Horsmanden:

> Who saith, that before ever Mr. Bacon went out against the Indians, there were said to be above two hundred of the English murdered by the barbarous Indians, and posts came in daily to the Governr, giving notice of it, and yett no course was taken to secure them, till Mr. Bacon went out against them. And that her husband had 3 men killed by the Indians before Mr. Bacon stirr'd, which was made known to the Governour, who notwithstanding was so posses't to the contrary, that he would not believe it to be any other than a meer pretence, for to make war against the Indians, and yt ye sd 3 men were alive and well, and onely shut up in a chamber to make the world believe they were murdered. She further affirmed that neither Mr. Bacon nor wth him had injured any English man in their persons or Estates, and yt ye country was generally well pleased wth wt they had done, and shee believed most of the councell also, so far as they durst show it.[33]

In the assembly that spring, Governor Berkeley tried to regain control of the situation by seeking to pacify the Southwest settlers and handle the raids. He invited Cockacoeske, suzerain/*weronsqua* of the tributary Pamunkey, to speak and asked for her help as part of the tributary agreement, help that she initially refused to provide.[34] It is important to consider how Cockacoeske's voice came to be heard at the council and how the English responded. Cockacoeske was important to Berkeley because he felt she could help navigate tributary assistance, but the council also sought her voice. As she tried to navigate her role as *weronsqua* and as a widow, she tried to reclaim power and remind the English of their obligations under the tributary agreement. Consider this quote from a contemporary English observer, John Clayton, who noted that Virginia Natives were seldom seen to be "affected w[i]th pleasure, or transported with passion [anger], and even among themselves they discourse . . . little[,] sit[t]ing several hours & perhaps not one word."[35] By this point Cockacoeske had led the Pamunkey for twenty years. When she appeared before the committee of the Governor's Council, she did so with a "commanding personage," as she "entered the chamber with a comportment gracefull to admiration, bringing on her right hand an Englishmen interpreter, and on her left, her son, a stripling twenty years of age," believed to be the son of Captain John West. She wore a black and white wampum peake on her head and dressed herself in a deerskin mantle with "deep, twisted fringe." She is described in the contemporary record as "majestic." Members of the council alleged that she spoke English well but insisted on communicating through an interpreter, an action likely taken to protect her interests.[36]

The council pressed Cockacoeske to provide men to serve as guides for expeditions against the Susquehannock, but she kept quiet. After further demands from the English, she broke her silence; the council records mention that she appeared close to tears and quite passionate. She launched into a fifteen-minute tirade, "often interlacing with a high shrill voice and vehement passion," in which she stated repeatedly, "Tatapatomoi Chepiack" (Totopotomoy is dead). This was a reminder and an accusation leveled at the council about the death of her husband and a hundred of her bowmen at the 1656 Battle of Bloody Run. Her people had not yet been compensated for these losses, and the colony's involvement in the Indian slave trade that escalated rapidly after the Westo victory had led to the enslavement of tributary peoples and the loss of their land to encroaching English settlers. For their part the council was not moved by her remarks: "Her discourse ending and our morose chairman not advancing one cold word toward asswaging the anger and grief her speech and demeanor manifested under her oppression, nor taking any notice of all she had said." She eventually agreed to provide 12 bowmen, although the council believed she had at least 150 under her command.[37]

On June 22 Bacon arrived at the statehouse in Jamestown and, backed by at least five hundred men, demanded his commission to pursue the Indians. The governor capitulated, at least initially, and promised Bacon the commission. Berkeley later recanted, stating that the commission, obtained by force, was void.[38] The June assembly outcomes are interesting for a number of reasons. At issue for the June assembly were the growing resentment of Native peoples and how to define an enemy Indian. The assembly decided that any Indian, tributary or not, that left his or her town without English permission was an enemy. As such, all of his or her lands were subject to confiscation. At this juncture, the assembly abandoned plans for frontier forts and instead voted to raise more troops—one thousand from several counties. The assembly sought to ease some of the hostility of the colonists by paying foot soldiers and horsemen a hefty sum of tobacco (1,500 pounds for foot soldiers and 2,250 for horsemen) and giving them rights to "plunder either Indians or otherwise." Thus they could take the Indians' guns, furs, and corn as well as enslave them: "Indians taken in warr be held and accounted slaves dureing life."[39] Bacon's Rebellion and the chaotic violence that erupted throughout the colony lasted through the fall of 1676, during which time, among other things, Bacon offered freedom to servants and slaves who joined his uprising, looted loyalist estates, and attacked Indians throughout the colony, killing and enslaving indiscriminately.

Of particular interest is his attack on the Pamunkey and Cockacoeske. His violent assault was symbolic of a total disavowal of the entire tributary system. For her part, Cockacoeske believed the English would eventually come to their senses and thus instructed her people "that if they found the English coming upon them that they should neither fire a gun nor draw an arrow upon them."[40] Bacon located the Pamunkey in the Great Dragon Swamp between the Mattaponi and Pianketank riversheds in New Kent County. He and his men looted the tribe of their fur, trading cloth, and wampum. They captured forty-five Indians and killed at least eight.[41] According to contemporary accounts, the captured Indians "were some of them sold by Bacon & the rest disposed of by Sr. Wm. Berkeley, all but five w'ch were restored to the Queen by Ingram who was Bacon's Gen'll."[42] Cockacoeske, by her account to the royal commissioners, was chased by the rebels off into the "wild woodes where shee was lost and missing from her owne people fourteen days." She, along with a ten-year-old boy, stayed alive by "gnawing sometimes upon the legg of a terrapin" that the boy found.[43] While in the woods she saw a Pamunkey woman lying dead in the road, which "struck such terror in the Queen that fearing by that gastly example" she plunged farther and farther into the woods.[44]

To capture and kill Cockacoeske would have been an important strategic coup for Bacon in his assault on the tributary system. In an effort to find Cockacoeske, Bacon and his men captured a female Pamunkey relative who was close to Cockacoeske, in the hopes that she would lead them to Cockacoeske. Instead of doing so, however, the colonists alleged that she "led the quite contrary." Realizing this, Bacon ordered his soldiers to kill her by a blow to the skull. At this point the rebels were wandering through the swamps, which continued until they found the main trading path and found the Nansiatico. There they took a young woman hostage, "half starved, and so not able to escape." Many of the Nansiatico attempted to flee, but they were soon discovered, and the English "killed two or three Indian men and as many women."[45]

Symbolic of his rejection of the entire tributary system and his effort to dehumanize Native people writ large, Bacon marched to Jamestown with his captive Indians on display. He burned the city on September 19, and Berkeley fled to the Eastern Shore. To celebrate his victory, Bacon returned with Byrd to Gloucester County to loot the Berkeley supporters. Byrd took charge of handing off loyalist items to the rebels. According to a witness, "whenever he mett with any fine goods, as silk fine Hollands, or other fine Linnings, silke stockings, Ribbond, or the like he sent them into Bacons roome." After a time Byrd passed out, drunk on cider and wine, but the divvying up of goods continued. Since Byrd had the keys to the chests attached to his body, the looters merely hoisted him and carried him around as they "tooke such goods as best liked them."[46] Initially William Byrd had firmly held views opposing Berkeley's Indian policy, and while he supported Bacon in May 1676, his support by that fall proved lukewarm at best. Byrd acted as a follower of Bacon who wanted revenge for perceived slights in the Indian trade but did not want to destroy the Indian trade and disagreed with the burning of Jamestown. Byrd also cared little for the economic and social problems of the lower classes. The rebellion ended that fall with the October death of Bacon from bloody flux. But repercussions of the Indian slave war and the attack on Cockacoeske, for both Byrd and his aunt Sarah, were far from over.

Retaliation against the rebels would be quick and violent on the part of the loyalists. While Berkeley would have to answer for his actions, he took no small part in ensuring a vindictive counterstrike against the rebels. The new assembly met in February 1677 and sought to punish, focusing on women in particular. In accordance with gender norms of the era, women were not held responsible for most crimes, since it was assumed that the woman's husband controlled her actions. One exception to these attitudes was treason. Therefore "the Virginia Assembly must have thought that the women involved in the Rebellion would slip through its fingers because of these provisions and accordingly tried to make married women liable for seditious libels." The new law specifically targeted women like Sarah Grendon and Mrs. Haviland, whom the assembly called "the fore runners of tumult and rebellion."[47] For example, charges for seditious libel for men were fines—one thousand pounds of tobacco for the first offense, double that amount for the second—as well as standing at the pillory for two hours. But married women, unless they could pay the fine, were subject to twenty lashes for a first-time offense and thirty lashes for the second offense. While it was common for women to endure physical punishments because they could not pay fines, one scholar, Julia Cherry Spruill, argues that the 1677 law "invited husbands to maintain social order by not paying their wives' fines and therefore subjecting them to flogging." She also points out that the assembly might have sought to "intimidate married women with the possibility of humiliating punishment for future misbehavior."[48]

After the rebellion waned, the royal commissioners wrote that Bacon had utilized these women to "preach Rebellion." It is clear in most narratives of the events of 1676 why Mrs. Haviland stepped into such a role: she played the role of helpmeet because her husband went on the Occaneechee excursion with Bacon. But Sarah Grendon's motivations are less clear, and it seems likely that she acted on her own initiative. Little is known about the life of Sarah Harris Stegg Grendon, aside from her marriages. Her first husband, George Harris, a merchant in Charles City County, died in 1663, and she remarried Thomas Stegg, a merchant, commissioner, and trader in Charles City County, in 1664. Stegg died in 1670, and Sarah later remarried Lieutenant Colonel Thomas Grendon, another commissioner in Charles City County. Regarding her marriages to Stegg and Grendon and their influence on her politics, it is important to note that Thomas Stegg's father, also named Thomas, was a Commonwealth supporter against the royalist Berkeley during the English Civil War and Protectorate. Early on, then, there is evidence of problems between Sarah's household and the governors, problems that likely led to her allegiance to Nathaniel Bacon in the rebellion. When the rebellion started, her husband at the time, Thomas Grendon, was not in the colony. Yet Sarah was deeply committed to the rebellion, and the reason may be found by examining the Indian trade and issues of Indian enslavement in the southwestern counties—an issue deeply tied to the roots of the rebellion itself. Sarah was a manipulative and savvy individual who likely played a role in her second husband's trade in slaves and skins and saw Berkeley's regulations as prohibitive.[49] According to Kathleen Brown, the royal commissioners "denied that women were capable of wielding the power Berkeley ascribed to them," choosing instead to label all women involved in the rebellion as victims, including the "good Queen of the Pamunkey."[50]

At issue for Sarah Harris Stegg Grendon in 1677 was the warrant against her. Sarah was the "only woman excepted from the pardon in the act of indemnity and free pardon passed by the Assembly in February, 1677."[51] Her husband, Thomas Grendon, spoke with the royal commissioners in an effort to defend his wife from the accusation of treason, asking them to try her themselves, since Berkeley had refused to pardon her. In Sarah Grendon's case, the commissioners (Moryson, Berry, and Jeffreys) criticized Berkeley, arguing, "Some mens Estate being taken away for the indiscreet tattle of their Wives here, and while they were absent about their lawfull affaires in England."[52]

Questioned by the commissioners, Sarah readily admitted to providing gunpowder to Bacon's force but claimed she thought it would be used only against enemy Indians. In order to receive a pardon, she claimed her words and deeds were that of "an ignorant woman."[53] The commissioners ruled against Berkeley: the warrant, they argued, was not properly executed, the estate seized was that of Sarah's husband and not hers, and "the speaking of some foolish words by a simple woman (thought tending to disturbance in those ill times) was no pretece sufficient to seize the estate of a husband so far absent, especially without due proof and conviction."[54] Scholar Pierre Marambaud contends that Sarah was likely expressing opinions similar to Byrd's by involving herself in the rebellion and agitating against Berkeley's control of the trade.[55] An emerging politician, Byrd survived the melee unscathed and was elected as burgess of Henrico in 1677. On May 10, 1677, the commissioners heard the allegations against Sarah Harris Stegg Grendon and dismissed them. That very same day, in a separate hearing, the new governor, as well as the attorney general of the colony, found no evidence to try Sarah for her life because she had done nothing more than many other colonists had during the rebellion.[56]

While sorting out the issues of rebels and loyalists among the colonists, the royal commissioners also sought to rectify the situation with the tributaries. In negotiations with the tributaries and in the Treaty of Middle Plantation, one can see the extent to which Cockacoeske attempted to turn the tragic events of the rebellion to her favor. The arena in which she was most successful was with the royal commissioners. The royal commissioners labeled Cockacoeske a victim of the event and called her the "faithfull friend to and lover of the English," recommending that she be compensated for her suffering and losses with gifts. It has been well documented that Cockacoeske "exerted considerable influence over the treaty's architects" as she attempted to regain control over the former Powhatan chiefdom. Herbert Jeffreys reported on June 11, 1677, about the treaty and the signing process, noting that the Queen of Pamunkey signed "on behalf of herself and Severall Nations now reunited under her Subjection and Government as anciently."[57] In what was clearly an attempt to regain power over the smaller Native nations of the Tidewater, Cockacoeske sought a return to the paramountcy.[58]

By October 1677 the Lords Commissioners of Trade and Plantations recommended an expansion of the treaty to include Maryland, and the king commissioned gifts for the Indian leaders who signed the original treaty, namely the *weronsqua* of the Weyanoke, the *weroance* of the Nottoway, the *weroance* of the Nansemond, and Cockacocske, "queen" of the Pamunkey. As a sign of the English Crown's goodwill toward his Native tributaries, the king commissioned crowns and royal robes for the four Native leaders. Fashioned for each of the four were crimson velvet hats trimmed with ermine and "small crowns or coronets of thinne silver plate, gilt and adorned with false stones of various colours, with the inscription 'A Carolo Secondo Magna Brittaniae Rege.'" Cockacoeske and her son, John West, however, received additional recognition as well.

The king's commissioners, Sir John Berry and Francis Moryson, asked for a "crown and robe, together with a stript [striped] Indian gown of gay colours and a Bracelet of falce stones" in addition to a bracelet of false stones and a silver pendant to be made for Cockacoeske. They hoped these gifts would make up for the loss of her "rich matchcoat." Her son was to receive "a scarlett coate belayered with gold and silver lace, with breeches, shoes and stockings, hatt, sword and belt suitable, and a pair of good pistols."[59] The gifts arrived with Governor Thomas Culpeper in June 1680 but the Executive Council of Virginia objected to them, as the treaty had expanded to include some twelve Native leaders who represented seven Indian groups.[60] The council asked that the gifts be delayed, "fearing those people may be heightened thereby especially by such Marks of Dignity as Coronets, wch as they conceive ought not to be prostituted to such mean persons." The council further explained their reasoning on behalf of the colonists who suffered "fatal returnes for considerable presents given unto" Native peoples, arguing that presents of this nature were "a wrong way of manageing of those people they esteeming presents to be the effects of fear, and not kindness." Importantly, the council also took issue with the preferential treatment of Cockacoeske, alleging that there were several other neighboring and nontributary Indian groups that "deserved of the English at least as well as the called Queen of Pomunkey" and that they "will shew their Resentment at least against them which is almost as bad."[61] By refusing to acknowledge her importance, her loss, or her role in maintaining peace, settlers disregarded Cockacoeske's leadership role.

It was not only the Executive Council that took exception to the adornment of Cockacoeske and the power granted to her and the Pamunkey in Articles 12 and 18 of the treaty. Article 12 gave Cockacoeske dominion over "several scattered Indian nations," and Article 18 placed several of the tributaries under Pamunkey rule.[62] Martha McCartney posits that Cockacoeske attempted to return the Pamunkey leadership to the "chiefly dominance" of the era before Opechancanough's death.[63] The Chickahominy and Rappahannock greatly resented this intrusion, and the colonial secretary, Thomas Ludwell, indicated in his letters regarding the second version of the treaty that the several nations under Cockacoeske were "dissatisfied" and "contemptible at their new subjection."[64] Indeed, in a list of grievances compiled by Cockacoeske and her son, Captain John West, she alleged on June 5, 1678, that the Chickahominy were refusing to pay tribute and obey her commands. Among the nine grievances, Cockacoeske accused the Chickahominy of poisoning one of her great men, while the Chickahominy alleged that Cockacoeske "cutt off soe many Chickahominy heads." Later that month Cockacoeske wrote to Colonel Moryson that the Rappahannock and Chickahominy were both "very disobedient to my commands."[65] According to McCartney, "government records suggest that the Chickahominy and the Rappahannocks retained their independence, though they continued to uphold their groups' commitment to the treaty itself."[66] Despite her efforts, Cockacoeske did not successfully re-create the Powhatan chiefdom paramountcy.

Both Sarah Harris Stegg Grendon and Cockacoeske began to shift out of the public record in the aftermath of Bacon's Rebellion. Thomas Grendon remained an important person in Byrd's life, and therefore, so did Sarah in the immediate years after the rebellion. In the county court of Henrico, on April 1, 1678, Byrd gave Thomas Grendon and Abel Gower, his "trusty and well-beloved friends," full power of attorney.[67] In 1684 Thomas Grendon died, and Sarah remarried quickly. William Byrd wrote derisively of this marriage in his correspondence. First he wrote to his suppliers, Perry and Lane of London, a further indication that his aunt had some involvement in his merchant endeavors. On March 29, 1685, he wrote, "Mr. Brain (who hath married Mrs. Grendon) pretends great matters though I cannot conceive what encouragement they found this year, comeing into the Country in Sept. with 30 servants and 1000 or £1200 worth of Goods." He wrote of the marriage again to Father Horsmanden, "[M]y Aunt was marryed again in about the latter end of Jan'ry to one Mr. Edward Brain a stranger to all here, but pretends to bee worth money, if not the Old Woman may thanke herself Capte Randolph and my self are Exrs. For the Estate in Virginia, and they are now about Sue us for the £1500 Jointue Mr. Grendon made her."[68] It appears that with her last marriage, Sarah Harris Stegg Grendon Braine wore out the patience of her nephew. Byrd alleged that his aunt remarried because she could not stand to "lie alone," indeed that she was not able to "be alone." There is some evidence that Byrd harbored seeds of patriarchal anxiety over the power of women. It is likely that Byrd objected to Sarah's role in his uncle's trade and her power outside of her expected role, a woman whose control over financial decisions and households subverted the natural order of things. He also feared the influence the outsider, Edward Braine, had on his aunt. Her inability to remain independent posed a possible threat. According to Byrd, in a letter to Thomas Gower, Sarah Harris Stegg Grendon Braine had the power to "sweep away all the Virginia estate."[69]

As for Cockacoeske, George Smith, the Pamunkey interpreter, informed the governor on July 1, 1686, that Cockacoeske was "lately dead" and that her heir was her niece, not her son, Captain John West, confirming that a matrilineal inheritance line was still in place in the Pamunkey community. References in 1702 name the niece as "Ms. Betty Queen ye Queen," and in 1708 there was a Pamunkey leader named "Queen Ann."[70]

Women were at the heart of the social, economic, and political machinations of Bacon's Rebellion.[71] As noted above, white English women played the role of propagandists and purveyors of secret intelligence for the public relations campaign needed by Bacon to whip the countryside into a frenzy of support for his genocidal Indian campaign. And the reshaping of Indian tributary relationships in the Treaty of Middle Plantation in 1677 was due in large part to the plans of Cockacoeske. She likely knew that the English believed she would pass her power on to her son, John West, and attempted to use the unfortunate circumstances to her advantage.

The conclusion of Bacon's Rebellion and the death of Governor Berkeley in England would not end the questions about the role of tributaries in the settlement. The conflict over fundamental issues of trade, Native

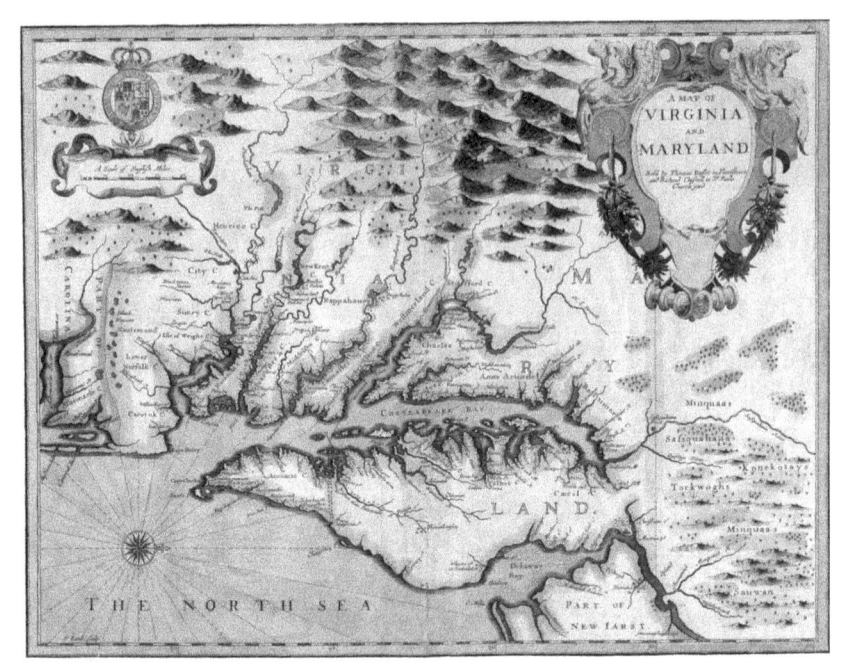

Figure 3. Map of Virginia and Maryland by John Speed, 1676. Courtesy of the Maryland Historical Society, Item ID # [Map 1676].

land rights, the role of the nontributary and tributary Indians, and settler expansion in the plantation economy all remained at issue. The so-called Indian problem combined with settler anxiety over taxation, labor, political representation, and the threat of imperial war. The colonial leaders in the era following the Treaty of Middle Plantation would have to face rumor, upheaval, and the greater problems of regulation of Native affairs in an increasingly violent expansion into the piedmont by both Anglo settlers and Native traders.

4 / In the Wake of War: Tributary Obligations

With the intention that "the peace and quality may be a lasting one, founded upon the pillars of reciprocal justice, confirming to the Indians their just rights and redressing their wrongs," the royal commissioners drafted the 1677 Articles of Peace at Middle Plantation to re-create the tributary alliance and reestablish the trade. The 1677 peace agreement following Bacon's Rebellion again promised to protect the land rights of the tributaries (Pamunkey, Chickahominy, Nansemond, Nottoway, Meherrin, Saponi, Stuckanock, Occaneechee, and Tutelo) while exercising caution toward nontributary Indians.[1] As settlers and tributaries sought to reconfigure their relationships in the aftermath of the treaty, English settlers took opportunities to expand south of the James River into the territory of the Nottoway, Tuscarora, and Meherrin. Land was a continuing source of conflict and asymmetry was a general problem in Virginian-Indian relationships. Official Anglo attempts to secure borders and control Native movement while settlers constantly pushed south of the Blackwater became a point of contention as rumors and violence dominated the discussions of the day.

Adding to the anxiety and upheaval of the era was the Indian slave trade. Violent actions and rhetoric precipitated Bacon's Rebellion, with enslavement and execution of Indian peoples at the forefront of Bacon's genocidal attacks. As mentioned in the previous chapter, the June 1676 laws effectively legalized most Indian slavery by stating that all Indians taken in war were slaves for life.[2] Should differences arise over who had rights to slaves, the 1676 law allowed for "the cheife commander of the party takeing such slaves or plunder [to be] the sole judge thereof to make equall division as hee shall see fit."[3] War prisoners transformed into slaves became payment for loyal soldiers. The House of Burgesses affirmed this practice, allowing soldiers to keep all plunder, including Indian slaves, as payment for their services.[4] There is some evidence that importation and exportation of Indian slaves continued as well. On July 2, 1678, a resident of Surry County, Robert Caulfield, received 350 acres of land from the county court for importing four white servants, one African slave, and one Indian named Jacob into the colony.[5] In 1679 the assembly extended the law by allowing Indians taken in war to be free purchase for soldiers, thus legalizing most Indian slavery.[6]

The legality of enslavement was far from resolved. The assembly not only decided in 1682 that Indians captured as prisoners of war outside the tributary zones should be considered slaves, as agreed to in 1676 and 1679, but it also legally recognized any and all Indian slaves sold by neighboring Indians (tributary or nontributary) trading with the Virginians.[7] This meant that any Indian could be enslaved if he was sold by an Indian friendly to the English, thus allowing for an influx of legal Indian slaves. Yet in May 1683 the assembly reversed its position, outlawing the entire practice by stating that no Indian could be a slave.[8]

The available record shows that the populace of Virginia did not obey the law. Colonists continued to utilize forced Indian slave labor and to trade in Indian slaves. On April 14, 1685, a Mr. Crawford filed a petition against Roger Jones for harboring three Indians—a boy, girl, and woman—whom Crawford had legally purchased and used as slaves. No record remains of the outcome of the Crawford case, though evidently he valued the investment in Indian slaves well after the law outlawing Indian slavery had been established.[9] Recognizing that the trade in slaves continued, however, and acknowledging the role of slave labor in the growing plantation economy, the legislature eventually passed an act in October 1705 making all slaves, African or Indian, real estate. Thus Indian and African slaves' legal status converged and their rights within the colony diminished greatly. The assembly also forbade all Africans and Indians from holding any public office in Virginia and fined offenders upward of two hundred to five hundred pounds currency.[10] The council approved the 1705 act on February 5, 1707, and again on January 12, 1712. The House of Burgesses discussed repealing the act in November 1712 but chose not to.[11]

Virginians' wills indicate some of the other ways colonists sought to define the status of their Indian slaves. On occasion Indian slaves were inheritable. Benjamin Hatcher of Henrico County in the piedmont, for example, bequeathed an Indian boy named Ben to his son William. John Miller bequeathed to his stepdaughter an Indian girl named Sue in the summer of 1682.[12] The will of Amy Bevill of Henrico County gave two Indian girls to her children when the children came of age.[13] On the Eastern Shore, the December 1691 will of Mrs. Mary Scarburgh of Accomack County bequeathed to her grandson and his wife "my two slaves named Lingo & Mole an Indian woman and her increase forever only the first child she shall have I give as a Legasey to Matilda the Dafter of Anth. West," until the death of said Matilda, at which point "my said slaves and their increase shall revert and be ye proper intrust and estate of ye children."[14]

There is also some evidence that Indians took advantage of the intercolonial trade in humans to benefit themselves. On July 6, 1692, William Byrd complained of strange Indians stealing one of his African slaves and selling her to an inhabitant of Philadelphia. Byrd was especially concerned about the precedent that Indians selling Africans would set among the Native population, saying that should Indians buy and sell Africans, it would "soe incourage the Indians to steal from one Govrnmt and sell to another," not only making it difficult to keep a servant but discouraging English settlement in the regions where their estates could not be protected.[15] Another example of an intercolonial trade in Indians is available in a 1693 letter from Virginian James Blair to New York governor Nicholson, in which Blair states in a postscript, "I put Mr. Bowlin in mind of an Indian for your Hon'r, but he has not yet found any to his mind."[16]

The level of anxiety and fear over the threat of violence, both real and perceived, played an important role throughout the Chesapeake. The stories that people tell about violence, both real and imagined, matter. In Virginia this was coupled with lopsided and asymmetrical power relationships based on a reliance on Indian trade, hunger for land and staple crops, and the competitive nature of expansion. *Ad terrorem* violence, through the strategic placement of conquered foes' body parts in public places, such as the spiking of heads on pikes, was a product of English settlement throughout their colonies. Indigenous raiders incited fear through their destruction of outlying settlements and captivity raids. English settlers and Native peoples, with differing perceptions of fairness and just practices, fell into direct competition with one another over resources, often leading to violent confrontation.[17] A trade in guns, coupled with the raids of enslavers, contributed to the development of the shatter zone and a market economy of desire coupled with anxiety.

As the trade escalated and further settlements moved into the piedmont, guns provided the most material advantage, although a robust trade in other items was important as well. John Lawson commented on the Indians' use of guns and their ability to "learn anything soon," stating, "I have known an *Indian* stock Guns better than most of our *Joiners*, although he never saw one stock'd before."[18] William Byrd I wrote to his suppliers about the discriminating tastes of his targeted consumer in 1685: "Pray speake to the gun smith that the dogs of all the guns locks have good hold otherwise the Indians will not buy them."[19] Later his son, William Byrd II, also commented on the importance of guns, opining that Indian men used European firearms almost exclusively. Byrd II considered the gun trade a benefit to everyone, stating that it made tributaries entirely dependent on the English for trade and survival. He even argued that guns made the Indians less likely to cause harm to the English, as he found that "they were really able to do more mischief while they made use of arrows, of which they would let silently fly several in a minute with wonderful dexterity, whereas now they hardly ever discharge their firelocks more than once."[20] Interestingly, neither Byrd mentioned which groups they traded with, despite the importance of Indigenous trade to their livelihoods. Tributaries and nontributary Indians alike also bought cotton broadcloth. Native tributaries wore matchcoats to show their allegiance to the Virginians, and matchcoats allowed the tributaries safe passage through colonial territory, particularly to hunt deer and make their way to trade forts. English manufactures began to supplant Indian-made utensils. The trade lists of men like Byrd and Wood frequently mention cooking utensils as must-have items. Truck also included hoes, knives, scissors, guns, powder, and shot, and John Lederer wrote that nontributary and tributary customers were adept at bargaining, or "higgling."[21]

The 1677 treaty with the tributaries reestablished trade and restored the tributaries. The General Assembly frequently tinkered with the idea of opening the Indian trade to all colonists but often closed the trade to only a few licensed traders. Yet in June 1680 the assembly approved a free and open trade for all persons at all times and at all places with "our friendly Indians," meaning those tributaries of the Virginia government.[22] In 1682 the issue emerged again when William Byrd I, along with Robert Smith, Joseph Bridger, Philip Ludwell, John Page, Nicholas

Spencer, William Cole, and Richard Lee, petitioned the Executive Council for a monopoly of the trade, only to be denied. Byrd even attempted to offer the king a sizeable portion of the profits, to no avail.[23] In 1691, with the expiration of the 1680 free trade act, the Executive Council voted again to prohibit trade except for necessary arms and ammunition that tributaries might need for their own subsistence.[24] In April 1691 the assembly voted to repeal all laws restraining trade and called for a free and open trade in skins, furs, and ammunition with all Indians whatsoever. This act would be renewed in 1705 and again in 1733.[25] William Byrd I complained of this repeated opening and closing of the trade in the spring of 1691 in a letter to his London suppliers. Byrd wrote that he would have had more skins and furs to send had it not been for the prohibitions. He lamented that although the assembly had reopened the trade, it had placed a great imposition on it and he feared "itt can never bee worth while onely those goods wee have by us must bee sold."[26] On June 4 he wrote again to the suppliers that he did not have the quantity of skins and furs that he wished he could provide, because of the imposition of the assembly.[27]

Expansion west, and at times south, was still on the minds of the traders. Cadwallader Jones patented 1,443 acres on the south side of the falls of the Rappahannock River in the northern half of colonial settlement in 1673 but quickly set himself up as a trader to the piedmont, trading west and south with the Occaneechee and Tuscarora in the aftermath of Bacon's Rebellion. He wrote in February 1682 that he had "an inland trade about four hundred miles from here S.S.W. This year the Indians will need Roanoke and I have a considerable trade with them." He also spoke of the threat of the Seneca to the trade as he acted as ranger for the territory. As a trader, however, he was not very successful, as he overextended his credit.[28] In January 1699 he wrote a missive to Governor Nicholson proposing to extend the trade farther south and west. Jones's main concern was the fur trade and his desire to open the trade west to Louisiana. Jones argued that extending west would benefit the English in their trade rivalry with the French. Referencing a possible trade levy for the new College of William and Mary, he wrote that an expansion would be highly beneficial: "In five yeares according to the Law now Establish'd as to ye Indian Trade the Colledge would be Saluted wth near the Sum of Two thousand pounds Sterlg per year and all waies Increaseing."[29] Nicholson was not moved by Jones's plans, but later administrations would utilize Jones's efforts. There is some evidence that the House of Burgesses considered some of Jones's ideas—namely, an idea of establishing western trade through a monopoly—and his thinking was likely the impetus for the later Virginia Indian Company under Lieutenant Governor Alexander Spotswood.[30]

Jones ultimately failed, but William Byrd traded extensively south and west and frequently wrote of the threat to the English posed by hostile Indians, not considering the role his own trade in guns and slaves had in the upheaval of the Southwest. In an incident set to circumvent Abraham Wood's power in the interior, Byrd allegedly executed seven Native men accused of murder, then "took away their wives and children," likely to sell.[31] Highlighting Byrd's influence in the colony, Governor Lord Francis Howard, Baron of Effingham, appointed Byrd as commissioner to the Seneca who were raiding in Virginia in November 1683. That fall a Seneca raiding party took several captives from Virginia tributaries.

Byrd quickly took advantage of his position to bolster his own political aspirations and arranged for a treaty with the Seneca in Albany, and then in 1685 he went north again to negotiate for a lasting peace. Referencing the theft of one Indian girl and three Appomattox boys from one English settler, Byrd demanded that the Five Nations "renew the Covenant Chain" and "Deliver up all Christian, Indian, or Negro Servants and Slaves, that are amongst you." An interesting dialogue emerges from Byrd's accusations, as the Indigenous leaders gave wampum, beaver pelts, and explanations of the events. Carachkondie, a leader of the Onondaga, responded that he did not know of the "heathen girl" taken while washing "linen in front of the door." He continued, "it could have happened" but added that their men had not yet returned from their raids. He confessed that the three boys now lived in the towns of the Mohawk and Oneida. Adopted and accepted into the community, he doubted that they could be returned; the girl, however, if found, should be returned. The Seneca spoke next, denying any break with the 1684 covenant, and alleged, "If any evil has been committed, the four nations who sit here must have done it. We say so right in their faces [which the four nations did not deny], and we will keep to your orders steadfastly." The Cayuga asked for Taggohergos, an Oneida, to speak for them, and he agreed that the boys were in Oneida and Mohawk towns. He told Byrd "that a great deal of trouble" would come from trying to release the boys but that "we will come in the spring and repay what has been charged to us now. In the meantime, we will make a place for the boys, this being in the way of a preparation to handing them back." And finally Canondodawe spoke for the Mohawk: "We declare for ourselves that we have had no part in what happened to the Virginians. But you, Cayugas, and

Oneidas, I have to tell you and punish you, for you are slow in hearing, and therefore I will sing to you, to admonish you to follow your duty better. You Cayugas, you think that you cleared yourselves thoroughly by laying down the beavers, but we have to say to you, you did not do your duty."[32] Lasting peace was not to be. In 1689 Byrd complained that his traders were having a hard time in the interior—two were killed, several lost their horses, and upheaval led other traders to "leave their goods abroad." He was concerned about Indian attacks when he wrote about "several strange Indians" near his plantation who caused him alarm.[33] A month later he wrote to merchant Arthur North that the Indians on the periphery were "very troublesome" and killed daily a number of cattle and hogs and had occasionally shot at some of the colonists.[34] In 1690 he wrote to his suppliers Perry and Lane that while he was well stocked with goods, he had a hard time trading since the Indians were "att war with each other, & troubles on all hands." This statement does not consider Byrd's own role in the upheaval, but it is very likely that an increased gun trade and demand for Indian slaves led to the attacks and war throughout the region.[35]

Indian warfare disrupted colonial trade, and this is central to understanding the Virginia colonial world. Traders like Byrd actively sought the chaos of the Indian slave trade for profit. Haudenosaunee mourning wars, on the other hand, affected Byrd's bottom line. Even tributary Indians understood the complex geopolitics of the trade and shared the anxieties of their English neighbors, particularly as Haudenosaunee people ranged south. In the peripheral settlements, where large numbers of Haudenosaunee-Iroquoians moved through on their raids south, both settlers and tributaries lived in a state of anxiety and fear. William Byrd I considered Indians, particularly nontributary ones, a major threat to the colony.[36] Despite his efforts in Albany, or perhaps because of them, Byrd felt especially concerned by the threat posed by the Five Nations. On April 26, 1689, false alarms raised in Stafford and Rappahannock Counties told of a plot by the French and ten thousand Seneca to attack the region. Several colonists responsible for raising the alarm were later jailed.[37] On July 25, 1690, Byrd wrote to his relative Daniel Horsmanden and friend Nordest Rand about a man killed by unknown Indians.[38] In Stafford County near the Maryland border, on June 15, 1694, George Mason reported to the council that nontributary Indians, likely Haudenosaunee, killed an African slave near Brent Towne. Mason related that he persuaded the English colonists to return to their settlements after the alarm but felt that a local militia of rangers was necessary to maintain order. The council agreed.³⁹ In 1695 other rangers requested tributary Indian assistance in their pursuit of a James River Indian accused of killing an Englishman, calves, and hogs. They promised to pay tributaries in arms and ammunition for their assistance. There is no record of the outcome of this expedition.⁴⁰

In the fall of 1697 a number of Occaneechee killed a Carolina trader, Robert Stephens, who was traveling through Virginia. The colonists questioned the suspected killers at Appomattox Town, but after the suspects left, a group of "strange" Indians killed the suspect Indians.⁴¹ This death led one of Byrd's traders, Richard Traunter, to pen a journal that lends insight into the Occaneechee in the trade and the rearrangement of power after Bacon's Rebellion, especially the role of English traders moving into the Catawba territory. Traunter was an established trader who understood and spoke the language of the Tuscarora, Wateree, and Waxhaw. There are two journals from his travels through the interior in 1698 and 1699, where Traunter writes of "the disposition of the Inhabitants . . . [and] my making peace with several Nations of Indians to the great advantage of the Indians Traders."⁴² In his introduction to the journal, Traunter makes clear that his motivations came from a "natural" desire to travel but also to provide information for traders on how to get to Carolina safely. The latter was a direct result of the murder in 1697 of Stephens. Another member of Stephens's party, John Herne, went to Byrd and told him of the attack. Later Byrd heard of another surviving member, Indian Jack. Byrd, "acquainted with the miserable condition of this poor Indian," immediately sent for a doctor and then Indian Jack lived with and worked for Traunter.⁴³ Traunter promised Indian Jack that he would see him returned to Carolina and his people, the Wateree, but warned him that there were threats against him, likely inspired by the hostilities of the Indian trade, particularly the slave trade. Other traders informed Traunter that the Occaneechee had promised to kill Indian Jack and any who traveled with him, but Traunter, perhaps foolishly, stood resolute once Indian Jack told him he would go home on his own if necessary. Traunter asked Byrd for assistance in getting an expedition together. According to Traunter, "When he [Byrd] saw my resolution and that all his persuasions could not divert me from going," Byrd agreed to provide him with goods and provisions, as he also desired safe passage for his traders to Carolina. Byrd warned Traunter that the Indians would likely kill "by Treachery" instead of attacking him openly and that Traunter should be prepared.⁴⁴

Traunter left with four other Virginia traders, who by his estimation "had more courage than the rest," on August 15, 1698. There were twelve men total in his party, and in his journal he spoke frequently of their fear of attack and death by the southern Indians as they set out from Appomattox. Traunter, for his part, spoke firmly of the need to show strength when confronting Indians, as they would respect the traders more if they showed courage. While the trading group saw signs of Indian traps for beaver and otter along the way, they did not get close to Occaneechee Town until August 30. On the trip there, however, in one incident one of the traders discharged a gun at night to scare off any prospective Indians but had overloaded his gun so much that he was knocked senseless by the discharge.[45] On August 29 Traunter discussed an attack on the Enoe by the Tuscarora, and the following day, upon seeing memorial stones at Occaneechee Creek, he began to ready his men for entering Occaneechee Town. When the English arrived, the Occaneechee showed no sign of battle but instead brought the English food and the English gave back tobacco, beads, powder, shot, and some salt.

Traunter saw this as a lesson for the traders, saying, "I could not forbear laughing att the Traders, and told them that I hoped that they were now Sensible how Indians might be managed, provided a man be not afrayd of them."[46] Traunter spoke directly to the Occaneechee about the rumors his traders had brought him about the threats against Indian Jack and asked for Enoe Will, the man who first told the traders of the threat. Enoe Will, being brought forth, asked Traunter for a "Soc-ca-hick" that would make him "king of the Occaneechee." Traunter describes the "Soc-ca-hick" as a commission, a sign of respect that the Enoe and Occaneechee understood as "something extraordinary in this piece of paper." He alleged that it gave Enoe Will much respect among the Occaneechee and that the Carolina Indians also understood it as powerful.[47] It is very likely that Traunter was exaggerating the importance of the document, but control of and access to trade would have made the "Soc-ca-hick" a much desired item.

During his further travels into Carolina, Traunter hunted extensively and described the impact of trade and interaction, particularly the role of disease. A smallpox epidemic had ravaged the Suteree and the Waxhaws that Traunter visited. He included a detailed description of sweating houses and the death of a Waxhaw child, the mourning process, and the burial, adding that the Waxhaw believed that "they doe not dye but sleep for a time."[48] Diseases like smallpox, bubonic plague, influenza, and measles moved through the interior. These crippling diseases had high fatality rates.[49]

Traunter arrived at Captain James Moore's in Carolina on October 1. For his part, Traunter was rather pleased with himself that he had figured out a way to handle the Occaneechee that his traders had not thought of before. Basically, Traunter alleged that he had the upper hand. His second journal, however, shows otherwise.

In his second journal, from March 1699, Traunter wrote that he hoped to find a quicker overland passage than the first. Arriving at Occaneechee Town, however, he found that his plans to circumvent the Occaneechee via Enoe Will had fallen apart because Enoe Will lost the piece of paper, the "Soc-ca-hick."[50] In his discussion with Enoe Will on the outskirts of Occaneechee Town, Traunter promised another commission, but Enoe Will demurred, saying that, "[while] he would not be afrayd to goe to the Occaneechees . . . He'd never be king of such Rogues again" and that he hoped in time "he should be powerful enough to goe and make Warr upon them, vowing to kill every man, woman, and Child of them, calling them all the ill names he could think on."[51] Further discussion of the events surrounding Robert Stephens's death and the threat of the Occaneechee persuaded Traunter to give Enoe Will another "Soc-ca-hick," but this time he was sent to the Tuscarora for assistance in killing the Occaneechee "if they should hurt the English or disturb them in their Trade, since they had been such Rogues as to say they would kill the English."[52] Enoe Will and his men then accompanied Traunter into Carolina as hunters for the party, capturing a number of Occaneechee to sell as slaves in Charleston, likely bound for the sugar islands. By enslaving and raiding prominent Occaneechee towns, Traunter and his allies weakened the Occaneechee's dominance in the piedmont.[53] By 1704 the Virginia traders continued to compete with Carolina traders, working with many Carolina Native groups, including Peedee, Waccamaws, Waywees, Wynways, and Cape Fear Indians.[54] Despite Carolinian attempts to dissuade customers from the Virginia Indian trade, a competition continued over quality of truck and prices.

The journals of Traunter's expeditions into the interior make it clear that deerskins were in abundance throughout the interior, as were those of beaver, otter, and panther. The skins trade quickly accelerated in the years following the first expeditions, and trade correspondence provides insight into the skins and slave trade. In the winter and spring months, Byrd sent his traders for skins and furs and paid them in profits from the treated skins.[55] Robert Beverley, a contemporary of Byrd, wrote about the new practice of slaughtering large numbers of deer for the skins trade in

1705. Beverley noted the indifference the Indians now had for the deer carcasses, stating, "They make all this slaughter only for the sake of the skins, leaving the carcass" to rot in the woods.[56] To illustrate the sheer number of skins involved in the trade, a trader and friend of Byrd's, Robert Hix, had a cache of fifteen hundred skins seized from him by Carolinians in 1707.[57]

As the market economy expanded, naturally so did colonial settlement. Between 1677 and 1701, one of the most important land issues involved the settlement of the Pamunkey Neck and Blackwater Swamp. At issue was the problem of multiple surveys and overlapping claims to the land. In an effort to resolve colonial concerns over what to do with the land below the Blackwater Swamp, the council reduced tributary lands in the region on May 1, 1688, in part because the council argued that the Pamunkey were now a population "wasted and dwindled away." The council felt that it would be in the best interest of the colony to fortify English settlement in the area in order to protect the tributaries from incursions from the Five Nations. Importantly, petitions started coming in from tributaries to move to the south side of Blackwater Swamp because of Haudenosaunee attacks.[58]

In 1690 the council decided that remnants of surveyed lands in the region should go to the tributaries.[59] Two days later the council made inquiries into illegal surveys taken by English colonists who sought to patent the land for themselves.[60] On April 3, 1693, the council called in colonist James Minges to discuss his alleged illegal patents and to bring with him all the pertinent papers.[61] He arrived on April 27, 1693, and claimed no knowledge of the survey of Pamunkey Neck.[62] Almost two years later, on December 6, 1695, the council heard testimony from unnamed colonists concerning deserted lands in the region and, considering it a matter of great importance, ordered the land to be immediately surveyed.[63] The hearings continued for some time. On December 13, 1695, the council determined that it was in the best interest of the colony that the vacant lands be surveyed and quickly settled by the English. But it took several years to survey and settle them. In August 1696 the council decided that ten thousand acres of the land would go to William and Mary College. In August 1701 the surveys were completed and the College of William and Mary received most of the surveyed land.[64]

English encroachment on Native land raised several options: Indian assimilation into colonial society, Indian escape into the interior, violence, or any combination of the three. Many Native groups attempted peaceable interactions with the English by either voluntarily vacating their lands completely or petitioning the English courts for their rights. These efforts had varying degrees of success. In 1678 the Rappahannock left the region because of English encroachment and finally, in 1684, merged with the Nansiatico.[65] The Wicomico complained of settler John Smith's land encroachment to the council on April 29, 1693. The council reprimanded Smith.[66]

What is particularly interesting and important about these various council meetings is the level of tributary involvement in petitioning for land rights and filing grievances. The council heard Pamunkey and Chickahominy land grievances against English settlers on October 24, 1690.[67] The Chickahominy initially sought refuge from English settlers on their lands by moving in with the Pamunkey in 1680, but by 1689 relations with the Pamunkey had soured. The Chickahominy petitioned for protection from the Pamunkey and sought leave to move to Ricahock. They finally successfully received new lands and moved to them in 1694.[68] In the fall of 1694, however, the Chickahominy complained of poor land quality and the assembly granted them additional new lands in 1701. The following summer the assembly reduced the land allotted to the Chickahominy, a move that only heightened the pressure on the Chickahominy to move once again.[69]

On November 1, 1697, the council sought interpreters to go to all the tributaries to report on their land usage and needs.[70] By expending a sizeable amount of energy, labor, and money to send these interpreters as well as to hear tributary petitions and grievances, the colonial administration showed their desire to abide by the treaty. Having read the interpreters' reports, the council agreed on July 10, 1700, to protect tributaries' lands by prohibiting land sales, specifically declaring that all tributary lands should be protected under the 1677 Treaty of Peace. This meant that land protected by the treaty should not be granted to any English settlers and that patents for other lands should be drafted in the exact same manner as grants to English settlers of non-Indian lands. Finally, it also meant that the tributaries did not have the right to grant or lease lands to anyone except their own people.[71] Almost immediately, the council broke this agreement by allowing the Pamunkey to sell large parcels of land. While some English settlers legally purchased lands through the courts with the approval of the tributaries, the sales effectively encouraged mass settlement and, as the following evidence suggests, violence.[72]

The council heard the petition of Arthur Whitehead on May 24, 1699, regarding an assault by the tributary Nottoway.[73] At its meeting of September 5, 1701, the council was read the letter of Major Peter Field describing "two strange Indians taken somewhere upon Swift Creek & brought hither Prisonrs." The council decided to lay the matter before the House of Burgesses.[74] The threat of Indian attacks was not a matter of little concern for the colonists. Those living in the periphery, surrounded by Indian settlements, feared attacks constantly. Those Indians living near the settlers often had to deal with the ramifications of the hostile attitudes resulting from these fears and themselves lived in fear. A growing uneasiness about close proximity with the Indians came to typify the English colonists' vantage point.

A variety of settler responses emerged as they faced with Native violence in the era of the tributaries. In both trade and settlement, there was a threat of violence. At times both accommodating and threatening, settler responses to Native agency and strength provide a lens through which to understand divergent understandings of power. Microaggressions on a regular basis, coupled with the threat of slavery and captivity, certainly contributed to the general anxiety of the era.[75]

The Nansiatico had been tributaries of the English government since 1646 and lived in the Northern Neck of Virginia, north of the settlements of Jamestown. Like the Piscataway, these Indians settled along the Maryland boundary near an area where the English had begun to encroach on Indian land. Troubles between the Nansiatico and colonists had been brewing for decades. On October 1, 1681, the council deliberated on a request by Maryland for the extradition of a tributary Nansiatico, Nehemin, suspected of a "barbarous murder" in Point Look Out, Maryland. The council appointed Secretary Nicholas Spencer to determine the validity of the accusations. If Spencer could not clear Nehemin of the charges, the council wanted him to take Nehemin to Maryland himself.[76] There is no record of the outcome of the Nehemin investigation, but this was not the last time a Nansiatico was accused of murder.

The 1704 Nansiatico incident likely began with English land encroachments onto Nansiatico lands. In April and May 1704 the Nansiatico complained that settler Thomas Kendall of Essex County forced them off their land.[77] In September the council read a letter from William Tayloe, a colonel with the militia in Richmond County. Tayloe reported that ten Indians came to the house of John Rowley and killed Rowley, his wife, and his son. His mother and a girl escaped. Tayloe insisted that the Nansiatico Indians were the killers, as they had threatened the family before.[78] An additional letter from Tayloe reported that the Nansiatico had confessed to the killing of John Rowley and his wife and son and asked for directions from the council on what to do with them.[79] The council decided quickly that the Nansiatico must be taken to Williamsburg for trial.[80]

The council then decided that it would be too costly to bring them all to Williamsburg and decided that a court of oyer and terminer at Richmond County would suffice. The council ordered interpreters for the Meherrin, Nottoway, and Nansemond Indians as well as the interpreter to the Pamunkey and Chickahominy Indians to attend. Asking the interpreters to bring two to three men of each nation with them, the council hoped that this would show the tributaries that the Indians received equal justice in the court system and that they would report such information back to their nations.[81] It is unlikely that the accused received justice, as the colonial government in Williamsburg wanted the punishment of the Nansiatico men to be "harsh and thorough-going."[82]

The court determined that the acts committed by the Nansiatico were so heinous that they divided the Nansiatico children among the English and sold the adults into servitude in England or the island colonies. The assembly wrote, in part, that it believed the Nansiatico had been in contact with other nontributary Indians and posed a grave threat to the colony; the latest occurrence being the last straw, the Nansiatico therefore should not be left at liberty to produce further depredations in the colony.[83] The assembly provided for all Nansiatico over the age of twelve to be sold as servants overseas, never to return to Virginia, on "pain of death." Children under the age of twelve were to be sold to Virginians, for whom they would work as servants until they were twenty-four years old, but they would never be free to resettle into an Indian town.[84] It is highly likely that the children, dispersed throughout the colony, became lifelong slaves and that the adults were sold to Antigua.[85]

The council's request for Indian observers at the trial had a multifaceted intent. The colonists may have wanted to use the incident to show that they treated the accused with justice. It is also likely that the colonists hoped to publicize their judicious handling of the situation to the Lords Commissioners of Trade and Plantations. Perhaps, however, they were using the trial to show other Indians in Virginia that they, too, could face enslavement and banishment from the colony if they killed English settlers. Unfortunately, there is very little record remaining on the Nansiatico except for the incidents of their land being encroached upon by the English and their violent reaction and subsequent enslavement.

In its efforts to control the Meherrin, the Virginia government sought to protect Meherrin interests *because* they were tributaries and a lucrative trade ally, even though there was clear evidence that Meherrin were attacking English settlements. The relationship between Virginia and the Meherrin was unlike the colony's relationship to other peripheral groups, like the Piscataway and the tributary Nansiatico. The problems in the southwestern periphery of colonial settlement were different from those in the northern border areas, and the colony repeatedly attempted to accommodate the Indians in the northern border area, in part because they provided them with lucrative trade goods.[86]

The council first dealt with the Meherrin on April 29, 1687, when it discussed the Meherrin's departure from their residence along the North Carolina border and their attacks on outlying colonial plantations. The council sought to get information about the Meherrin from the neighboring tributary Nansemond even as it pursued diplomatic relations with the Meherrin themselves. Council journals indicate that the Meherrin had never had any claims to land on the north side of the Blackwater Swamp, located to the south of the James River residents. Since arriving in the area, they had injured English settlers by killing their stock and "by their Insolent Carriadge, terrifye, and affright the Inhabitants." Nevertheless, the council agreed that if the Meherrin had already planted corn in the area, they would be permitted to remain until the harvest. After the harvest they were to leave the region, return to the south side of the Blackwater Swamp, and desist from injuring English livestock.[87] For the next fifteen or so years, it appears that the Meherrin accepted the offer and did no further damage to Virginia plantations, living as tributaries of the Virginia government.

However, in 1703 the council received a complaint from North Carolina regarding damages caused there by the Meherrin. The North Carolinians alleged that the Meherrin were a tributary of the North Carolina government. The Meherrin sought assistance and protection from the Virginia government, which was happy to acquiesce if the Meherrin became tributaries. Virginians responded that the North Carolinians had no right to demand tribute from the Meherrin, as the Meherrin lived near the Blackwater Swamp, which was not within the bounds of Carolina, and thus were tributaries of Virginia. The Virginians did, however, concede to pay the North Carolinians for damage to their settlements.[88]

As they had done to other tributaries, the Virginians moved the Meherrin settlements farther north, toward the Nottoway, and between April 18 and May 12, 1705, the colonists set new boundaries for the Nottoway and Meherrin.[89] However, despite the Virginians' pretenses at control over Meherrin settlement, the Meherrin continued to have disagreements with North Carolina. The council returned to the dispute between North Carolina and the Meherrin on June 22, 1706, stating that the Meherrin should not be disturbed from their land until the boundary between the two colonies could be agreed upon.[90] The North Carolinians claimed their right to the land the Meherrin lived on, while the Virginians claimed that since the Meherrin were dependent on the Virginia government as a tributary, the North Carolinians should not bother the Meherrin until the Virginians determined the rights concerning the land.[91] Late the following spring, the Virginians sent out surveyors again to allocate Meherrin lands in the hopes of finally settling the issue between Virginia and North Carolina, an issue that would emerge again a few years later.[92]

The Nansiatico and Meherrin are examples of the larger issue—that violence underlay much of the interaction between the English settlers and the Indians. The courts attempted to uphold tributary rights to land and made efforts to create a system for land sales and surveys. Despite these efforts, violence played a key role as settlers increasingly encroached upon Indian land, attacked Indian stocks, and killed Indians attempting to trade, work, and travel throughout the colony. Indians retaliated in kind and also instigated violence. All of which led to continual dispossession of Indian land as well as the sale of Indians into slavery.

In a 1691 letter to Stephanus Van Cortlandt, the governor of New York, William Byrd informed Cortlandt that two Indians in Tuscarora Country could be purchased from the Tuscarora for wampum, especially of the black variety, at a price of fifty to sixty pounds sterling, suggesting an expected rate for Indians.[93] Men from the upper towns of the Tuscarora also complained to the Executive Council on January 26, 1691, that two Indian men were missing, and the Tuscarora alleged that the English had killed them. Instead, the council discovered that a Virginia colonist, Daniel Pugh, had sold these men, along with two other Tuscarora, into slavery and shipped them to Barbados and another sugar island. At a council held in York County in January 1691, William Duckingfield of North Carolina alleged that "a Maherin Indian being present told them that Danll Pugh of Nansimond County . . . had sent tme to Barbados, on which they threatned Revenge"[94] Again in York County, in February 1691, Thomas Tyler, master of the brigantine *Swallow* of Barbados, was summoned to give an account of the Tuscarora Indians. Tyler produced a "bill of Lading Signed to Danll Pugh of Nansimond County for the said Indians, and the said Pughs Instructions for the disposall of them."[95] Pugh did not appear before the council despite the summons requiring his presence, and the council ordered him taken into custody.[96]

With the upheaval brought on by the trade, a continually shifting understanding of revenge and justified violence emerged. Naturally, despite their status as tributaries of the Virginia government, the Indians of Virginia held their own beliefs regarding boundaries and law. Revenge and retaliation for deaths were deeply held values for many southern Indian groups, and it is likely that by this time the colonists recognized that they might create a cycle of violence by wantonly killing Indians. On the other hand, if the colonists did indeed understand this cycle and knew what an attack on an Indian group would lead to, they may well have incited violence intentionally in order to harass their Indian neighbors. With trespassing and raiding at a constant level, one of the most serious responses was to simply kill the offender. For southern Indians, killing often required revenge or a redress of grievance through compensation.[97]

Evidence that at least some colonists understood something about blood revenge can be found in a 1708 case of an argument between the Nottoway and the Saponi, both living near newly established English settlements on the south side of the James River at the time. On October 30, 1708, the council heard a request from some Nottoway for permission to pursue the Tutelo Indians, whom the Nottoway claimed had murdered both English colonists and Nottoways. The council granted their request.[98] On July 14, 1709, the Surry County Court heard from trader Benjamin Harrison regarding quarrels among Saponi, Nottoway, Tuscarora, and Tutelo. The Saponi complained that the Nottoway and Tuscarora had killed two of their people and demanded the capture of the killers. The Nottoway complained that the Saponi had killed three Nottoway men and wounded two more prior to the killing of the Saponi men, and the Nottoway, according to the principles of blood revenge, thought it reasonable that they should be allowed to kill two Saponi. The Saponi asked the Nottoway to pay for the loss of the men; the Nottoway agreed but said they would pay only if the Saponi paid for the three men they had killed. According to Harrison, he told them that they could "make Bargains amongst them selves," but he had no say in the matter, as it was not the English "law to sell mens lives for money."[99]

The Saponi countered that it was not they who had killed the Nottoway, but the Tutelo. The Nottoway replied that the Saponi and Tutelo came together and they were "all as one people," and they further alleged that the Saponi originally promised to help the Nottoway against the

Tutelo but, "instead of helping them, they had betrayed them and given the Tutelos notice of their coming."[100] The Saponi denied the Nottoway allegations that they had betrayed them. Instead, they countered they were owed a substantial amount of roanoke for their troubles.[101] The council stepped in and rebuked the Nottoway. The council wrote that the Nottoway Indians had killed two Saponi on Benjamin Harrison's plantation and forbade the Nottoway from going out in the future painted for war or from "lying in wait" to attack any Indians near the plantation. They also ordered the Nottoway not to harbor any Tuscarora or other nontributary Indians.[102] It would appear that the Nottoway complied with at least a portion of this order, as they informed William Byrd II of threats of an Indian conspiracy on December 17 and 19, 1711.[103] Implicit in this discussion is an English acceptance of Indian retributive action. This case is likely an anomaly, and, as we will see, other cases highlight that while the English likely understood Native actions, they also employed a deliberate misunderstanding of those actions and fomented fear of Indian raids to dispossess the Indians of their land.

Captivity was once a form of social control with defined purposes related to kinship and mourning. The shift to economic purposes for captivity created new ways for violence to emerge with the constant threat of raids. Robert Beverley wrote of a Towasa Native named Lamhatty who fled from the Shawnee in 1707 to an English plantation owned by Andrew Clark on the north side of the Meherrin River. Native slavers (either Tuscarora or Creek) stole the twenty-six-year-old Lamhatty from his town near the Gulf Coast and eventually sold him to the Shawnee. Beverley's rendition of Lamhatty's experience is quite brief but remarkably telling of Indian slavery. Lamhatty traveled with his captors for six weeks to Abica, then spent a week at Jabon before taking a five-day journey to Tallapoosa, where the slavers had him work "in the ground" for three to four months. They then took Lamhatty on a six-week overland trek to Opponys before crossing the mountain over the course of a month to sell him to the Souaoukas (Shawnee). Lamhatty stayed with the Shawnee for six weeks before running away. He arrived at Andrew Clark's house near Christmas, stark naked and frightened. His arrival terrified the colonists, who "seized upon him violently & tyed him tho' he made no manner of Resistance but shed tears & shewed them how his hands were galled and swelled by being tyed before." Clark and company then tied one arm and brought Lamhatty to Lieutenant Colonel Walker of King and Queen County. Interestingly, Beverley stated that Lamhatty was quite comfortable at the Walker homestead but that "noe body can yet be found that understands his language." Instead Lamhatty tried to draw his story in the dirt. In a postscript, however, the story changed, as Beverley explained that Walker had other Towasa Indian servants or slaves (or those who spoke a similar language, at the very least) and that Lamhatty was "sometimes ill used by Walker." He added that the man became "very melancholy after fasting & crying several days together sometimes using little Conjuration," and when the weather improved with spring, Lamhatty made his escape.[104]

Lamhatty was but one victim of the Indigenous slave trade. In 1709 John Lawson described the manner in which raiding Indians marked slaves for the fields in Carolina and Virginia: "When they take a Slave, and intend to keep him to Work in their Fields, they flea the Skin from the Setting on of his Toes to the middle of his Foot, so cut off one half of his Feet, wrapping the Skin over the Wounds, and healing them. By this cruel Method, the Indian Captive is hinder'd from making his Escape, for he can neither run fast or go any where, but his Feet are more easily traced and discover'd."[105] In this same journal, Lawson also mentions a young Indian woman from the mountains whom he heard was sold as a slave in Virginia.[106] Lamhatty was just one of thousands of southeastern and Ohio Valley Indians taken captive in the English-sponsored slave raids.[107] The economy that ushered in this commercial trade in Indians slaves and skins led not only to upheaval and violence between settlers and Indigenous peoples but to intercolonial rivalries for dominance of the trade and Native alliances. Carolinians and Virginians would soon become embroiled in a number of violent conflicts that their trade had directly contributed to.

5 / The New Paradigm: Alexander Spotswood's Trade Policies

Long has the furious priest assayed in vain. With sword and faggot, infidels to gain, But now the milder soldier wisely tries By gentler methods to unveil their eyes. Wonders apart, he knew 'twere vain t'engage The fixed preventions of misguided age. With fairer hopes he forms the Indian youth To early manners, probity, and truth. The lion's whelp thus, on the Libyan shore, Is tamed and gentled by the artful Moor, Not the grim sire, inured to blood before.

—WILLIAM BYRD II, PROSE WORKS

The passage quoted in the epigraph, Byrd explains, was "not published during his [Spotswood's] administration for fear it might then have looked like flatter," making a sarcastic jab at his political enemy, Lieutenant Governor Alexander Spotswood. Byrd is probably referencing Spotswood's origins in English Tangier, Morocco, referencing the lion as representative of England. Spotswood represented a direct threat to Byrd's trade ambitions. With the 1710 arrival of Spotswood and a trade war with the Tuscarora, the tributary system began to crystallize as a means of expanding Virginia's influence beyond the trade and as Enlightenment-inspired leaders began to seriously consider proselytization as a way to influence and control Native allies. Native peoples of the Eastern Woodlands also saw opportunities with Spotswood's plans. But older traders, particularly William Byrd II, saw ways to monopolize the trade as Carolina traders moved north into the Chesapeake and piedmont. Conversion, expansion, and revision of the tributary system worked side by side with Virginia's rivalry with Carolina. Although the North Carolinians would ask for Virginians' assistance in the Tuscarora trade war, it is clear that there was no semblance of intercolonial alliance.[1] By the early eighteenth century, the Carolina settlers were firmly establishing themselves and extending their own skins and slave trade networks into the piedmont. Virginians had to determine where they fit into the trade, and between 1707 and 1711 a variety of problems arose between the traders of Carolina and Virginia. Eventually the rivalry made its way into the Virginia Assembly, which sought to protect its traders' interests. At the center of this discord lay the Virginian Robert Hix, who frequently traded south of the James River near Carolina settlements.

Hix consistently encountered problems with Carolina government officials, who were angered by activities of Virginia traders to the south and west. This culminated in the seizure of Hix's goods and his imprisonment by Charlestown authorities in 1708. Carolina traders viewed the Virginians as foreign competitors and sought to drive the Virginians out of the region and establish their control over Native allied trade.[2] The Virginia Executive Council visited this issue on April 28, 1708, when it heard the complaints of Hix, David Crawley, and several unnamed traders regarding what they viewed as the illegal seizure of their goods by the Carolinians. On November 2, 1708, the Virginia Council asked Hix to draw up an account of his seized furs and skins, with the intent of demanding reparations from Carolina.[3]

The disagreements over Carolina's treatments of Hix were minor compared to Virginia's involvement in hostilities between the Tuscarora and the Carolinians when the Tuscarora began attacking not only Carolina settlements but also residents of New Kent County in Virginia. The Executive Council suggested a ban on all Native trade on June 4, 1708, because of the Tuscarora's refusal to cooperate in a murder investigation and trial regarding the killing of Jeremiah Pate of New Kent County. The council required the Tuscarora to deliver members of their town—Charles, Stephen, and Will Mason—for trial; however, the Tuscarora continued to refuse.[4] The council extended the prohibition on October 26, 1708.[5] It did not work. Carolinian traders continued to provide the Tuscarora and other Southside Indians with guns. By banning all Native trade, the prohibition hurt the tributaries and Virginia traders, and eventually the Council lifted the order in 1709. This was partially in response to a petition from the Nansemond, Virginia's tributary ally, regarding a dire need for trade, especially trade in guns and powder. To address the Nansemond's concerns, the council sent Colonel Benjamin Harrison to all the tributaries to determine their needs. Naturally, of great importance were the demands of the traders, who feared their goods would "perish on their hands while the Inhabitants of North Carolina enjoy the benefite of the Indian trade."[6]

Virginia traders often ignored the tensions in the council regarding the Tuscarora and bans on trade and continued to make plans to trade Southwest. William Byrd II petitioned the council asking to open the Indian trade in the Southwest near Carolina in February 1709.

The council rejected the request, prohibiting trade with inhabitants of Carolina because of the Tuscarora murders and because hostilities were beginning to emerge between the Carolinians and the Tuscarora.[7] Other traders continued to request permission to trade in Carolina, asking for "free liberty to trade with all Indians whatsoever."[8] Taking matters into their own hands, Virginia traders often ignored the council's bans and consistently traded in what Carolinians believed was their territory until eventually both colonies petitioned to England for help in solving their quarrel. On June 16, 1709, William Byrd II learned that the queen had forbidden the Carolinians from meddling with the Virginia traders.[9] Consequently, the Virginia Council finally granted free passes to all Indian traders "at all times, in all places" to trade with the southern tributaries and the Tuscarora, thus supporting the expansion of the Virginia trade south toward Carolina.[10] Byrd remarked that skins sold for very little on August 31, 1709. The influx of skins was in part a result of the competitive trade between the two colonies.[11]

Under the leadership of the newly appointed lieutenant governor, Alexander Spotswood, the council met in 1710 and forbade the South Carolinians from interfering with Virginia traders, ordering reparations for an illegal bond the Carolinians had extorted from Robert Hix as well as the return of his goods.[12] This had no effect, and by September 5, 1711, Spotswood informed the council of the illegal actions of the colony of Carolina in preventing Virginians from entering its territory to trade with the Indians. The Carolinians, for their part, claimed that the Virginians illegally traded with Carolina Indians, mainly the Tuscarora, by supplying them with guns during a time of war.[13]

By the fall of 1710 the recurrence of trouble between the Meherrin and North Carolina led to Spotswood and his council seeking a permanent solution. A consistent point of tension between the Meherrin and North Carolina settlers was the southwestern border and Native alliances. The Virginians decided to determine the boundary between Carolina and Virginia by conducting an extensive set of interviews with Indians of the area about the bounds of the colonies. This discussion is particularly interesting because neither the Virginians nor the North Carolinians agreed to the boundaries of their colonies. The Virginia government sought depositions from the Weyanoke, Nottoway, Meherrin, and Nansemond.[14] This project lasted several years and coincided with the Tuscarora War and North Carolinian complaints about the Meherrin in February 1711. Colonel Edward Hyde, governor of North Carolina, alleged that the Meherrin disturbed the North

Carolina colonists between the Meherrin River and Wiccons Creek, a settlement three miles from the Indian town.[15]

Under the leadership and influence of Spotswood, the Virginians protected their tributary ally, saying that the Meherrin had reason to complain about the behavior of the residents of Carolina. Spotswood alleged that the North Carolinians were the aggressors, "disturbing the antient possessions of the Indians by their new encroachments." In addition, the Virginians insisted that the government of North Carolina respect Meherrin land claims. This, the Virginians argued, was a crucial portion of the presumption of tributary rights under the Articles of Peace and had to be maintained.[16] Why the Virginians chose this path is highlighted not only by intercolonial conflict but also by the expansive nature of the tributary system under the Spotswood regime. The Meherrin issue would continue to percolate through the next several years.

As Spotswood sought to reinvigorate the tributary system, he shifted his concerns from dealing with the Carolina governments to trying to entice several of the Tuscarora towns to become tributaries of Virginia, thus ensuring they would remain loyal customers of Virginia traders. On October 24, 1711, friendly Tuscaroras arrived at Nottoway Town. They asked to renegotiate for peace, offering six blankets for each enemy they killed and the "usual" price for slaves. As tributaries they promised to deliver children to be educated as Christians as a sign of fidelity. Nottoway Town was a site for many of the Iroquoian speakers; the Tuscarora were comfortable going there to find trade and allies. Later the Five Nations would also go to Nottoway Town. That being stated, the Nottoway stayed faithful to the English during the Tuscarora War and were subject to attacks by the Tuscarora for that stance. The Nottoway and Meherrin settlements acted as "buffers" for the colony along its southwestern border.[17]

The council drafted an agreement for a league of friendship with the friendly towns of the Tuscarora, since their spokespeople desired "nothing more than to continue in peace with this Government" and had intended to honor their agreement by providing children to the colonists. The Tuscarora spokesman explained that they were frightened because of recent hostilities that something might happen to the children along the way to colonial settlements.[18] The council believed the Tuscarora spokespeople and agreed to give them their asking price. As part of the peace negotiations, William Byrd II went to Nottoway Town. There he and the militia of the colony received the governor and showed "some part of our strength to the Indians."[19] Several of the tributary Indians arrived in town to meet the governor, and about thirty mounted militia volunteers went on to Saponi Town to meet the Tuscarora delegation.

Byrd's diary account of this event not only illustrates the efforts the Virginians made to show their supremacy to the visiting Indians but also Byrd's importance in the trade. On the day of his arrival he pursued Indian women "with which we played the wag." Depicting his own sense of self-importance, he tried to prove English superiority, writing that "when all the militia was drawn up he caused the Indians to walk from one end to the other and they seemed very much afraid lest they should be killed." After the show of English strength, Byrd, alongside Spotswood, enjoyed "a war dance by the men and a love dance by the women" as well as other displays from the Indian children. Later, after a hearty supper, the company of men raped an Indian girl named Jenny.[20]

This sexual violence speaks to the ways in which the overland English traders increasingly crossed intercultural borders as well. While many traders lived among the Indians and at times took Indian wives who volunteered themselves as cultural mediators, Byrd's actions highlight his sinister and domineering view of his trade.[21] Using Indian women as cultural brokers became a common practice in trade relationships between the English and the Indians of the Southeast. According to John Lawson, the Indians often provided the prettiest women to traders, and he further wrote that Indian traders working in the interior lived among the Indians, at times for years, often taking Indian women as wives. These women instructed the traders "in the Affairs and Customs of the Country." Indeed, Indian women of the Eastern Woodlands had a great deal of responsibility in the southeastern trade. As interpreters and advisors, the women utilized their power in the trade to gain status within their communities, and the children of marriages between English traders and Indian women often went on to positions of power in both English and Native communities. Through intermarriage, English traders gained intimate knowledge about the community and access to trade. An Indian wife also held a position of responsibility. Women became sources of information for foreign relations as well as trade because they could advise on what the traders were up to.[22]

The rape of Jenny speaks to Byrd's and the others' attitudes toward the rights of Native peoples. Byrd and his ilk were schemers and opportunists. So it should come as no surprise that diplomatic and trade relations with the Tuscarora failed by November 28, 1711, and the council declared war against all of the Tuscarora towns.[23] Diplomacy with the Tuscarora was tied directly to Spotswood's ambitions regarding trade regulations, and although his efforts failed in the short term, the hostilities provided him with the excuse to secure further regulatory measures. Spotswood wrote to the Council of Trade in 1712 regarding his plans for defense against the Indians and his attempt to resurrect the policy of limiting of trade to only those licensed.[24] The council agreed, suggesting that trade be limited by having traders post a three-hundred-pound bond and promise not to trade with the Tuscarora.[25] By July 1712 the only traders allowed to trade in the Southwest were Robert Hix, John Evans, David Crawley, Richard Jones, and Nathaniel Urven. In October 1712, for suspicion of trading with the Tuscarora, the council fined Gilbert and Adam Ivy ten pounds sterling apiece.[26]

By the end of 1712 the disagreement with North Carolina and the Meherrin remained unresolved. The Virginia Council received multiple reports of the Meherrin engaging in theft, killing of livestock, and firearms trade with the Tuscarora. However, a surprising report from Thomas Pollack, a colonist living on the Meherrin River, supported the future of the Meherrin as tributaries. Pollack felt that prior "misdeeds" should be forgiven, and he doubted the Meherrin would do further mischief to the Virginians.[27] His prognosis proved wrong when, on October 16, 1713, the council accused a Meherrin, Mister Thomas, of providing information regarding the English to the Tuscarora. Mister Thomas alleged that he was held by the Tuscarora against his will, and the council then allowed Thomas to be delivered to the Meherrin settlement until further proof could be found of the allegations against him.

Eventually the eight upper towns of the Tuscarora sought peace, but the talks stalled when the Virginians argued that the Tuscarora must deliver children to secure the peace. With the Carolinian defeat of the Tuscarora in March 1713, large numbers of Tuscarora fled to Virginia and allegedly began to attack settlements along the Roanoke River almost immediately.[28] The friendly upper towns of the Tuscarora continued to refuse to send hostages, and Spotswood sent trader Robert Hix to meet with the hostile Tuscarora. Assisting Hix was the Nottoway *weroance*, the Tutelo *weroance*, and a Saponi leader.[29] Reporting to the Lords Commissioners of Trade and Plantations on November 16, 1713, Spotswood reported that Hix found the Tuscarora "in very miserable condition, without any habitation or provision of Corne for their Subsistence" and in a state of despair.[30]

Two leaders of the Tuscarora (Haweesaris/Basket and Naroniackkos/George) returned with Robert Hix and requested tributary status that would include a trade agreement with the Virginians and a promise to provide children.³¹ The Virginians and the Tuscarora agreed to terms for peace on February 27, 1714. The Nottoway and Saponi who lived near the Tuscarora towns and who may have been involved in the late war also signed a separate treaty. Each group received a six-square-mile reservation in the hopes of consolidating Indian groups for settlement near trading forts.³² Spotswood had high hopes for this treaty, believing the Tuscarora needed Virginia's trade and fearing that they would return to Carolina.³³

Spotswood took this opportunity to forge new treaties with the Stuckanock and Occaneechee as well.³⁴ While it would appear that Spotswood had unbridled power in these negotiations, it is important to note that the Nottoway, Saponi, Tutelo, Occaneechee, Meherrin, Tuscarora, and Stuckanock all had a choice to make. Accepting the English tributary system brought with it promises of protection from Haudenosaunee raids and the violent slave trade in the Carolinas. In providing that protection, however, Spotswood altered the status of existing tributaries and added new ones by merging smaller groups, determining where the Indians could live, limiting their travel, and forcing the newly accepted tributaries to learn English and accept Christianity. Spotswood settled the Saponi, Stuckanock, Occaneechee, and Tutelo in southwestern Virginia as one village, describing them as a people speaking "much the same language but still different."³⁵ Similar motives led to the unity of other Siouan groups in December 1711 when the Saponi, Occaneechee, and Stegaraki petitioned for a tract of land north of the Meherrin River and the Tuscarora trading path. By April 1712 the Tutelo chief joined them at the new location, and the records referred to the nations collectively as the Saponi.³⁶ In contrast to previous policies, Spotswood did not immediately reopen trade with surrendering Indians, choosing instead to focus on restructuring the trade. The Tuscarora treaty eventually failed, but Spotswood allowed the remaining Tuscarora friendly to Virginia to merge with the Nottoway by an act of council on May 1, 1714.³⁷ The Virginians also continued to support the Meherrin's claims against North Carolina. When the Meherrin reported that North Carolina still expected tribute from them, the Virginia Council ordered the Meherrin to ignore the Carolinians' request.³⁸ The council moved to merge the Meherrin with the Nottoway, Saponi, Tutelo, Occaneechee, and Stuckanock and granted them some of the Tuscarora towns' tributary lands north of Blackwater Swamp on January 27, 1714.³⁹ The council formally merged the Meherrin with the Nottoway and the Nansemond with the Saponi on March 1, 1714, eventually moving them all to the site at Fort

Christanna.⁴⁰ This discussion highlights not only the Council's efforts to accommodate Indian allies but Spotswood's efforts to ensnare them within the sphere of influence he created by expanding the numbers of Virginia's Indian tributaries. The Meherrin fit into the machinations and schemes of the imperialist Spotswood and thus were necessary as partners in his Fort Christanna and Virginia Indian Company experiment, a part of his larger Atlantic goals for the British Empire.

It appeared to Spotswood that the late war with the Tuscarora had stemmed from their encouragement by the Haudenosaunee Five Nations to attack the southern colonies. Writing to the Earl of Dartmouth, Spotswood related the tale of Tom Blount, the chief man of one of the neutral Tuscarora towns. Blount had no desire to join the rest of the Tuscarora in war against the colonists and looked forward to the reopening of trade with Virginia.⁴¹ According to Spotswood, Blount confessed that during a Seneca attack, one of the Seneca "after having robb'd our Traders as they were going to the Western Indians, came to his Town and endeavour'd to perswade him and the other Neutral Towns, to joyn in attacking the So. Carolina Indians and raising the Siege." After this attack, a party of Virginia tributaries met the Seneca, killed several of them, and alerted Spotswood to the threat. Spotswood wrote to the governor of New York that "to endeav'or to discover these Robbers and obtain a reparation for the damages sustain'd by our Traders, which am't to upwards of a thousand pounds Sterling without that sett of Trader will be utterly ruin'd." Spotswood wrote the Earl of Dartmouth again on June 10, 1713, regarding the same subject, this time asserting that the "Mohacks and other Northern Indians" attacked the traders and took their cargo of goods.⁴²

The aftermath of the Tuscarora War saw a rearranging of Indian settlements south of the James River and along the piedmont at the urging of Lieutenant Governor Alexander Spotswood. The war also led to a further restructuring of Virginia's defense system under Spotswood's plan to create an Indian trade site at Fort Christanna.⁴³ Devastating Indian raids led to the overhaul of the military defense structure, employing rangers and Indian guides to police the borders. Concerned that the Seneca and Tuscarora posed a problem not only to the Carolinians but also increasingly to the Virginia tributaries and colonists, Spotswood sought to create a permanent buffer of tributaries to the south to protect the colony against further hostilities. The resettlement began with the return of the Saponi to Virginia and eventually led to the creation of new tributaries and the merging of various groups in Virginia and

Carolina. After the attacks by colonists on local Indians during Bacon's Rebellion, the Saponi had retreated to the mountains, but by 1708 they lived as tributaries under the Virginia government along the foothills of the mountains and subsequently moved to the Meherrin River for better protection from the Tuscarora.

Spotswood endeavored to win the confidence of a number of small groups fearful of the Tuscarora as well as slave raids and persuade them to move to Fort Christanna, a site on the Meherrin River, and to send their children to the College of William and Mary while he secured funding for a school at Christanna. The arrangement must have seemed mutually beneficial for the Saponi to agree to it; after all, Spotswood promised the safekeeping of their children and the benefit of direct trade with Virginia alongside protection from raids. Spotswood sought funding from the Society for the Propagation of the Gospel in Foreign Parts and the bishop of London, but since the endeavor fulfilled a trade and military function, he saved money by replacing the rangers on the south side with the fort of tributaries, funded in part by trade.[44] Spotswood pushed through the Act for Better Regulation of the Trade in 1714, creating the Virginia Indian Company and the settlement of Fort Christanna, intended as a borderlands buffer, trading post, and a place of education for friendly Indians.[45]

Spotswood had two goals in mind for his project: to regulate the English traders and to control the Indians. In part, Spotswood hoped to curb the traders' worst abuses of the Indians. He wrote to the Lords Commissioners on May 9, 1716, that regulation would keep Indians from "rambling amongst the English plantations," and by fixing the trade in one location where "all unjust and fraudulent dealing might be discovered," it would also encourage the recovery of the trade with the nontributary Indians, a trade hindered by the recent wars in the Carolinas. Spotswood engaged in a feud with the status quo of trade and Native affairs in the colony, particularly with William Byrd II. Spotswood also created a new court of oyer and terminer and sought to have stronger control over the London agent Nathaniel Blakiston.[46] Spotswood raged against the mistreatment of the Indians by unscrupulous traders, arguing that the Indians never attacked without provocation and frequently attacked only the plantations that they traded with—in short, contending that the traders caused these problems.[47] Virginia's control over its traders was something wholly new. Although the assembly had passed efforts to control traders before, they had been largely ignored, as traders sold guns and slaves and "laughed at efforts to stop them."[48] Spotswood argued that protection of the colonists must include keeping trade away from English settlements. This was partially in response to the Tuscarora War and unrest that would eventually lead to the Yamasee trade war in Carolina, but it was also in response to abuses by Virginia traders that Spotswood feared could cause strife in his own colony.

Although the assembly and county courts tried to restrict trade with Indians to designated markets and times of year, the Indians and their colonial neighbors frequently ignored these regulations. The traders increasingly grossly mistreated the Indians, placating them with liquor and swindling them in trade deals.[49] Chief among Spotswood's complaints against the traders was that they used alcohol to cheat the Indians and pay them unfair prices for skins. This, Spotswood alleged, caused the Indians to retaliate by murdering the traders who had treated them unjustly or by attacking the nearest English settler.[50] Spotswood felt that establishing a settlement of Indians away from the colonial settlements would prohibit Indians from gaining too much knowledge about the colonists and would also prevent the abuse of Indians, thus diminishing the threat of Indian retribution. He further hoped that a fort at Christanna would alleviate the threat posed to the periphery settlements by the Seneca and Tuscarora and would also reestablish Virginia trade.[51]

An overhaul of Indian affairs included the issue of Native conversion, focusing first on the nascent College of William and Mary and then the new fort. Education and proselytization in Virginia can best be described as an afterthought. Although some minor effort to convert Indians began with the settlement of Jamestown, the colonists focused on "civilizing" their Powhatan neighbors primarily by setting boundaries to settlements. Some discussion of teaching captive Indian children the English language as they learned useful trades such as carpentry or cobbling was a thinly veiled attempt to justify captive taking and the forced labor of Native children. As noted in previous chapters, Indian children became more readily available for English households after the 1646 peace. While agreements dictated that Indian children were not to be kidnapped, treated as slaves, or transferred to other families, the reality remains that Virginians blatantly ignored the law.[52]

Ten years passed before the colonial assembly further codified laws related to the taking of children and what should happen to those children brought into English homes, cautioning English settlers to "do their best to bring them up in Christianity, civillity and the knowledge of necessary trades."[53] In September 1656, as part of tributary agreements and as a sign of faith between the two parties, colonists and local Indians in Rappahannock County agreed to have Indian orphans sent to the English to be trained in Christianity.[54] By 1660, in order to encourage families to take in Indian orphans, the legislature allotted a twelve-hundred-pound allowance for each English family for the maintenance and education of Indian children.[55] Despite the guise of legality and repeated discussions of preventing the abuse of hostage children and regulations for their treatment, genuine efforts at educating Indian youth were sporadic.[56] The tributaries were coerced into giving up their children, and when given the opportunity to speak, they told of their pain in realizing that many of these children were sold into slavery.[57]

A renewed interest in conversion began with shifting concerns about the tributaries' fidelity to the colony and fear of Indians following the series of wars and skirmishes throughout the southeastern colonies. One proposed solution, intended to remove the threat of Indians, was to convert the existing Indigenous population, beginning with tributaries but extending to nontributary Indians as well. This changing perspective was coupled with a general rise in religious activity in the colony due to the arrival of a charismatic missionary and educator aligned with the bishop of London, who sought to bring spiritual vitality to the American colonies. The arrival of Reverend James Blair in 1685 marked a change in Virginia toward revitalizing the colonial Anglican Church and led to Virginia's first successful formal efforts at educating and converting hostage Indian children whom colonists hoped would become missionaries to their home communities.

Blair acted as the catalyst for the founding of the College of William and Mary in 1693, which eventually enrolled somewhere between two and twenty-four tributary Indians a year in its first fifteen years of existence.[58] At the college, the English instructors not only intended to teach the Indians the rudiments of reading and writing English but also sought to train these students as missionaries to convert the Native populace.[59] Blair later wrote a proposition for the "encouragement of the Christian Education of our Negro and Indian Children," which stipulated that the training of Indians should cover the Creed, the Ten Commandments, and the Lord's Prayer.[60] The philanthropist Robert Boyle, a director of the East India Company who contributed funds to missionaries throughout the British colonies, created a relatively large fund for Indian education at William and Mary. Yet despite his generous bequest, the colonists anticipated that they would need to find supplementary ways to finance the college. In October 1693 legislators sought to bring levies against the Indian trade in order to finance the school.[61] In addition, the colonists had to reapportion tributary lands in order to make room for the college by allotting twenty thousand acres of land from Pamunkey Neck and Blackwater Swamp from the Chickahominy.[62]

Despite efforts by the colonists to create a school where Indian children could be educated, tributaries were not eager to send their children to the college. Additionally, little evidence exists to support the claim that a majority of colonists supported the plan. At least one historian has argued that the college never seemed to have "a workable plan" for the education of the Indians.[63] According to the contemporary observer Reverend Hugh Jones, many of the young Indians, procured by the colonists with "much Difficulty," died, "often for want of Proper Necessaries and due Care taken with them."[64] The Brafferton estate records tell an optimistic story of hope for the college, indicating a desire to keep "soe many Indian children in Sicknesse and health in meat Drink Washing Lodgeing Cloathes Medicines Bookes and Educacon from the first beginning of Letters til they are ready to receive Orders and be thought Sufficient to be sent abroad to preach and Convert the Indians."[65] Tributaries feared the Indian slave trade, particularly the trade in children. Although Boyle endowed the college for the education of Indian children, most scholars agree that while some Virginians made clear attempts toward education, many children were sold into labor or died, never returning to their communities to proselytize. Thus Virginians had to coerce tributary Indians into turning their children over, and they bought nontributary children outright; the Boyle fund purchased "half a Dozen captive Indian Children Slaves and put them to the College."[66] Little is known about these first pupils of the college and whether they even survived, let alone successfully became missionaries.

Spotswood's plan to educate and convert the Virginia Indians was ambitious, and he intended to reach beyond the current tributary groups. In a letter to the bishop of London on November 11, 1711, he expressed hope that educating and converting the tributaries close to the colony would give the English a good start toward "a greater progress among those more remote, when they see the advantages these reap by it." He then described the negotiations with the upper Tuscarora towns and his plans for expanding Virginia's sphere of influence through tributary peace agreements that would bring more children into his school. Spotswood desired a plan of conversion and wanted to bring all Indians interacting with and moving through Virginia into peace agreements with the Virginia government, peace agreements that were contingent upon captive exchange. First he had to convince the tributaries to bring their children to the school, and he did so by focusing on halting the illicit Indian slave trade.[67]

Spotswood's plans to curb the abuses of the Indian slave trade inspired trust from the tributaries, and the Pamunkey sent twice the number of children required. Spotswood hoped that a complete overhaul of the trade would convince tributaries to send their children and to allow Native missionaries to proselytize to their communities.[68] In 1711 Spotswood decided to employ a different tactic. He remitted tribute of skins and furs to encourage attendance; if the tributaries sent their children, he would consider their tribute paid in full for the year. This persuaded a few tributaries, including the son of the *weronsqua* of the Pamunkey, to attend. The Nansemond, Nottoway, and Meherrin began to send children, and Spotswood anticipated that the Chickahominy would send their sons soon. So successful were Spotswood's "recruitment" techniques that the school had twenty-four Indian students in 1712 and soon depleted the Boyle endowment and Indian trade taxation funds. Spotswood hoped to eventually pay for the school by public levy: forty pounds of tobacco levied against every tithable person.[69] In the interim, Spotswood tried to solve the problem of funding by appealing to the General Assembly and then to financiers in England, including making a plea to the Society for the Propagation of the Gospel in Foreign Parts (SPG).[70]

In the spring of 1712 Spotswood needed external funds. He drafted exuberant letters about instruction of Indian children to the bishop of London, Henry Compton, and the archbishop of Canterbury. Although his plan to generate funding through a public levy had failed, he insisted that he had not "for that reason slackened my endeavors for the conversion of that people."[71] He informed the bishop of the current enrollment of fourteen students, with expectations of six more. Certainly this news should guarantee support from the SPG and the Anglican Church, which could not "imploy their Charity to better purpose than by laying such a Foundation for bringing a great many Souls to the Christian faith."[72]

While the bishop supported Spotswood's plans and attempted to influence the SPG on his behalf, Spotswood did not receive immediate funds and support. He tried again. Anxious and enthusiastic, he explained his master plan: each tributary town should send two sons of their "Chief men" to William and Mary. Once there, "instructed in Literature and the principles of Christianity, at the expence of the College," they would become missionaries to their own people. To encourage tributary involvement, Spotswood discontinued the required yearly tribute, "so long as their Children continued with us." Spotswood insisted that the children and their parents and other observers seemed "pleased" with this positive incentive to send children and expressed "much satisfaction with the care that is taken of them, and frequently lament their own misfortune in not having like advantages in their Youth." Despite his best efforts, Spotswood warned that the depletion of his funds threatened his lofty plans for the future. Monetary assistance from the SPG was essential to the conversion of the entire Virginia Indian populace, and he alluded to other SPG funding efforts in other colonies: "Every other plantation has been in a manner supplied [with monetary assistance for Indian conversion] at their charge."[73]

Spotswood's letter to the archbishop of Canterbury was no less impassioned in requesting assistance. In order to convert the entire Indian populace, Spotswood asserted, he would need one or two missionaries, of "good lifes and zealous in their Offices" to place at the largest of the Indian towns, where there "would be no hard matter to bring them all over in a generation or two from their own Pagan Superstitions to the true faith." Once settled there, missionaries could build churches and schoolhouses where they would not only teach the inhabitants of the town but also assist in teaching the Indians throughout the interior. Spotswood intended for all the legal trappings of English settlements to exist at these towns, allowing the missionaries to be the justices of the peace. This was an essential provision because the remoteness of the Indian towns from the English often caused their "frequent injurys [to go] unredressed, w'ch, in a great measure, irreconcile the Indians both to our Religion and Government." Spotswood rationalized that his system would prevent further injuries to the Indians and help in settling their disagreements with English settlers.[74]

Despite these elaborate plans, Spotswood had to put everything on hold when the colony became embroiled in the Tuscarora War in 1711. John Lawson, who eventually met his death at the hands of the Tuscarora, lamented the trade's effect on Native peoples, highlighting the ways the settlers and traders "let them walk by our doors hungry, and do not often relieve them. We look upon them with disdain and scorn, and think them little better than beasts in human form; while with all our religion and education, we possess more moral deformities and vices than these people do."[75] Poor trade relationships, the enslavement of the Tuscarora, and encroachments on their land led directly to the Tuscarora War.[76]

Ever the opportunist, even though he failed in his external fundraising efforts, Spotswood saw the trade war as an opportunity to cut costs and raise funds by himself by consolidating military rangers. Next he

Figure 4. Seal of Virginia, 1714 (Queen Anne).

hoped to use tributary settlements on the Carolina border as buffers. This buffer policy involved voluntarily and forcibly resettling tributary and nontributary Indians. He planned to use any excess funds for education efforts. Conditions in the region favored Spotswood's policy because many smaller Indian groups desired to move closer to colonial settlements for protection from raiding Indians in the piedmont.[77] While enrollment at William and Mary declined during the Tuscarora War, Spotswood continued in his efforts to regulate the Indian trade and develop a new frontier policy that would further his plans for Indian education, plans that would push the limits of his administration. In 1714 Virginia adopted a new seal that visualized Spotswood's goals for his colony under Queen Anne.

At Fort Christanna, Spotswood hoped to use tributary settlements as buffers against hostile Indian raiders. They, in turn, would benefit from the protection of the English militia and a robust trade. Even though the Tuscarora threat was subdued with their migration north after the Tuscarora War, in late 1713 the House of Burgesses approved Spotswood's plan. The Tuscarora War had inspired fear within the colony, but Spotswood hoped Fort Christanna would provide a remedy for these concerns and reinvigorate the trade. Spotswood insisted that his buffer plan would work to reorganize trade, protect residents and Indians on the south side of the James River, and create a better working relationship with Indians in Virginia.[78] To Spotswood, who was desperate to rein in the traders and develop his ideal, the education of Indian children would prepare the way for the conversion of the whole Native populace, which would, in turn, ensure the fidelity and compliance of Native elders. The colony had successfully built Fort Christanna by October 14, 1714.[79] To encourage the Indians providing children for education, Spotswood suggested to the bishop of London, he intended to combine trade with education, allowing Indians moving to Christanna or sending their children to William and Mary privileges to trade within the Virginia Indian Company, "which, by former Laws of the Colony, they were prohibited to do."[80]

In 1714 Spotswood himself visited the fort and successfully persuaded the Saponi, Tutelo, Occaneechee, and Nahyssan to occupy a tract on the south side of the Meherrin River. The relatively small size of Siouan polities in the Virginia piedmont made it difficult for them to defend themselves from raids, and thus an alliance with Virginia offered them a chance to find security and coalescence. By this time the Saponi included remnants of other, smaller Siouan towns devastated by Haudenosaunee-Iroquois and slave raids.[81] Despite the draw for some groups, other Indigenous polities resisted Spotswood's plans. In August 1715, after the Nottoway refused to hand over twelve of their children, the council held the Nottoway Great Men hostage until they sent their boys to Fort Christanna.[82] Emboldened, Spotswood added Carolinian Indians, the Sara and the Esaws (later known as the Catawba), to the list of Indians he intended to settle at Christanna.[83] That Spotswood would resort to kidnapping, violence, and bribery to get his way indicates his desperation to ensure the success of his plans.

The College of William and Mary sponsored the school at Christanna, and so desirous was Spotswood to succeed with his education schemes that he initially paid teacher Charles Griffin, a Quaker settler from North Carolina, fifty pounds a year out of his own pocket.[84] By all European accounts, Griffin had great initial success. Writing after the fact, the Reverend Hugh Jones recalled that the Saponi "adored" Griffin and that he was often lifted up into their arms as they hugged him with exclamations that they "would have chosen him for a King of the Sapony Nation."[85] Spotswood wrote a glowing report to the bishop of London. Indian children, he said, could now read and write "tolerably well" and repeat the catechism, and they knew "how to make their responses in ye Church" and showed "a great desire" to be baptized. Spotswood departed from previous policies by not requiring individual godparents for each child but instead allowing the schoolmaster to act as the godparent for the Indian children. Anticipating approval from the clergy, Spotswood was surprised by their refusal to grant permission to baptize the Indian children, on the grounds that they were not born to Christian parents. Hostility to Indigenous baptism reflected the colonial concept that Indigenous peoples were not capable of conversion because of their "hereditary heathenism," as described by Rebecca Anne Goetz with reference to Virginia. Goetz explains that the belief in "hereditary heathenism" was endemic among the locally born colonists but not among English-born men like Spotswood and Blair.[86] The contemporary observer Reverend Hugh Jones felt that objections to Native baptism could easily be "refuted, if the Persons be sensible, good, and understand English, and have been taught (or are willing to learn) the *Principles of Christianity* . . . [for] *Christianity* encourages and orders them to become more humble and better Servants." Jones was likely speaking of tributaries only, for he advised against baptizing "wild Indians" because it was "prostitution of a Thing so *sacred*."[87]

In early June Spotswood determined that the Saponi were in "good disposition" to have their children educated at the fort and believed "there is all human probability of the Success" of securing an alliance that benefited all while removing "their Savage principles and Heathenish Superstitions."[88] By October 26 many of the children could say the Lord's Prayer and the Apostle's Creed. A ten-year-old girl died before her baptism and Spotswood took it quite personally, as he had promised to be her godfather and was with her at the end, when "she seem'd to express her self with much concern that she could not see us." He opined, "I look upon the education of these Indians to be so feasible that I should be very sorry if it miscarry for want of a suitable support."[89] In 1716 he was happy to report to the Board of Trade that there were one hundred students at Fort Christanna.[90] Spotswood obviously had an agenda, but other observers of Christanna also utilized the site to push their own perspectives.

John Fontaine traveled with Spotswood in April 1716 for ten days. Fontaine, an Irish Huguenot who hoped to purchase land in the colony, provides some of the most detailed descriptions of regular trade and education activities at the fort and in the piedmont Southwest. Ultimately, Fontaine's assessment reveals his relative inexperience with Indigenous polities and the trade.[91] While it is unclear what Fontaine hoped to see, his assessment of the interior suggests his disappointment at the lack of influence the trade had on Virginia's tributaries. Clearly out of his element, he wrote, "We have no roads here to conduct us, nor inhabitants to direct the traveller." This was simply not the case. His journal referenced Indian settlements throughout the journey and encounters with Indians who all spoke English and had English trade items in their homes. Once at Christanna, Fontaine quickly gravitated to Charles Griffin, who impressed the naïve Fontaine with stories of his success. Learning of the lieutenant governor's arrival, the Saponi Great Men came to the fort. A large delegation—approximately two hundred men, women, and children—brought several skins to spread at the feet of Spotswood.[92] More comfortable speaking in Siouan, the Saponi asked for an interpreter so that they could discuss their grievances with the colony and other Indigenous groups, highlighting what they wanted out of Spotswood and the English.

Utilizing the trade and their position as tributaries, the Saponi hoped to bolster their own polities and ensure their safety and protection from enemies, both colonial and Native. Spotswood paid for damages from fraudulent English traders but the Great Men were particularly concerned about the "Genitos." Likely a Haudenosaunee raiding party, these warriors had killed fifteen members of a Saponi hunting party. This was not the first run-in the Saponi had had with Five Nations raiders and explains in part the Saponi desire for Virginian tributary protection. In 1701 a Saponi hunting party captured five "Sinnagers or Jennitos," likely northern Iroquoian raiders, described by one Saponi as "a Sort of People that range several thousands of Miles, making all Prey they land their Hands on." While the Saponi hoped to execute the five men, their allies, the Tutelo, had recently reclaimed several Tutelo prisoners from the Seneca, and in hopes of maintaining that peace, the Saponi agreed to return the five men. This exchange with Fontaine certainly indicates that the peace did not last. Spotswood refused to retaliate against the Genitos with colonial militia but instead promised the Saponi powder and shot so they could seek their own revenge.[93]

When younger members of the Saponi arrived later that day, Fontaine found himself continually surprised by their dress and mannerisms and again showed his utter lack of experience with Indigenous peoples, his tone vacillating from shocked awe to disgust throughout his journal. When describing the men, he said their outfits, hairstyles, and face paint made them appear like "so many furies." Spotswood appeared unfazed and comfortable with his Native tributaries, yet Fontaine, perhaps because of his newness to the area, seemed surprised by the young women, who were naked from the waist up with deerskins draped across their shoulders. As he looked the men and women over from head to toe, he thought their skin was ugly because they applied bear skin oil, but in other ways he seems oddly fascinated, writing that they were "straight, well limbed, good shape and extraordinarily good features as well the men as the women." Emboldened by his gaze, he apparently even tried to touch the women but was rebuffed: "They look wild and are mighty shy of an Englishman and will not let you touch them." This might result from previous English interactions with Saponi women, particularly Jenny, whom William Byrd and some other Englishmen raped during the Tuscarora War by getting her drunk, which Byrd said made her "good sport." Knowledge of this event would certainly affect Saponi responses to English men, and Fontaine would not have dared to boldly grope an English woman he was meeting for the first time.[94]

On April 17 Fontaine and Spotswood went to Saponi Town outside Fort Christanna. The settlement, although larger than previous Saponi dwellings, followed Saponi, not English, desires. Built in a cleared field along the Meherrin River, palisaded walls protected a circle of houses with a tree stump in the center.[95] Returning to the fort the next day, Fontaine had one more chance to be awestruck yet disturbed by the Indigenous people he encountered when Spotswood organized an archery event culminating in a "war dance." A musician sat in the middle of a ring playing a board with two sticks while singing a "doleful tune," sometimes "shrieking hideously, which was answered by the boys," as the Saponi danced in a circle to the rhythm of the music. Fontaine believed that the dance showcased the inhuman and barbarous nature of the Indians' war practices, by which the Saponi might surprise their enemies, and their "inhuman way of murdering all their prisoners, and what terrible cries they have when they are conquerors."[96]

One of the most important elements of Fontaine's journal is his description of trade. On April 20, ten Meherrin came to trade at the fort, bringing beaver, dear, and bear skins. Once the skins were delivered to the fort, the Meherrin refused to stay, opting instead to stay in the woods overnight.[97] Relating to the trade is Fontaine's glossary of Indian words, possibly in the trade language Robert Beverley alluded to in his 1705 history, which Beverley called "a sort of general Language."[98] Many of these words and phrases were necessary for the simplest elements of dialogue in a trade relationship, such as greetings, "Jog de log" (How d'ye do?), "Kihoe" (Come here); numbers, "Nacout, Tock, Nos," (one, two three); and names for trade items, "Mahinkt" (shot bag), "Tabike" (powder horse), or "Mosnukhe" (otter). However, the nature of this list is telling in and of itself. It is a trade list at first glance, but it also reflects the nature of social interaction, especially concerning sexual relations within a multiethnic trade town. Such phrases as "Ke ly pomerin" (Will you kiss me?), coupled with "Conopana" (Come to bed) and "Mihu mima mikito" (my dear wife), speak to exchanges other than trade.[99]

Spotswood and Fontaine left the fort on April 21, to the sound of cannons firing, and several Indians from Saponi Town assured Spotswood that they were sorry to see him go "but that they would guard him safe to the Inhabitants."[100] Spotswood's official letters to the bishop of London and to the Lords of Trade make no mention of this journey with Fontaine, yet by May he was writing to the bishop about his successes at Christanna, expanding settlement in the region, and its positive effects on his proselytizing efforts, adding that he could not fathom an endeavor more worthy of funding and support than the conversion of the Indians in Virginia.[101]

Despite his proclamations of great successes at Christanna, ultimately the fate of the fort and its Indian inhabitants became mired in the discourse on the Virginia Indian Company and Spotswood's enmity with William Byrd and his Executive Council. In an April 16, 1717, letter to a William Popple of the Council on Trade, Spotswood related the precarious nature of south side settlements and again related the need for conversion and ordered Indian settlement at the fort. This time, however, Spotswood emphasized the threat of individual English traders inflaming the South Carolina Indians and the Seneca. Spotswood again became passionate regarding his beloved project as he described the death of a number of Catawba and others who brought eleven children to Christanna. A party of Seneca attacked the Catawba at night, killing five of them, wounding two, and carrying off an additional five prisoners. The Catawba were "highly enraged at this insult," feeling that the English had some part in it, and it was "with abundance of difficulty, and not without running some hazard in my person," that Spotswood was able to persuade them to leave their children at the fort.[102] The Catawba were part of Spotswood's trading and diplomatic strategies to further lure southern Indians into the tributary system. Describing his efforts with the Catawba, he wrote that he convinced them to send children for education as part of a promise to live in peace with the Virginians. He blamed the English traders for this attack, describing them as "some loose fellows" who, while carrying on an illegal trade with the Tuscarora, informed the Seneca of the Catawba arrival at Christanna, which then "thereby encouraged the one to fall upon the other." He included this information to show that he was not at fault for this failure, to persuade the Lords of Trade of the necessity to back him on the Virginia Indian Company and Fort Christanna, and to take aim at his foes, the English traders, to show "how little regard [they] have to the Peace of this Country."[103]

Byrd, a powerful Indian trader, member of the Executive Council, and Spotswood's greatest foe in the colony, had quite a bit to say. Byrd led the charge against the company and became the one with whom Spotswood most frequently came to vicious verbal blows over the Virginia Indian Company and the Christanna experiment. While Spotswood envisioned an orderly Indian settlement at Fort Christanna and a regulated Indian trade company, Byrd (likely angry that he was repeatedly denied trade monopolies) sought to destroy Spotswood's visions that were directly contrary to Byrd's desires. Reflecting on the total effect of Spotswood's efforts, Byrd agreed that tributary students knew how to read and write and understood some of the principles of Christianity but argued that the conversion was only skin deep. Tributaries did not serve as missionaries to their own people, as Spotswood had hoped.[104] Instead, after they returned home, Byrd believed, they almost immediately relapsed into what he referred to as "infidelity and barbarism." Byrd felt that Griffin enthusiastically took to instructing his pupils and was met with affection from his pupils. Yet Byrd also lamented that in the end, "all the pains he had taken among the infidels had not other effect but to make them something cleanlier than other Indians are." Education could even prove dangerous, as the Indians learned instead to dislike the English and, so aggrieved, became "more vicious and disorderly than the rest of their countrymen." Considering it prudent to keep an eye on Native tributaries in order to prevent any hostilities, Byrd likely was reflecting on his own mistreatment of Native peoples as well as the trade wars of the past.[105]

Byrd, for his part, felt that Spotswood's efforts were too little too late and that the only way to really succeed at converting the Indians was through intermarriage. He also apologized that he could not provide a better account of the "poor Indians." This says quite a bit about Byrd's self-perceived ownership over the bodies of his Native traders and the tributaries. He felt that all men had the "same natural dignity" and that Indian wives "would have made altogether as honest wives for the first planters as the damselfs they used to purchase from aboard the ships." Byrd completed his thought by disparaging the English women sent to the colonists as wives, writing, "'Tis strange, therefore, that any good Christian should have refused a wholesome, straight bedfellow when he might have had so fair a portion with her as the merit of saving her soul."[106]

Unhappy with the idea of regulation and wanting to wholly control the enterprise themselves, the traders balked at the purchase of Virginia Indian Company stock. Desperate, Spotswood had to convince members of his council to buy shares.[107] Ultimately, the Virginia Indian Company failed because of opposition within Virginia, especially from Byrd, who went to London and with the help of merchant Micajah Perry agitated against legislation supporting the company. Additionally, the counties of Surry, Isle of Wight, Charles City, King and Queen, Norfolk, Prince George, Nansemond, Henrico, and Warwick all sent grievances to the House of Burgesses in 1715 against the Act for Better Regulation.[108] Spotswood enthusiastically petitioned the Lords Commissioners of Trade and Plantations on behalf of his company and argued to the Lords Commissioners that the company would benefit Virginia, the trade, and the Crown.[109] He boasted that since the inception of the Virginia Indian Company and the settlement of Fort Christanna, there "has not been one murder committed on the Frontiers, and scarce a Complaint of any Injury on either Side." Spotswood argued that the success of the company was in the best interest of the colony and would allow better intercourse between Virginia and South Carolina, allowing Virginia to reclaim trade with the southwestern Indians and have recourse against the Carolinians for seizing private traders' goods. The Lords Commissioners were not swayed by his argument.[110] In the document "Advice to the freeholders of the several Countys in Virginia in their Choice of Representatives to serve in the Approaching Assembly," the anonymous author makes it clear that "Spotswood's schemes were a general assault upon Virginia rights."[111]

The Lords of Trade proclaimed that trade companies never contributed much to the conversion of Indians, as evidenced by the Royal African Company, the Dutch East India Company, and others. Instead, the Lords of Trade wrote, these companies had a history of instigating wars in the name of private gain that in the end proved to be a great dishonor to the name of Christianity. Spotswood hoped to stave off the closing and dismantling of the fort, writing to the Lords of Trade that the fort at Christanna had been "so usefull to the Security" of the tributaries and English settlers in the region that "the slighting therof would have proved of ill consequence." He argued that it would be dangerous to disperse the Indians, in part because of threats by the Five Nations to the safety of the peripheral settlements. Spotswood related that he planned to maintain the fort until at least April 23, 1718, when the assembly could meet to decide a course of action.[112] Even so, in May of that year the House of Burgesses determined that the fort was no longer necessary for the maintenance of the colony's borders and resolved that the government should send home the Indians of Christanna with trade goods in order to preserve their friendly relationship to the Virginia colony.[113]

The demise of the Virginia Indian Company and the closing of the fort left Spotswood to secure the safety of Virginia colonists and Indians by seeking diplomatic relations with the Five Nations. A treaty whereby the Five Nations agreed not to travel west of the mountains further made Fort Christanna obsolete, and the Virginians made plans to return Catawba children to their homes and to disperse the other Indian settlers. Local histories of the area allege that the Saponi and Tutelo remained there until 1740, when they moved to Pennsylvania and joined the Haudenosaunee.[114]

Virginia Indians were in a strained position regarding their interaction with the English. Clearly they were ambivalent at best about receiving an education from the English and moving to places such as the College of William and Mary and Fort Christanna. The colonists forced the tributaries to provide Indian children as hostages as part of the process of negotiating tributary relationships. Certainly there was an economic incentive motivating Indians to sign tributary agreements that offered to access to trade goods and protection from their enemies. Learning the English language and converting to Christianity provided Indians with abilities to navigate the English world, skills that would help them secure employment as traders and interpreters—increasingly lucrative professions. Another factor that needs to be considered is why piedmont Indians who were autonomous from Virginia agreed to move to Christanna in the first place. The answers lie in the slave trade and the shatter zone. With the arrival of the English Carolinians, piedmont Virginia and North Carolina Indians were surrounded by slavers and were very vulnerable to attacks by armed raiders as well as to disease. It is very likely that Christanna provided a place of refuge from these attacks and diseases. The Indians relied on the promise of Spotswood that their children would be educated and not enslaved. But when what they saw as a way to avoid the slave trade ultimately resulted in their children's enslavement, Spotswood's plan lost its appeal.

6 / Peace at Albany: 1722

The Tuscarora War (1710–14) established Carolinians as the primary Indian agents and traders, yet Virginians under the leadership of Spotswood still tried to maintain and build new alliances with local Indians through the Virginia Indian Company and later through intercolonial negotiations for peace. One can see that Indigenous peoples attempted to utilize colonial frameworks to their advantage, while colonial leaders sought to use Native alliances to exploit and gain power in order to rise in the ranks of colonial society. Haudenosaunee-Iroquoian paths cut south through the fall lines east of the Appalachians on their way to Catawba country. Before Bacon's Rebellion, Maryland aligned itself with the Susquehannock, leading to Iroquoian attacks on Tidewater settlements. Realizing that alliances with a smaller group could not ensure their protection, colonists eventually sought to come to terms with the Five Nations. With their defeat and incorporation into the Five Nations, the Susquehannock became the southern door of the Longhouse, keeping the raiding path open.[1]

Through intercolonial cooperation, the goal for the colonial governments was to end the mourning wars' devastation of trade and settlements. The English repeatedly failed to understand Haudenosaunee motivations, nor could they understand that the Five Nations were "not an empire, nor was it a monarchy," but an alliance of migrants with varying degrees of control over its members. Eventually Shawnee migrants from the Carolinas moved north to Pennsylvania and joined this alliance.[2] For many smaller groups, "voluntary absorption" held the promise of a better future, without the expectation of "harassment and servitude among the English."³ They too had reason to raid south, mainly to attack the Catawba in South Carolina. Shawnee natives newly settled along the Susquehanna River in Pennsylvania took advantage of the opportunity to raid and exact revenge in retribution for Catawba slave raids against the Shawnee in the Carolinas.⁴ With a pluralistic set of Indigenous entities, each with their own motivations for engagement in mourning raids, one can see that an effort by multiple colonies and Indigenous groups was necessary to ensure peace.

In 1677 Virginian representative Colonel Henry Coursey went to Iroquoia to ask the Haudenosaunee to stop their attacks on Virginia and Maryland. Treaties of peace and friendship with the Five Nations Haudenosaunee were signed throughout the colonial period, most notably with the 1677 silver Covenant Chain.⁵ The efficacy and enforcement of these treaties showed that agreements with the English held little power over Indigenous militarized polities, as the Five Nations and their allies ignored them and raided south through the piedmont with ease and frequency. A sustained interest in greater control over the English empire and in intercolonial cooperation led to a rise in new leadership in the American colonies in the postrestoration era. Alexander Spotswood and his generation of colonial leadership typified the increased interest by the Lords Commissioners of Trade and Plantations. All along the Atlantic seaboard, English colonists fought the peripheral wars of the empire, particularly with France: King William's War (1689–97), followed by Queen Anne's War (1702–13), and then King George I's War (1722–24). With the French utilizing Native alliances to attack English settlements in the wars of empire, coupled with colonial Indian trade conflicts such as the Tuscarora War and the Yamasee War, an era of fear highlighted the need for intercolonial cooperation for protection against Indian threats.

In this age of anxiety and violence, Spotswood once again sought to exploit his advantage. One could make the argument that this typified Spotswood's viewpoint of Virginia as a whole, that he was not a visionary idealist but an opportunist, one who saw the need for intercolonial cooperation and a new system of governance that would fit the maturing colony in the new age of empire. From his first entrance into Virginia politics, Spotswood made clear that his primary goal was to secure the borders and, as noted in prior chapters, he met with great opposition from the Virginia Council in his efforts to organize the trade and reorganize protection of the borders. Intercolonial cooperation proved necessary to facilitate a new system and Spotswood, ever the persuasive politician, once again undertook a vigorous letter-writing campaign against his detractors and in search of support for his ideas. In defense of the Virginia Indian Company and his rearrangement of the ranger system, Spotswood wrote to the Lords Commissioners of Trade and Plantations on February 7, 1716, to answer allegations leveled at him by Virginians. Of interest is the third query, accusing Spotswood of a "high Misdemeanour" for building two expensive forts, one on the James River and one on the Rappahannock, "only to support two private Interests, in both which he is principally concerned."[6]

In characteristically emotional and superfluous Spotswood fashion, the lieutenant governor responded vehemently to the "Querist" by correcting the writer on the location of one fort: "Had he been witness of the many painfull Marches I have taken through the uninhabited Woods to contrive for the Security of the Frontiers, he might have known that the ffort he speaks of stands above an hundred Miles from where he places it." Spotswood conceded that he did build a fort on the Meherrin River, one he felt was necessary to "oppose the incursions of the Northern Indians," namely, the Five Nations. He also argued that his undertaking of the fort was "by my frugall Contrivance, been defray'd by little more than the sum which the Assembly had usually given for one year's defence of the Country." At issue for Spotswood was that the old system of protection was cumbersome, expensive, and simply did not work. In a frustrated, exasperated, and at times annoyed tone, he makes it clear that the traders and Virginia politicians who lobbied against him were not considering the larger picture. By employing rangers only, the Virginia colony was "continually alarmed in all quarters" by murders and violent attacks. In 1713 alone more than twenty people were killed or taken by the Indians, and Spotswood joyfully boasted that his project had stopped this violence: "Our outward Inhabitants have not been disturbed with so much as one single alarm." He also argued that to "procure this Tranquility to the Country," he gave up his own safety and comfort to traverse the countryside to see where the fort should be built and to observe how the fort progressed.[7]

Further on in the letter he answers allegations about Fort Christanna as well and claims that he furnished his own funds "without receiving or expecting any gratification for the same." His only concern was "putting this Country in a better posture of defence," in response to the late wars in Carolina and the upheaval in the piedmont.[8] The forts along the borders responded to the Tuscarora War and the Yamasee War. They were intended "to bring those Pagans to our Terms," he said, by letting them see "our Demands back'd with a Force."[9] Indian affairs and the safety of the colony were the subjects of yet another letter to the Lords of Trade in September 1716, where he wrote about the resolves of the House of Burgesses. In response to an accusation that "ye People have more at heart than I the safety and Dignity of this Colony," he states not only that his intentions are contrary to these accusations but "'tis very notorious" that he had voluntarily gone "when the Frontiers were most infested by the Indians" to several counties and tried to muster the militia. He gathered only two hundred willing men, at great hardship, for "even upon great pay . . . notwithstanding their Wives, their Children, and all they had, lay then at Stake, even tho' I called to some whose Father's Blood had been newly spilt by those Savages," many still refused to muster.[10]

All of Spotswood's impassioned posturing to the Lords Commissioners of Trade and Plantations related back to the failing Virginia Indian Company and his grand designs for the colony. Late in the experiment with the fort at Christanna, as mentioned in the previous chapter, a number of Catawba and other Natives arrived with eleven of their children to enter into education and trade agreements. A party of Seneca attacked, killing five adult Indians, wounding two, and capturing five as prisoners. While the Natives who were attacked initially were angry at Spotswood, he convinced them it was no fault of the English. Spotswood wrote to Secretary of State Paul Methuen that despite a peace agreement signed in 1685 between the Virginians and the Five Nations, the mourning wars and raids continued along the piedmont. In the year 1713 alone, the Seneca robbed Indian traders of their goods on numerous occasions, murdered a "Gent'n of Acco't" in the outer plantations, stole slaves, and "now threaten to destroy our Tributary Indians." In short, Spotswood concluded that the relationship with the Seneca required "Reparation" and "that those Senequas [need to] be made to understand that those presents that have on diverse occasions been made to them at a very great expence to the Crown" were given not only on behalf of the people of New York but on behalf of all the colonies.[11]

The repeal of the Act of Trade and Virginia Indian Company along with the planned closing of Fort Christanna left the Virginia piedmont in a perilous condition, in Spotswood's opinion. Although his tenure of office was insecure and his successors might not agree with his intentions, his plan for posterity was a permanent answer for Indian affairs.[12] To that end, Spotswood had to figure out a way to handle the Haudenosaunee raids. Spotswood's last major act regarding Indian affairs as lieutenant governor of Virginia was to make one final attempt to secure the piedmont by endeavoring to enter into a new agreement with the Seneca, in collaboration with Pennsylvania, New York, and Maryland. He wrote of this project to another of the secretaries of state, Joseph Addison, in August 1717. Writing that the colony had had a break from the problems of the pirates (namely, Blackbeard), he opined that the only danger the colony faced was "from the Northern Indians."

Spotswood intended to travel to Philadelphia to meet with the governors of the three other colonies affected by Five Nations raids, with the approval of the Executive Council of Virginia.[13] To illustrate the need for this meeting, he wrote again that same month to the Lords Commissioners of Trade and Plantations about the Catawba incident. In this particular letter, he gives further insight into the event that a few Virginia traders, "some loose fellows" who were carrying on an illegal trade with the Tuscarora towns, had told the Five Nations about concerning the arrival of the Catawba. Spotswood punctuated his remarks by again bringing up the regulation of the trade, noting that men such as these had "little regard" for the "Peace of this Country."[14] In 1717 Spotswood traveled to Philadelphia and New York to stop the Iroquois from moving south through Virginia Native territory. Spotswood suggested that the Haudenosaunee might carry official passes and travel only west of the mountains, while the Virginia Indians would stay in the east. He believed that the New Yorkers were "insufficiently attuned to Virginia interests," and thus he proposed negotiations at Swift Run Gap instead of Albany "as the official center of contact with the Iroquois." Unfortunately, "the new rendezvous point had yet to be built" and the Haudenosaunee, the colony of New York, and the Board of Trade rejected the idea.[15] Writing later of this conference with the governors of Maryland and Pennsylvania, Spotswood remarked that they were in complete agreement "that there could not be a more proper Season to bring those Indians to reasonable terms than now," since the English were at peace with the French.

Captain Christopher Smith of Virginia went north to the Haudenosaunee and got them to admit to their attack on the Catawba but could not get them to agree to any sort of reparations.[16] While Spotswood did not have an opportunity to speak directly to the sachems of the Five Nations, Governor Robert Hunter of New York intended to speak with them that spring, and Spotswood hoped for positive results.[17] On May 9, 1718, the House of Burgesses discussed a letter from Spotswood in which he spoke of the attack made on the Catawba, the 1677 Middle Plantation Treaty with the Virginia Tributaries, the original Covenant Chain with the Haudenosaunee, and how the Treaty of Middle Plantation entitled tributaries to the English government's protection from the northern Indians.[18] Here Spotswood was campaigning for support from the assembly.

Later that month the House of Burgesses discussed a Catawba woman reclaimed from the Five Nations. The Virginians had sent Christopher Smith to Albany to reclaim her, but she had escaped from the Haudenosaunee on her own and hid "upwards of five Months in the Woods she came in almost famished to a Plantation on the head of James river." A man named John Hughes took her in and protected her, and he had petitioned the House of Burgesses for a reward.[19] On May 20, 1718, the burgesses resolved that the governor and council should set forth to "determine what further measures shall be taken" to preserve a peace and "friendship" with the northern Indians.[20]

The topic was revisited again May 22, when the House of Burgesses ordered a letter be sent to Spotswood saying, "Wee return yor Honour our hearty thanks for yor goodness in giving this House Such Early notice of the motions of the Indians to the Norward against the Tributarys of this Government."[21] When the Executive Council met on May 28, 1718, to "determine what Measures shall be taken to preserve the Friendship of the Northern Indians," they resolved to put the decision off until the opinion of the House of Burgesses could be known.[22] At their May 31, 1718, meeting, based on discussions with Spotswood about the meeting with the governor of Pennsylvania, the burgesses advised that "since the said Northern Indians have given some satisfaction for the breach of their former Treaty and have also given assurances for their future observance thereof," there was no need to enter into a new treaty with the northern Indians. It was also at this meeting that the council discussed the dismantling of Fort Christanna and the need to send back the Catawba Indian children housed at the fort.[23]

Despite their beliefs that problems with the Haudenosaunee were at an end, the June 27 meeting indicates otherwise. With the chaos of dismantling the fort at Christanna arrived reports that the guards were acting in a "mutinous and disorderly manner, refusing to do the Duty of Sentinells." This was a concern because "the Northern Indians are on the Frontier & seem to have a Design on that Place." The council ordered Captain Robert Hix of the late Virginia Indian Company to apprehend the former guards.[24] The Haudenosaunee had allied themselves with the

Tuscarora in the recent war in North Carolina. They also frequently sided with the Meherrin and Nottoway against the Saponi, whom Spotswood sought to protect as tributaries of the Virginia colony. Thus the 1717 raid on the Saponi and others at Fort Christanna was a genesis of Spotswood's Iroquoian plan but not the only stimulus.[25]

In September news arrived at the Virginia council of rumors in North Carolina that both Seneca and Tuscarora Indians planned to attack a number of settlements in Bath. This story came from an Indian slave owned by a Mr. Worseley, whose plantation was alleged to be a target. With this advance warning, the settlers exchanged some fire with the Seneca, leaving the plantation unharmed. Relating to events in Virginia, the council heard word that the Seneca were demanding the Saponi Indians housed at Christanna be delivered to them. Spotswood advised the council that he had had the Saponi "taken into the Fort for their Protection." In response to those actions, Spotswood related that "the Senequas had made Overtures of Peace and the Saponies have accordingly made a kind of Treaty with them whereby they are to cease all hostilitys on both sides." He asked the council to advise whether a meeting of the assembly was necessary to reflect on the recent events, but they were of the opinion that it was a bad time of year to meet and that with the recent agreement with the Saponi and Seneca, there was no pressing need to meet.[26]

In his August 1718 letter to the Board of Trade, Spotswood related news of the meetings of the council and warned that the northern Indians were likely to bring "disturbance, w'ch may be expected, that their Partys being very numerous in our Frontiers."[27] Later in that same letter he opined on the defense of the borders from Indians who lived to the west and around the Great Lakes. In his expedition over the mountains in 1716, he related, he found Lake Erie to be but five days' march from the western edge of the foothills. Spotswood encountered "a great Nation of Indians living on a River w'ch discharges itself in the Lake Erie." With this information, Spotswood informed the Board of Trade of the threat of French-allied Indians in the Great Lakes and piedmont and the importance of establishing settlements in the Great Lakes to block the passes through the mountains.[28]

In a letter dated September 27, 1718, Spotswood informed the Board of Trade that the security of the borders was of the utmost importance, especially since the fall of the Virginia Indian Company. The Five Nations, allied with the Tuscarora, had murdered a man at one of the outer plantations and posed a grave danger to the colony of North Carolina. Spotswood levied allegations against his council in this letter, writing that "whatever may befall this Government of its Neighobours from those Indians, w'll be imputed to the obstinacy of Virginia." Highlighting his increasing frustration, he added, "I must plainly charge it on y't factious party in the Council here who rather chuse to ruin their Country than to Second any Measures I project for the King's Service, or the publick benefit."[29]

The Seneca appeared again in the discussions of the council in April 1719, when Spotswood related an allegation made by the Great Men of the Nottoway against an English colonist from Henrico County. According to Spotswood, the Great Men alleged that one of their nation had been killed by an unknown English man, but upon his investigation he found that the dead man had likely been drinking alcohol and had accidentally fallen into a creek and drowned. Spotswood thought it necessary, however, to promise to the Nottoway that he and his council would make further inquiries into the man's death, because the Seneca were at Nottoway Town and "it may not be fitt to give the Nottoways any cause to believe themselves Slighted herein, least they Should persuade the Senequas to revenge the Quarrel by the murder of some of the English." The council voted unanimously in favor of Spotswood's plan as the "most prudent answer," pledged a speedy inquiry into the matter, and promised to give due satisfaction to the Nottoway if they found any indication that the man's death was the fault of the English. They called the Great Men of the Nottoway in to relate this and the Nottoway then informed the council that the Seneca desired "a passport for their more Convenient travelling through the Inhabitants of this Country in their return home." Spotswood and his council related to the Nottoway that they would be pleased to provide the Seneca with papers if they would come to Williamsburg and "Satisfy him of their being in Friendship" but added that Spotswood could not provide the passport and "permit any Indians to pass through the Inhabitants of this Country of whose friendship and Peaceable condition he was not well assured."[30]

It appears that the Seneca did not comply with this request, as by May 28, 1719, the council heard the complaint from Essex County of Mr. Lawrence Tallafero, who on May 10 encountered fifty Seneca at his residence. The Seneca "took away all the Provisions they found there" and informed him that 350 more Indians were in the foothills of the mountains, on their way back north after raiding the southern Indians. The governor responded that he could not take action against the Seneca because of the resolution of the council dating back to May 31, 1718, which provided "that no measures should be entred into with the

Northern Indians untill they should Commit actual Hostilitys on the Inhabitants of this Colony and he did not know whither the Gent who were of that Opinion then would judge the Plundering a House such an Act of Hostility." One has to wonder here what the colonists would define as "actual Hostilitys" if the destruction of a household and theft of provisions was not. The meeting was complicated by the arrival of Wittmannitacighkee, chief man of the Catawba, and five of his nation. He had not brought an interpreter, but the council sent for one in order to learn what he needed and put aside the Seneca issue until further information was known.[31]

Almost in answer to Spotswood's query, petitions arrived later that spring of 1719 from New Kent and Henrico Counties, where the inhabitants felt they were in "great and eminent Danger" from the northern Indians marching south on raids. Spotswood also included a letter from the governor of Pennsylvania, William Keith, relating that the Five Nations, along with some tributaries of Pennsylvania, intended to "Try the Strength of the English at the fort of Christanna." According to Keith, the Cayuga Nation "plainly declared That they expected a Free recourse for their People through the English Plantations while they were making Warr on their Enemys." Spotswood asked the council what measures the colony should take for the protection of its outlying settlements. One might imagine that he was a bit terse in this discussion, as he related that the methods he had pursued—namely, the founding of the Virginia Indian Company and the construction of Fort Christanna—had kept the colony protected and "Free from any Disturbance" for "five or six years past" but that these measures "were faulted by the last General Assembly" and the council had yet to come up with new protective measures.

The council, for its part, considered these new developments a threat to the colony and proposed a series of responses to Haudenosaunee actions. First, should the northern Indians attack Christanna, the governor should order the neighboring counties' militias to repel them by force in order to protect the tributary Indians still settled at the fort as well as the colonists in the area. Second, in regard to Haudenosaunee passing through the area on their raids south, the militia should protect the colonists but not attack unless the Haudenosaunee "begin Hostilitys," and the militia should provide themselves with arms and ammunition. Third, the militias of the various outer counties should endeavor to meet with the parties of Indians marching through and advise them, in a friendly manner, not to go near English settlements. Should the Indians not take heed of these warnings, the militia officer should send word to the governor immediately. Fourth, given that the Nottoway often housed the Haudenosaunee and were tributaries of the Virginia government, they should advise the governor immediately if the northern Indians arrived. Additionally, the council asked the Nottoway to advise the Haudenosaunee not to go near English settlements and ordered the Nottoway to provide no further trail guides to the northern Indians. Finally, the council advised the governor to write to the governor of New York, a task that Spotswood noted he had already undertaken.[32]

William Thornton of Richmond County reported sighting eight northern Indians in July 1719, informing the council that the Indians had been "for some time Skulking about" and had raided several houses. No mention was made at this council about a redress of settler grievances on this issue.[33] The council met again that fall to discuss a report from a commission on Indian affairs at Albany that intriguingly related an allegation by the deputies of the Five Nations that "one of the principal Men of Virginia desired them to fall on the Indians Settled at Christanna" and had paid them with powder and lead for their troubles. Spotswood asked the council to again consider a full diplomatic proposal of peace with the Five Nations, but again the council deferred consideration until more members of the council could be present.[34]

Steps to secure a peace agreement progressed slowly. At its November meeting the council considered the needs of the Virginia tributaries—namely, the Nottoway, Meherrin, and Saponi. They directed the Great Men of these three groups to attend a December council meeting and in the weeks leading up to that meeting to "forbear Hostilitys on one another on any pretence whatsoever." At issue was the enmity between the Saponi and the Tuscarora. The council ordered an interpreter sent to the Saponi and Henry Briggs to the Tuscarora to inform them of the council's knowledge of Tuscarora activity against the Saponi. The Great Men of the Tuscarora were also to attend the December meeting, and the governor promised "Protection in their coming and returning" to the Tuscarora. Henry Briggs was to inform any leaders of the Five Nations that he found present at the Nottoway or Tuscarora towns as well.[35]

On December 9, 1719, Spotswood reported that he had written the governor of North Carolina requesting the presence of the Tuscarora at the meeting with the Native groups but neither the Tuscarora nor the Saponi had arrived in Williamsburg to meet with him. The Seneca, Nottoway, and Meherrin were present, however, and Spotswood had a number of items to present to the council. Six northern Indians were present at the meeting, one of whom claimed to be a Great Man of the Onondaga. On behalf of the northern Indians, they agreed to neither attack the Saponi in English settlements nor go nearer to Fort Christanna than some twenty miles away on the Meherrin River at the Great Creek, but, interestingly, "both partys [Saponi and Five Nations] being still at Liberty to attack each other at any place without the Inhabitants or beyond the Distance above mentioned." Spotswood also agreed to provide the Five Nations with a belt of wampum, given to the Onondaga representative as a token of peace to return to New York. Colonel Nathaniel Harison was to provide the belt. The council ordered a "stroud water Blanket flap" be given to each of the northern Indians in Williamsburg and a "laced hatt" given to the Chief Man and the interpreter, to show their respect and keen interest in attaining a lasting peace.[36]

At a council held the next day, the Nottoway and Meherrin were brought in for interrogation about their complaints against the Saponi and the issue of the Five Nations. Regarding the Five Nations, the Nottoway and Meherrin informed the council that eight Nottoway and twelve Meherrin had joined the Seneca and Tuscarora in the attack on Fort Christanna. Motivations for this attack are not clear, but one cannot discount the lure of trade or revenge. Retributive cycles of violence permeate the trade era, as insult required insult, often instigated by desire for trade goods. Although they were tributaries of the English in Virginia, the Nottoway and Meherrin were Iroquoian speakers who likely had sustained contact with Haudenosaunee raiders throughout the piedmont. One also cannot discount the impermanence of ties with English colonies. Connections with any colonial government at this time were a matter of convenience, particularly for powerful groups allied with the Haudenosaunee. In an effort to establish its legitimacy and power, the Virginia Council decided that the militia should apprehend the alleged attackers and bring them to Williamsburg for trial. The council proclaimed "that they be then made Sensible their making War upon any of his Majestys Subjects and their firing upon his Majestys Fort is a Crime for which their Lives are forfeited but that in Compassion to their Ignorance, the Government is willing for this time to passover their Office," but should it happen again, the penalty would be death. The council further moved that the northern Indians could stay at Nottoway Town until January 10, 1720, and that an interpreter should inform them that they should pose no further threat to the Saponi. On January 10 they would receive word to come to Williamsburg to receive their belt of peak and have leave to pass through the settlements of the English on their return north.³⁷ But in a February letter to the Board of Trade, Spotswood related his frustration with New York, particularly Colonel Peter Schuyler, mayor of Albany. Spotswood alleged that Schuyler had not "acted w'th that Integrity and Regard to the Neighbouring Colonys" and that his insistence on holding all negotiations at Albany was "too low a Condescension to the humours of those Savages and such is more likely to create in them a Contempt of the British power than a fondness for our Friendship." For his part, Spotswood was insistent that the colonies must act in a cohesive manner.³⁸

Eleven months passed without mention of the Five Nations in the council records until October 15, 1720, when the records include a letter from Governor William Keith of Pennsylvania regarding a council at Conestoga proposing peace between the Indians of Pennsylvania and the tributaries of Virginia. Spotswood ordered an interpreter sent to the tributaries asking each nation to send four of their Great Men to Williamsburg the following month to receive "such measures as may most effectually establish a peace."³⁹ A message from Governor Keith was read on November 3, 1720, to the House of Burgesses:

> I remark to you the naked State both of your harbours and ffrontiers, the disarmed Condition of your Militia, the Inconvenient length of many Counties, and I leave to your consideration whether the giving Encouragment for Extending your Out Settlements to the high Ridge of Mountains, will not be laying hold of the best Barrier that nature could form, to Secure this Colony from the Incursions of the Indians and more dangerous Incroachments of the French.⁴⁰

On November 12 Great Men from the Nottoway, Meherrin, Nansemond, Saponi, Tottero, Stukanoe, and Occaneechee attended the council to hear of the plans for peace from Governor Keith of Pennsylvania on behalf of the Conestoga, Ganowass, and Showanoe. The deputies of the Virginia tributaries agreed heartily that they "were very desirous on their part to live in Peace" and pledged to prevent future hostilities by refusing to pass over the "great Mountains nor pass to the Northward of Potomack River." To seal the peace, a belt of wampum was to be made by the Nottoway, Meherrin, and Nansemond and another by the Saponi, Tottero, Stuckanock, and Occaneechee for the governor of Pennsylvania.⁴¹ The House discussed these plans on November 21.⁴²

On December 15, 1720, the House prepared an address to Lieutenant Governor Spotswood in which it raised concerns over obtaining a peace with the Five Nations, given their history of breaking agreements. The House made clear that it appreciated Spotswood's efforts, stating, "The many Instances of your great penetration and your Indefatigable application to the Indian Affairs in the frequent Occurences which have hapned thro' the whole Course of your Government convince us." Yet they also made clear their frustration with previous treaty relations at Albany: "That you must know as well as any man the nature and Strength of the Indians and their Scituation as well as that of this Country and how ineffectual It must be to treat with those Nations at Albany." The House also mentioned that Virginia tributaries had never broken the previous treaties, with no mention of settlers breaking their promises, but concluded that there could be no further peace agreements with the Five Nations until a firm agreement was reached that would prove lasting and effectual.[43] The council responded to the House on December 17, 1720, agreeing that Spotswood had worked tirelessly to achieve a peace with the northern Indians and that it was in the best interests of all the English colonies to cooperate toward lasting peace in Anglo-Indian relationships but contending that certain stipulations must be met first.[44] During all these discussions, the leaders of Virginia were also considering threats from pirates and the Spanish along the southeastern coast and from the French along the southwestern coast and from the mountains. Fear of the French and the Five Nations contributed to the creation of Spotsylvania and Brunswick Counties during these sessions to act as buffers along the border.[45]

To publicize the new peace accords and to encourage an understanding of the seriousness with which the respective governors would forge ahead in intercolonial cooperation, a report of the July 5, 1721, meeting between the Five Nations and Sir William Keith was published in Philadelphia on July 26, 1721. This report covers the speeches made by Keith and the Five Nations delegates in great detail. Keith spent some time reminding the Conestoga of the wisdom of William Penn and related that Penn did not "approve of wars among the Indians whom he lov'd, because it wasted & destroyed their People, but always recommended Peace to the Indians, as the surest way to make them rich & strong, by increasing their Numbers."[46] Keith also informed the Conestoga that he had recently undertaken an exhaustive journey to meet with the Virginia tributaries in order to establish peace and that he wanted his messages carried to the Five Nations as well. Governor Keith understood that peace with the Virginian and Pennsylvanian Indians could not be maintained without Haudenosaunee cooperation.[47] These relationships were disproportionate alliances in nearly all respects. The Haudenosaunee expected obedience from smaller Native groups, while the English, bolstered by a history of feudalism and hierarchical dynasties, expected that the Haudenosaunee could easily control other Indian communities.[48]

Intercolonial English efforts to solidify borders and establish peace began to cement with the development of Native alliances. On July 7 Keith met with Ghesaont, who spoke on behalf of the Five Nations. Ghesaont related that they had not forgotten the words of William Penn but complained that Pennsylvania traders carried liquor into the trade. Traders also "sometimes meet with their young people going out to War, & treat them unkindly," calling them "Dogs, etc," to which the young men responded that "if they were Dogs, then they might as such," and stole from the traders. Over the course of several conversations, Keith responded by arguing that the Natives had to be responsible for their own people, refusing to allow liquor in their towns or to buy it from the traders. He said that he must speak plainly and told them that the colonies, like the Five Nations, were united in defense and that an attack on one was an attack on all. The tributary Indians of Virginia and Pennsylvania would be protected, he said, and continuing down the path of war to the South was folly that would bring destruction of all:

> Your young men came down Susquehannah River, & take their road through our Indian towns & settlements, & make a path between us & the people, against whom they go out to war. Now, you must know, that the Path this way leads them only to the Indians who are in alliance with the English, & first to those who are in a strict league of friendship with the governor of Virginia, just as their our friends & children, who are settled among us, are in League with me & our people.
>
> You cannot therefore make war upon the Indians in league with Virginia, without weakening the chain with the English: For as we would not suffer these our Friends & Brothers of Conestogoe & upon the River to be hurt by any Persons, without considering it as done to ourselves; so the Governor of Virginia looks upon the Injuries done to his Indian Brothers & Friends, as if they were done to himself. And you very well know, that you are five different nations, yet you are but one People: so that any wrong done to one Nation, is receivd as an Injury done to you all.
>
> In the same manner, & much more so, it is with the English, who are all united under one Great King, who has more People in that

one Town where he lives, then all the Indians in North America put together.⁴⁹

Proving that Spotswood was not the only bombastic and emotional speaker, Keith sought to renew the bonds of friendship by mentioning that he wanted to polish the silver of the Covenant Chain. The two groups exchanged goods to show that they might now "be together as one people, treating one another's children kindly, & affectionably on all occasions."⁵⁰

Keith took issue with the recent wars and their destructive effects on the Native population, stating, "The Indians continue to make war upon one another, & destroy each other, as if they intended that none of their people should be left alive; by which means you are, from a great People, become a very small People; & yet you will go on to Destroy yourselves." He also made a point of saying, "If I were not your true friend, I would not take the trouble of saying all these things to you." Finally, he made clear that he was speaking on behalf of Spotswood as well.⁵¹ From the Indigenous perspective, the expectation that raids, ongoing for generations, must simply stop would require an entire shift of events. In an earlier meeting with the Shawnee in 1720, one leader said that "he counselled [the young men], but they would not obey; therefore he cannot answer them."⁵² It would take Haudenosaunee strong-arming smaller groups into obedience, vigilant enforcement, and agreement with the English for these changes to occur.

On August 10, 1721, word of the Conestoga meeting reached Virginia when Spotswood discussed a letter from William Keith in which he related that the deputies of the Five Nations had expressed their desire to come to Virginia to make peace and that they likely would arrive at Germanna. The Virginia Council pressed for them to treat at Williamsburg rather than Germanna or Nottoway Town. Of particular interest in this meeting, however, was Spotswood's discussion of securing the borders, particularly in the case of runaway slaves. Spotswood related that in pursuing a solution to the Haudenosaunee problem, he had also written to the governors of Maryland, Pennsylvania, and New York asking them "to give orders to their Indians to hunt for the said Runaways among the Mountains and had proposed a reward for bringing them in dead or alive."⁵³

In the final negotiations over the official treaty, the bulk of the work involved Governor Sir William Keith of Pennsylvania's efforts to unite the colonial response. It is clear from the minutes of the meeting with the Haudenosaunee at Conestoga that a new colonial policy of presenting a united front was emerging, as Keith warned the Five Nations that the English were all under the same king. Both Keith and Spotswood emphasized colonial interdependence in their discussions on the Five Nations raids. Of great issue as well was a concern over runaway African slaves who had been taken in and possibly harbored by northern Indians. Thus the securing of the border had wide-ranging implications. To Spotswood, a great issue was ensuring that northern Indians who were tributaries of Pennsylvania would return slaves. In a letter to Governor Keith, Spotswood wrote, "I have also a Demand to make of some Negro Slaves belonging to Virginia, which I understand are harboured among the Shuannoes and said to be set free and protected by those Indians. This is a proceeding that must so dangerously affect the Properties of his Majesties subjects in these parts, that I greatly depend on the Earnest Application of this Government to discourage your Indians from such a Practice."[54] Keith agreed with Spotswood that treaties of peace were necessary between the various tributaries but proved unable to convince his council. Spotswood, for his part, did not back down and offered wampum made by Virginia tributaries as tokens of their sincerity. He also indicated that one of the two belts of wampum indicated a request for a return of fugitive Virginia slaves. Keith sent Pennsylvania trader James LeTort to Conestoga bearing Spotswood's message. LeTort explained the recent treaty discussions at length and added a warning that Pennsylvania tributaries could not go south of the Potomac or east of the mountains, in order to "prevent all such mischief."[55] LeTort also translated the message about slavery, saying, "I must also further inform you that the ffive Nations have agreed in the same Treaty, that neither they nor you shall receive or harbor any Negroes on any accot. whatsoever, but if any of them be found by the Indians in the woods, they shall be taken up and brought to the Governour that they may be returned to their masters, for you know the Negroes are Slaves."[56] To ensure their compliance, "one Good Gun and two Blankets for each Negro" was offered, "and the same value you will receive, from time to time, for every Runaway Negro that you shall take up and deliver." As a reminder, LeTort closed his translation of Spotswood's message with, "But to entertain our Slaves is not only scandalous to the Indians but an injury to the English, and is contrary to the Treaty's already made."[57]

The council read the agreement from Albany at the October 20, 1721, meeting. The treaty renewed the Covenant Chain between the colonies and the Five Nations. The parties agreed to recognize the Blue Ridge

Mountains as the border between the Virginian tributaries and the Haudenosaunee, specifying that the Virginian tributaries could not go north of the Potomac or west of the mountains and the Haudenosaunee could not go south or east without licenses from the governors. It also put an end to the raids against the Catawba and Christanna Indians (Saponi) and the threats to Virginia settlers in the Shenandoah Valley and piedmont. The deputies of the Five Nations who came to Virginia returned north on a sloop provided by the Virginians to carry them to Annapolis. They each had as gifts of the treaty "a Coat of blue Broad Cloth, a Fuzil & as much Powder and Shott as they shall desire to carry wth them, and a Suit of Cloaths for each of the Widows of the Great Men that accompanied them hither and are since dead."[58]

While negotiations regarding the northern and western border were under consideration, Spotswood had not forgotten the Southwest and expansion of the trade. Regarding the southern border, delegates from the Chickasaw along with the Cherokee came to the council on October 23, 1721. They entered the room singing, "according to their Custom," and carrying a calumet and a package of deerskins. The Great Man of the Chickasaw took the deerskins and "spread [them] upon the Shoulders of the Governor and divers of the Council" before indicating that his nation was at war with the French and needed access to arms and ammunition. He stated that the English of South Carolina were incapable of supplying them, hence he came to Virginia. The record is incomplete, and all that remains is the following from Spotswood: "Tho Virginia be the first and Chief of the King of Great Britains Dominions in America yet he must understand," which likely referred to intercolonial cooperation, if the negotiations with New York and Pennsylvania were any indication.[59]

While the record on this meeting is fragmented, the discussion continued at the October 25 council meeting, and from that record one can see that Spotswood was hesitant to provide material goods to the Chickasaw. While he and the Virginia government were always "ready to treat the Chickasaws as Friends, but that the frequent Wars between them and the Neighbouring Indians renders it dangerous for our Traders to go among them, and will discourage any such Trade until the Traders can travel with safety." The Cherokee present professed a reopening of trade with the Virginians, "that wch they most desire." The council gave leave to the Chickasaw and Cherokee to gather arms and ammunition from Christanna, "provide they come thither in such manner as may give no uneasiness to the Inhabitants."[60] At the council as well were some of the deputies of the Five Nations, "and after some further Conference wth ye

Deputys of the Chickasaws and Chirokees Nation relating to their Making Peace with the Five Nations" in regard to the recent Albany accords, the Chickasaw and Cherokee left Williamsburg with promises that they would each receive one trading gun and as much powder and shot "as they shall have occasion for in their Journey home," to be delivered to Christanna.[61]

At the opening of the May 1722 session, Spotswood related, "The Answer which we have at length obtain'd from those Indians in a Solemn Conference held at Albany in September last will be deemed by you so satisfactory that you must think this Governments in the right to conclude upon Sending Commissioners to Albany."[62] The House replied on May 11, "We think ourselves oblig'd on this Occasion to Express the just Sence this House hath of the Extraordinary Care and application your Honor hath used in Setling the Preliminaries with the Indians of the Five Nations."[63] In June they heaped more praise on Spotswood, understanding that although it had taken him nearly twelve years and a great deal of effort, "as we have observed more particular skill and Dexterity in your Managing the Indian Affairs We think it will greatly conduce to the Establishing an honorable and lasting Peace" and that his efforts "will Redound to much to the Safety and Honor of this Country."[64]

A concern arose in March 1722 regarding the agreements. On March 7, in a report on the communications regarding the Albany treaty, word came from the Five Nations that only one of the five deputies had returned to New York. Along with this news was an allegation that the Indians tributary to Virginia, namely the Nottoway, had poisoned them. The Five Nations demanded "four boys as a satisfaction for the loss of their four Great Men; intimating that no other satisfaction would be accepted by them, and threatening in case of refusal to revenge themselves on the Inhabitants of Virginia." For its part, the council referred to the report from Spotswood that indicated that two of these men had died in Virginia but that these two men had arrived in bad health. The first died without coming into contact with the Nottoway and the second within a day after arriving at Nottoway Town. Of the other three deputies, two were also ill the entire time they were in Virginia, almost three months, and they "never expressed the least Apprehension of their being poisoned in this Colony, or by any of it's Indians, but on the contrary parted with the Chiefs of the Virginia Indians, will all the outward signs of friendship imaginable." Spotswood did say that there were some "expressions" that they might have been poisoned by Maryland Indians on their way to Virginia but that "no other regard was had here to that Suspicion of theirs, than to impute it to the natural Jealousy the Indians always have of one another." As to who might have committed the poisoning, Spotswood alleged that it might have been one of their party, Sketowass, a Tuscarora who, "having in all his behavior here, Acted the part of an Incendiary Rather than a Messenger of Peace, may be justly suspected guilty of destroying those of his Companions who would not joine in his Designs." The council agreed to examine the matter further and asked the governor of New York to send timely warning should the Haudenosaunee decide to avenge themselves.[65] No action on the part of the Haudenosaunee being forthcoming, on May 12 Spotswood announced plans to attend the treaty session in Albany that summer to cement the long-awaited peace.[66]

On May 31 the council allotted one thousand pounds to Spotswood for his expenses, twenty shillings per day for two commissioners (one from the House of Burgesses and one from the council), and five shillings per day (besides necessary charges) for Robert Hix, "an ancient Indian trader" who would also attend.[67] They set out for Albany on July 28 and met with the deputies of the Five Nations on August 29. The proposal was agreed to by all parties on September 6.[68] According to the treaty, it was lawful to kill any southern Indians who ventured north of the Potomac or passed west of the mountains, and any Five Nations Haudenosaunee who went south or east of the boundaries would be considered public enemies and killed or sold as slaves overseas.[69] The Virginia Council sent word to the tributaries (the Nansemond, Pamunkey, Chickahominy, Nottoway, Meherrin, and the Christanna Saponi and Catawba) on November 1, 1722.[70]

The Haudenosaunee hoped the English colonists would help them control the communities under their dominion. In the mid-Atlantic the agreement greatly infringed upon Shawnee, Conestoga, Lenape, and Conoy sovereignty. The peace and boundary lines were imposed by the Haudenosaunee and colonists onto these groups. Under threat of death or slavery, they agreed to abide by the treaty.[71] For a time, Virginia's contact with the Five Nations shifted to the Shenandoah Valley and Blue Ridge Mountains, where a lasting peace existed until at least 1738, when Haudenosaunee warriors marched south along the "back of the Blue Ridge, to do battle with the Cherokee and Catawba, [and] first committed casual outrages upon early settlers of Augusta."[72]

Alexander Spotswood returned triumphant, for, after many years fighting his own council, he thought had finally secured the borders. Yet there is evidence that he knew that his enemies in Virginia had conquered him in other ways before he left for New York in the summer of 1722. A royal commission dated April 3 arrived in Virginia on April 20, 1722, naming a successor, Hugh Drysdale, yet Spotswood did not learn of his removal until his return in October 1722. For his part, Spotswood had contingency plans, as he had lucrative land grants in Spotsylvania County and intended to retire and farm his acreage. According to a group of Virginia historians, "His land acquisitions ever since the truce with the Council in 1720 smack of the proverbial putting something aside for a rainy day."[73]

The 1722 treaty made Fort Christanna obsolete, and the Virginians made plans to return Catawba children to their homes and to disperse the other Indian settlers. Local histories of the area indicate the Saponi and Tutelo remained there until 1740, when they moved to Pennsylvania and joined the Haudenosaunee.[74] While the fort was slotted for abandonment with the demise of the Virginia Indian Company, there is evidence that it remained a site of trade. In his "History of the Dividing Line," William Byrd writes of the Saponi, "Christianna Fort, where these Indians live, lies three Miles from George Hixes Plantation. He has considerable dealings with them and supplies them too plentifully with Rum."[75] The Saponi did not formally abandon the land until May 1732, when they joined the Catawba and others settled near another Spotswood settlement, Germanna in Orange County. By 1753 the Cayuga had adopted the Saponi along with the Tutelo, thus joining the Six Nations Haudenosaunee.[76]

Conclusion

Even before the closing of Fort Christanna, the Indian trade in Virginia was rapidly declining. South Carolinians took the lead in developing a rich trade with the Indians to the south and west, particularly with the Creek and then the Cherokee. Eventually it became unnecessary for South Carolina to care about Virginia traders. The Virginia traders, in turn, became more interested in expanding their plantations and their other trade interests, including tobacco exports and African slave imports. The closing of Christanna was only one part of the continuing general decline in commerce between Indians and Virginians. Men like Abraham Wood and William Byrd I profited from the trade before the piedmont Indian populations became so decimated by disease, warfare, and slave raids that they could no longer supply pelts and the center of trade shifted to Charleston. By this time, William Byrd II, firmly ensconced in London, was more concerned with his profits in tobacco stores and the sale of African slaves. In part because of Virginia's proximity to other English colonies, the Virginians could not count on the Indian trade for long. Eventually the South Carolinians undersold the Virginians and emerged as the leaders in Indian trade. By 1725 Carolina trader George Chicken wrote that "the Virginia traders . . . I am certain can do no prejudice to ours in the Way of Trade there not being above two or three of them and their goods no ways Suitable or Comparable to ours."[1] This had not always been the case. Throughout the seventeenth and early eighteenth centuries, Virginia held control.

Figure 5. Westover Plantation, James River, Charles City County. Photo by the author, 2007.

One famous family symbolizes for most historians the Virginia gentry and the plantation complex: the Byrds. Looking at Westover Plantation (see figure 5), one of the finest examples of colonial architecture along the James River in Charles City County, Virginia, one sees an image of the Virginia elite and, given an understanding of colonial tobacco production, also a reflection of owners of African slaves. Digging a little deeper, one can see that William Byrd I and his son, William Byrd II, were educated men, their collection of nearly four thousand books representing the largest library in Virginia at the time. In hindsight the Byrds present an image of the consummate and excessive elite. But that's not the whole story.

From the perspective of their Indigenous allies, traders, and enemies, the Byrds were greater than and at times wholly different from the image of the gentlemanly planters. Byrd I built a trading empire while competing against Abraham Wood. This empire solidified the Byrd name among the Virginia gentry and allowed his son to enter into profitable arrangements with local Indians for skins and slaves, profits which he likely used to build Westover.

Access to European goods provided Virginia Natives with the means to expand their territorial domains and the leverage to oust enemies from the region. As trackers and traders alike, the tributaries became deeply entrenched in Anglo commodification of material objects. A desire for amicable relations with their neighbors played a role in their efforts to maintain trade relationship with their English partners. Rivalries with other Natives in the region also played a role in their efforts to secure supremacy in the region. Access to trade fundamentally changed the Virginia landscape through the hybridization that emerged from contact between colonists and Natives in the new exchange economy. Trade between Europeans and Natives was a reciprocal cultural exchange as well as a wholly economic venture. Indians thought that by giving gifts to the Europeans, they could bring them into kinship bonds but quickly learned that the Europeans would not act as proper kinsmen. At the same time, the most skilled European traders quickly learned that they had to understand Native ways of trade and act as kinsmen in order to gain access to Native slaves, skins, and furs. Trade with Indians naturally changed over time as the English population grew and more Natives became entrenched in the European market.[2] Indigenous interaction in southwestern Virginia and the piedmont had a central role in the larger narrative of the colonial plantation South. The Southeast cannot be understood without knowing Virginia, and one cannot understand Virginia without understanding the interaction between settlers and Indigenous peoples, between the goals of the tributary system and its realities.

Notes

Introduction

1. Byrd, *Prose Works*, 246–48, 284. Byrd discussed at length the religion of his Saponi tracker, Bearskin, during his survey of the Virginia and North Carolina boundary line in 1728, citing in two separate accounts his examination of Bearskin's religion. Byrd's assessment of the Saponi religion, as we now know, was erroneous.

2. Ibid., 391, 397.

3. See Billings, *Little Parliament*, for an understanding of the nuances of colonial Virginia's politics and politicking.

1 / Treaty of Peace: 1646

1. Gleach, *Powhatan's World*, 65.

2. Hening, *Statutes*, 1:322–26; Briceland, *Westward from Virginia*, 24. At Fort Henry were Abraham Wood, a noted trader, and Captain John Flood, an interpreter.

3. The exchange of children for the "compliance of adults" was fairly commonplace in the Early Modern era, and the English made similar exchanges with their children. English merchants and traders sent young boys to facilitate trade relationships throughout India, Indonesia, Japan, Portugal, and the Ottoman Empire, as well as in Virginia to learn "language skills and cultural knowledge that might further commercial relations." See Games, "Beyond the Atlantic," 684. It is important to note here that the practices of captivity and hostage exchange were widespread, not only in the Eastern Woodlands, as discussed throughout this work as mourning wars, but throughout the Atlantic world. Captive taking and Indigenous enslavement have been the subject of a number of recent works; see Rushforth, *Bonds of Alliance*; Brooks, *Captives and Cousins*; and Brooks and Martin, *Linking the History of Slavery*. For an understanding of English experiences, see Colley, *Captives*; for an understanding of English experiences with captivity and with the concept of slavery before the plantation economy, see Guasco, *Slaves and Englishmen*; for Anglo-Iberian experiences, see Voigt, *Writing Captivity*. The abuse of Native children in

Virginia through the hostage exchange as well as the advent of large-scale Native slavery are discussed in later chapters.

4. Robinson, *Early American Indian Documents*, 67–69.
5. Van Zandt, *Brothers among Nations*, 68–79.
6. Smith, "General Historie," 2:127; Strachey, *History of Travell*, 87; Rountree, *Powhatan Indians of Virginia*, 109.
7. Rountree, *Powhatan Indians of Virginia*, 144.
8. Gleach, *Powhatan's World*, 26.
9. For more on the general history of the Indian eras of southern history, see Wilson, *New Encyclopedia of Southern Culture*, 3:130–44.
10. Gleach, *Powhatan's World*, 4–5, 10–11.
11. For a more extensive ethnography, see Rountree, *Powhatan Indians of Virginia*. "The name 'Powhatan' is derived from a paramount chief's 'empire' . . . [that] covered most of the Virginia coastal plain and which was organized by the man Powhatan, who had in turn taken his name from his natal town, Powhatan, near the falls of the James River. In addition to these three Powhatans (the collection of coastal plain people, the 'throne name' of the chief, and the name of his hometown), the term 'Powhatan' is also applied to the closely related Algonquian dialects spoken in the region" (9–12).
12. Rountree, *Powhatan Indians of Virginia*, 9–12. The colonists took note of how many warriors were in each town to determine the population. They also typically listed the capital town by the name of the group. Rountree lists the capital towns geographically in terms of their present-day location and archaeological findings from the Eastern Shore to the Southwest bank of the James River, "down the northeastern bank of the James, and so on to the Potomac"; the names in parentheses indicate the anglicized version: Occohannock (Accohannock), 40 men, subchiefdom of Accomack, located in present-day Accomack County; Accomack, 80 men, name means "across the water," located in present-day Northampton County; Chesapeake, 100 men, located near south branch of Elizabeth River, exterminated by Powhatan by the time of Jamestown's founding; Nansemond, near modern-day Suffolk, 200 men; Warraskoyak, in Isle of Wight County or near Pagan River, 40–60 men; Quiyoughcohannock, 25–60 men, near Surry County; Weyanock, in Charles City County near Weyanoke Point and also at Powell's Creek in Prince George County, 100–200 men; Appomattoc, Appomattox River upstream of Swift Creek, 60–100 men; Powhatan, 40–50 men, east side of the James River falls at Richmond; Arrohattoc, ten miles downstream from the James River falls, Henrico County, 30–60 men; Chickahominy, capital towns in James City, Charles City, and New Kent Counties, 200–300 men; Paspahegh, west of the mouth of the Chickahominy in James City County, 40 men; Kicoughtan, Southwest of Hampton Creek mouth, 20–30 men; Chiskiack, near Indian Field Creek in York County, 40–50 men; Youghtanund, upper Pamunkey River in King William or New Kent County, 60–70 men; Pamunkey, several capital towns near Pamunkey River in King William and New Kent Counties, 60–70 men; Mattapient (Mattaponi), King William or King and Queen Counties, 30–40 men; Werowocomoco, Gloucester County, 40 men, capital of Powhatan's chiefdom in 1607; Piankatank, Middlesex County at Piankatank River, 40 men; Opiscopank (Piscataway), southwestern Rappahannock River in Middlesex County, no warrior count; Nandtaughtacund (possibly Nanzatico), Caroline County at the head of Portobago Bay, 150 men; Cuttatawomen, King George County on the

northwest side of Rappahannock River, and a site in Lancaster County, 20 and 30 men, respectively; Pissaceck, Westmoreland County, no warrior count; Rappahannock, two capital towns, Richmond County, 100 men; Moraughtacund (Morattico), Richmond County, 80 men; Wiccocomico (Wicomico), Northumberland County at head of Little Wicomico River, 130 men; Sekakawon (Chickacone, Coan), Coan River in Northumberland County, 30 men; Onawmanient (Nomini), western side of Nomini Bay in Northumberland County, 100 men; Patawomeck (Potomac), north of Accokeek Creek in Stafford County, 160 men.

13. Ward and Davis, "Tribes and Traders," 125.
14. Feest, "Virginia Algonquians," 253.
15. Benson, *Story of the Susquehannocks*, 6. The various groups associated with the Susquehannock include but are not limited to the Akhrakuaeronon (Atrakwaeronnon), Akwinoshioni, Atquanachuke, Attaock, Carantouan, Cepowig, Junita (Ihonado), Kaiquariegehaga, Ohongeoguena (Ohongeeoquena), Oscalui, Quadroque, Sasquesahanough, Sconondihago (Seconondihago or Skonedidehaga), Serosquacke, Takoulguehronnon, Tehaque, Tesinigh, Unquehiett, Usququhaga, Utchowig, Wyoming, and Wysox.
16. Fenstermaker, *History of the Conestoga Indians*, 5, 11; Van Zandt, *Brothers among Nations*, 166–86.
17. Hatfield, "Spanish Colonization Literature," 247.
18. Rountree, *Pocahontas's People*, 29.
19. Hatfield, "Spanish Colonization Literature," 246. Hatfield's article importantly argues that the initial English settlement was delimited by their perceptions of Tsenacommacah. Precontact political boundaries thus played a major role in Virginia.
20. Hatfield, "Spanish Colonization Literature," 270.
21. Rice, *Nature and History*, 56.
22. Hatfield, "Spanish Colonization Literature," 256. The Roman *tributarii* were superior in position to slaves yet inferior to the freeholders of land and houses called *ceorl*, who were also tribute payers. For an understanding of late Roman examples of tribute and their spread to continental Europe, see Mirković, *Later Roman Colonate*. John Smith's previous experience in Turkey and his theories on colonization are analyzed in Kupperman, *Jamestown Project*.
23. Gleach, *Powhatan's World*, 12; Rountree, *Pocahontas's People*, 38, 55.
24. Craven, "Indian Policy," 74.
25. Hatfield, "Spanish Colonization Literature," 281.
26. Nichols, "George Percy's 'trewe Relacyon,'" 259; Rountree, *Pocahontas's People*, 55. In a study of the limits and restraints of warfare in the Native Eastern Woodlands, Wayne Lee argues, "Blood demanded blood. The rewards and requirements of war were so thoroughly entwined in Indian societies that irrespective of the arrival of the Europeans, a nearly endemic state of war existed throughout much of the eastern seaboard and beyond. Equally thoroughly entwined within Indian societies, however, were structural and cultural limitations on the scale and devastation of warfare." Lee, "Peace Chiefs," 702.
27. Rountree, *Pocahontas's People*, 55.
28. Ibid., 38, 55, 61, 80; Gleach, *Powhatan's World*, 141. Oral history from the Mattaponi suggests that Powhatan *quiakros* played a role in John Rolfe's success with the strain of tobacco *Nicotiana tabacum*. They taught Rolfe harvesting techniques for

the local *Nicotiana rustica* favored by the Powhatans. Rolfe gained this knowledge through his marriage to Metoaka, and the Mattaponi argue that this exchange saved the English colony. Custalow and Daniel, *True Story of Pocahontas*, 73.

29. Gleach, *Powhatan's World*, 33; Rountree, *Pocahontas's People*, 66. Prior to his death, Wahunsonacock served as the peace chief, or *weroance*, in charge of internal affairs, while his brother, Opechancanough, served as the external war chief. There is some debate as to whether Opechancanough was Wahunsonacock's brother or his cousin. It is known that they were of the same kin network. Additionally, although Wahunsonacock was officially succeeded by Opitchapam or Itoyatan, Opechancanough's magnetic personality made him the real ruler.

30. Lee, "Peace Chiefs," 706.

31. Rountree, *Pocahontas's People*, 20; Washburn, "Seventeenth-Century Indian Wars," 95–96.

32. Washburn, "Seventeenth-Century Indian Wars," 95–96; Rountree, *Pocahontas's People*, 84.

33. W. Stanard, "Indians of Southern Virginia," 338–39.

34. Rountree, *Pocahontas's People*, 84; Hening, *Statutes*, 1:287. Six pounds of tobacco was levied for every tithable person in the counties of James City, York, Warwick, Elizabeth City, Northampton, Lower Norfolk, and Isle of Wight to pay for the cost of the march.

35. Hening, *Statutes*, 1:317–19.

36. Beverley, *History and Present State of Virginia*, 48.

37. Ibid., 48–50.

38. Rountree, *Pocahontas's People*, 86.

39. Beverley, *History and Present State of Virginia*, 50. Beverley does, however, comment on Oliver Cromwell's role during the English Civil War and the Navigation Act's impact on the colonial trade. Governor Sir William Berkeley, a Royalist supporter, returned to England after the restoration and appointed Colonel Francis Morison deputy governor (March 23, 1661–December 23, 1662). Under Morison's administration, according to Beverley, "all Indian affairs [were] settled." Beverley is referring to land allotments and trade. He adds, "Peace and commerce with the Indians was settled by law, and their boundaries prescribed" (53). Richard Bennet served as acting governor, April 30, 1652–March 1655.

40. Warren Billings opines in his edited volume of Governor Sir William Berkeley's writings that it is likely Berkeley took the lead in negotiations and drafting the treaty, "especially because the terms reflect his view of policies towards the natives, which was an outlook he consistently maintained for as long as he was governor." Berkeley, *Papers*, 73.

41. Rountree, *Pocahontas's People*, 90.

42. Hening, *Statutes*, 1:328. Flood was an interpreter fluent in Algonquian who was paid four thousand pounds of tobacco annually by the assembly for his services.

43. Ibid., 1:315.

44. Ibid., 1:293.

45. Robinson, *Early American Indian Documents*, 67–69.

46. Gleach, *Powhatan's World*, 181. Gleach suggests that this generic term also "would seem to be the basis for the blame and retribution against Powhatan Indians that would be exacted in response to the violent action of other Indians in the 1670s."

47. Billings, "Some Acts Not in Hening's Statutes," 64–65.

48. Robinson, *Early American Indian Documents*, 39.
49. Hening, *Statutes*, 1:402.
50. Ibid., 1:410.
51. Ibid., 2:149. Further discussion of land rights in the post-1646 era can be found in later chapters.
52. Billings, "Some Acts Not in Hening's Statutes," 68; Gleach, *Powhatan's World*, 185.
53. Hantman, "Monacan Archaeology," 116.
54. Ibid., 120.
55. Ward and Davis, "Tribes and Traders," 125, 130. The extent to which the English infiltrated the remote towns of the piedmont into North Carolina in the mid-seventeenth century is still under investigation by archaeologists, but Ward and Davis suggest areas they did reach, based indirectly on findings from the Mitchum Site along Haw River in modern-day North Carolina. There Ward and Davis found evidence of trade with other Indians such as "brass bells, rolled brass and copper beads, and small white and blue glass beads," but they found no signs of gun parts or iron tools. For a history of the early trade in the Potomac Basin, see the chapter "Peltries and 'Papists'" in Rice, *Nature and History*, 101. Rice states, "Though never of major economic significance, the fur trading activities of [William] Claiborne, [Henry] Fleet, and the Calverts [George and Cecilius] had the unanticipated effect of ensnaring Virginia and Maryland within an entirely Native diplomatic configuration."
56. Ward and Davis, "Tribes and Traders," 137.
57. Kelton, *Epidemics and Enslavement*, 90.
58. Merrell, *Indians' New World*, 5, 18, 29.

2 / Indian Trade and Upheaval: The Rise of Abraham Wood

1. See Gallay, *Indian Slave Trade*; Braund, *Deerskins and Duffels*; Hahn, *Invention of the Creek Nation*; Piker, *Okfuskee*; Saunt, *New Order of Things*; Ethridge, *Creek Country*; Merrell, *Indians' New World*.
2. Rountree, "Powhatans and the English," 173–205.
3. Bruce, *History of Virginia*, 1:68, 171.
4. Hening, *Statutes*, 1:314–15.
5. Ibid.
6. Scisco, "Exploration in 1650," 140.
7. Ibid., 169; Billings, *Sir William Berkeley*, 76–77. Wood also had the support of Berkeley. Billings suggests that Berkeley and Wood held a great respect for one another and participated in a "trusted, deep friendship that lasted until Berkeley's death."
8. Berkeley, *Papers*, 136n; Morrison, "Virginia Indian Trade," 234.
9. Bland, "Discovery of New Brittaine," 5–18; Scisco, "Exploration in 1650," 140.
10. Boyce, "Iroquoian Tribes," 286.
11. Bland, "Discovery of New Brittaine," 8; Powell, "Carolana and the Incomparable Roanoke"; Byrd, "Letters," 333. The Bland path later led to the Cherokee trade of the eighteenth century.
12. Bland, "Discovery of New Brittaine," 19; Briceland, *Westward from Virginia*, 44.
13. Bland, "Discovery of New Brittaine," 9.
14. Ibid.

15. Jennings, *New Worlds of Violence*, xxi. Jennings argues that "not only is violence 'historically transmitted,' but violent acts can be read as signs, even as they have different meanings for perpetrators, victims, and onlookers."
16. Bland, "Discovery of New Brittaine," 10.
17. Ibid., 11.
18. Ibid., 12.
19. Ibid.
20. Ibid., 17.
21. Ibid., 18–19.
22. Powell, "Carolana and the Incomparable Roanoke," 21; Briceland, *Westward from Virginia*, 44. Briceland suggests that Bland and Wood were less interested in trade than in exploration and encouraging European settlement of interior Virginia. However plausible the Briceland theory, trade contacts provided a likely reason for Bland's and Wood's efforts. Bland's discussions of the Nottoway, Meherrin, and Tuscarora are of particular interest to an understanding of the effect of trade on the interior and the impact of English expansion. While Lewis R. Binford makes the claim that "the general picture that the Bland account gives of the Nottoway and Meherrin in 1650 is one of relatively unmodified aboriginal life," I argue that a desire for control motivated the apprehensive behavior toward Bland on the part of the Meherrin and Nottoway. Binford, "Ethnohistory of the Nottoway, Meherrin and Weanock," 136.
23. D. Brown, *Sketches of Greensville County Virginia*, 5–11.
24. Hening, *Statutes*, 1:415; Juricek, "Westo Indians," 136; Bowne, *Westo Indians*, 53, 63; Ethridge, *From Chicaza to Chickasaw*, 90–97.
25. Juricek, "Westo Indians," 136; Bowne, *Westo Indians*, 53, 63; Ethridge, *From Chicaza to Chickasaw*, 90–97.
26. Meyers, "From Refugees to Slave Traders," 90. The area surrounding the James River falls served as a point of contention for interior and coastal Indians as well as colonists and is mentioned as a trading place during John Smith's first expedition into the interior.
27. Hening, *Statutes*, 1:415.
28. Ibid., 1:422; Kukla, *Speakers and Clerks*, 39.
29. Hening, *Statutes*, 1:422.
30. Coombs, "Building 'the Machine,'" 96–97. Coombs finds that "twelve of twenty-nine men who held office in Charles City between 1655 and 1665 employed Indians in some capacity, a higher percentage than can be documented for any other county during the same period." Bowne, *Westo Indians*, 53, 63; Meyers, "From Refugees to Slave Traders," 90.
31. See Robbie Ethridge, "Introduction: Mapping the Mississippian Shatter Zone," in Ethridge and Shuck-Hall, *Mapping the Mississippian Shatter Zone*, 25.
32. While stating a definitive number of Indian slaves is not possible due to the fragmented written colonial record in many of the counties where slavery took place, the physical record of the colony tells a different story. Based on archaeological evidence, the amount of movement, displacement, coalescence, and disease patterns suggests widespread enslavement throughout the Eastern Woodlands. See Ethridge and Shuck-Hall, *Mapping the Mississippian Shatter Zone*; Kelton, *Epidemics and Enslavement*; Gallay, *Indian Slave Trade*; Bowne, *Westo Indians*; Ethridge, *From Chicaza to Chickasaw*. It is particularly important to understand the longer history of captivity

and trade as it relates to a Mississippian past. See C. Snyder, *Slavery in Indian Country*, 5, 21, 55.

33. Ethridge, *From Chicaza to Chickasaw*, 98–99, 103; Everett, "They shalbe slaves for their lives," 84.

34. Robbie Ethridge, "Introduction: Mapping the Mississippian Shatter Zone," in Ethridge and Shuck-Hall, *Mapping the Mississippian Shatter Zone*, 25.

35. Worth, *Struggle for the Georgia Coast*, 15–18; Kelton, *Epidemics and Enslavement*, 112.

36. McIlwaine, *Journals of the House of Burgesses*, 15–17.

37. Woodward, "Faithfull Relation," 133.

38. Wood, "Letter," 214.

39. Warren, *Worlds the Shawnees Made*, 58–59.

40. In *Virginia Historical Index*, Swem painstakingly indexed roughly thirty years' worth of late nineteenth- and early twentieth-century academic journals devoted to Virginia history and genealogy, including the first and second series of the *William and Mary Quarterly*, the *Virginia Magazine of History and Biography*, *Tyler's Quarterly*, *Calendar of Virginia State Papers*, and the *Virginia Register*. In the first volume of Swem's index, the entries for the heading "Indian Servants and Slaves" run nearly two full columns, including eighty occurrences in these journals. These references included printed transcriptions of early Virginia records. From these citations, one can surmise that there was at the very least a strong demand for Indian labor in the seventeenth century and that Indian slavery posed enough of a problem to warrant several dozen laws and court cases.

41. Hatfield, *Atlantic Virginia*, 150–52.

42. Nichols, "George Percy's 'trewe Relacyon,'" 271.

43. Ibid., 448.

44. Tyler, "Indian Slaves," (1897–1898), 214–15; Tyler, "Indian Slaves," (1899–1900), 165.

45. Tyler, "Indian Slaves," (1899–1900), 165; Morgan, *American Slavery, American Freedom*, 232–34.

46. See Kelton, *Epidemics and Enslavement*; Ethridge, *From Chicaza to Chickasaw*; Bowne, *Westo Indians*; Meyers, "From Refugees to Slave Traders"; Gallay, *Indian Slave Trade*.

47. Hening, *Statutes*, 1:525.

48. McIlwaine, *Journals of the House of Burgesses*, 4.

49. Binford, "Ethnohistory of the Nottoway, Meherrin, Weanock Ethnohistory," 145.

50. Northumberland County, *Order Book*; Sparacio, *Order Book*; "14 February 1655/56," 58–59.

51. Hening, *Statutes*, 1:541.

52. Northampton County, *Orders, Wills, Deeds, Etc.*; Ames, *County Court Records*, 97.

53. Kelton, *Epidemics and Enslavement*, 110; Hening, *Statutes*, 1:525.

54. Hening, *Statutes*, 2:337, 350.

55. Ibid., 2:15–16.

56. Ibid., 2:237.

57. Ibid., 2:237.

58. Ibid., 1:322–26. Among the scholars contending that the law was frequently ignored are C. S. Everett, Maureen Meyers, and Robbie Ethridge.

59. Bruce, *Economic History of Virginia*, 54–55. Throughout his work, Bruce contends that regulations on Indian servants were "strictly enforced." Evidence provided throughout this chapter contradicts Bruce, and I argue that the ever-present laws and codes regarding Indian servants highlight how often these regulations were ignored by English colonists.

60. Vaughan and Rosen, *Early American Indian Documents*, 39.

61. Ibid., 40.

62. Hening, *Statutes*, 1:402, 1:393–96.

63. Ibid., 1:481.

64. Ibid., 1:455, 481.

65. Berkeley, *Papers*; Tyler, "Edward Hatcher Will," 91. The April 1, 1679, deed in Henrico County of Mary Platt to her daughter Mary, wife to Thomas Ligon, indicates ownership of at least one Indian girl, named Moll Wateres. The letter from Berkeley was received by the Charles City County Court on May 21, 1658; Charles City County, *Order Book*, 144.

66. Hening, *Statutes*, 1:546.

67. Northumberland County, *Order Book*; Sparacio, *Order Book*, 2:85.

68. Charles City County, *Order Book*; Fleet, *Virginia Colonial Abstracts*, 7:48.

69. Tyler, "Indian Slaves" (1897–1898), 215; Hening, *Statutes*, 2:155. Tyler theorizes in this record that "possibly as the reducing of Indians was justified on the same grounds as reducing negroes to that condition, viz: that they were heathen, the above action of the legislature contributed probably to the enactment of a law a few years late (1667) that baptism did not exempt slaves already such from bondage."

70. On May 28, 1697, in Northampton County, regarding the indenture of Assabe, an Indian servant to Captain Obedience Johnson, the court made void the indenture after petition of Toganaquato, Assabe's mother. Ames, *County Court Records*, 106.

71. Charles City County, *Order Book*; Fleet, *Virginia Colonial Abstracts*, 1:14, 43, 46, 2:5.

72. Charles City County, *Order Book*; Fleet, *Virginia Colonial Abstracts*, 12:42.

73. See the case of Robin, a Pamunkey shoemaker, and James Revell, a Metomkin overseer. Rountree, *Pocahontas's People*, 138; Rountree, "Powhatans and the English," 199; Palmer, *Calendar*, 163–64.

74. Lederer, "Discoveries," ed. Alvord and Bidgood, 145–47.

75. Ibid., 148.

76. Ibid., 136.

77. Harris thought at one point that he had found a tributary of the lakes to Canada but feared to venture northward because of the threat of "Mahock" Indians. He went on to abandon Lederer and boasted about his own abilities, about which Lederer opined, "Made him the bolder in Virginia to report strange things in his own praise and my disparagement, presuming I would never appear to disprove him." Ibid., 150–51.

78. Ibid., 151; Rights, "The Trading Path to the Indians," 403–26.

79. Lederer, "Discoveries," ed. Alvord and Bidgood, 154–55.

80. Ibid., 162; Kelton, *Epidemics and Enslavement*, 114. Though not the same site as visited by Lederer, a separate town has been excavated relatively recently and there archaeologists found some seventeen thousand European artifacts, most of which likely came from Virginia and later Carolina traders. See Davis, Livingood, Ward, and Steponatis, *Excavating Occaneechi Town*.

81. Lederer, "Discoveries," ed. Alvord and Bidgood, 165.
82. Ibid., 168.
83. Ibid., 169.
84. Lederer, *Discoveries*, ed. Cumming, 41–42.
85. Ibid.
86. Lederer, "Discoveries," ed. Alvord and Bidgood, 171.
87. Ibid., 155–56.
88. Briceland, "Batts and Fallam," 24.
89. Ibid., 183. There are two transcripts of the Fallam journal. The transcript cited here was completed by the Reverend John Clayton in either 1683 or 1684, when Clayton was the rector at Jamestown and a member of the Royal Society. It was read to the Royal Society in August 1688. Briceland, "Batts and Fallam," 27. Thomas Batts lived near Wood and owned 1,862 acres in Henrico County bordering the river and near the Indian towns of Appomattock.
90. Lederer, "Discoveries," ed. Alvord and Bidgood, 185.
91. Ibid., 192.
92. Ibid., 193.
93. Wright, *First Gentlemen of Virginia*, 312–13; Kukla, *Speakers and Clerks*, 35–36. The land at the falls of the James River was an eighteen-hundred-acre tract including three islands and a stone house with a chimney in the middle. Byrd, "Letters," 224, 279.
94. Woodfin, "Auditor Stegge's Accounts," 176. Stegge's accounts are the only available record of quitrents in Virginia prior to 1680. The Stegge family home, known as Belvidere, located on the present site of Richmond, Virginia, also known as Falls Plantation, in 1656 was located directly across the James River from the Battle of Bloody Run, which provides an intriguing coincidence. That the property sat directly across from Bloody Run placed Stegg at an advantage in the peace process with the Westo. In 1656 the council lifted the trade restrictions, allowing individuals to trade directly with both tributary and foreign Indians. Mentioned frequently, Westover Plantation plays a major role in trade papers of the seventeenth century, and the Indian trader Stegge and later his nephew Byrd likely became involved in various trades at the property.
95. Byrd, "Letters," 227, 233. Further discussion on Byrd and his aunt is in chapter 3.
96. Locke, "Journeys of Needham and Arthur," 209; Rights, "Trading Path."
97. Bowne, *Westo Indians*, 81–85.
98. Alvord and Bidgood, *First Explorations*, 79; Morrison, "Virginia Indian Trade," 234. See also Bowne, *Westo Indians*; Gallay, *Indian Slave Trade*; Everett, "They shalbe slaves for their lives," 82. The Westo initiated the trade alliance with the Carolinians by arriving at St. Gile's plantation on October 10, 1674, and leading Henry Woodward to the Westo town on the Savannah River. Woodward used this opportunity to determine the power of the Westo and to learn more about the interior. Woodward reached an agreement with the Westo that helped define the parameters of the emerging slave trade in South Carolina. One Native group, the Westo, would act as an intermediary between other Indians and the English settlers while procuring slaves for the English in return for trade goods, most notably guns.
99. Accomack County Court Records; McKey, *Accomack County Virginia Court Order Abstracts*, 2:18, 45.
100. Hening, *Statutes*, 2:283.

101. Alvord and Bidgood, *First Explorations*, 79–80.
102. Wood, "Letter," 210.
103. Warren, *Worlds the Shawnees Made*, 68–69.
104. Wood, "Letter," 211.
105. Ibid.; Warren, *Worlds the Shawnees Made*, 68–69.
106. Warren, *Worlds the Shawnees Made*, 70.
107. Wood, "Letter," 213; Briceland, *Westward from Virginia*; Stephen Warren and Randolph Noe, "'The Greatest Travelers in America': Shawnee Survival in the Shatter Zone," in Ethridge and Shuck-Hall, *Mapping the Mississippian Shatter Zone*, 166; C. Snyder, *Slavery in Indian Country*, 19.
108. Wood, "Letter," 214.
109. Ibid., 213; Stephen Warren and Randolph Noe, "'The Greatest Travelers in America': Shawnee Survival in the Shatter Zone," in Ethridge and Shuck-Hall, *Mapping the Mississippian Shatter Zone*, 166.

3 / The Rise of Indian Slavery: William Byrd and Bacon's Rebellion

1. There was an incident in 1663 in which Indians killed "2 or 3 but wounded more of such English as were nearest adjoining to [them]." Hening, *Statutes*, 2:193–94; Catlett, quoted in Billings, *Sir William Berkeley*, 200; Old Rappahannock County Orders; Sparacio, *Deed and Will Abstracts*, 57.
2. McIlwaine, *Minutes of the Council and General Court*, 488.
3. Thomas Ludwell, "Ludwell to Arlington, 12 Feb 1666/67," in Billings, *Sir William Berkeley*, 201.
4. Rountree, *Pocahontas's People*; McCartney, "Cockacoeske, Queen of Pamunkey," 172–95.
5. McCartney, "Cockacoeske, Queen of Pamunkey," 243–45. *Weroances*, and in the case of Cockacoeske, *weronsquas*, were typically related to one another. Cockacoeske's lineage and ties to power were Powhatan to Opitchapam in 1618, who was soon replaced by Opechancanough who oversaw the last of the two armed conflicts. Upon Opechancanough's death at the hands of his English guards, a Pamunkey warrior named Necotowance took over and the former chiefdom disintegrated with the treaty of 1646. Totopotomoy ascended to power in 1649, and the records clearly indicate the disintegration of the chiefdom at this time.
6. Byrd, "Letters," 226.
7. Ragan, "Brief Survey of Anglo-Indian Interactions," 23.
8. Spotswood, *Official Letters*, 1:125.
9. McIlwaine, *Executive Journals of the Council*, 3:198.
10. Byrd, "Letters," 227, 233.
11. Meyers, "From Refugees to Slave Traders," 92; Wright, "William Byrd I and the Slave Trade."
12. Wright, "William Byrd I and the Slave Trade." Byrd had stakes not only in the Indian slave trade but also in the African slave trade. He owned principally at least one ship, the *William and Jane*, captured by French privateers off the coast of West Africa in March 1699. The French Senegal Company seized the ship and took it to France, claiming it had the sole right to trade off that particular coast and the African Company could trade only in Guinea. Byrd petitioned the Commissioners of Trade and Plantations asking for reparations and release of this ship.

13. Henrico County Miscellaneous Court Records; Weisiger, *Henrico County Virginia Deeds*, November 17, 1673, 134. Thomas Harris was the brother of Major William Robert Harris of the 1669–70 John Lederer expedition and the brother-in-law of Thomas Ligon, another owner of Indian slaves, particularly children. See chapter 2.

14. Clayton, "Aborigines of the Country," 194.

15. Ewan, *John Banister*, 91, 130, 382. John Banister's writings related the capture of prisoners and the torture processes of the Indians of the Southeast, citing that "lying in wait for men as they do for wild beasts, & are like Nimrod mighty hunters: yet when find them must die, do it very resolutely. The prisoners they take, at night where they take up their quarters, the lay them on their backs with their arms & legs stretched out, & tied to 4 steaks. Their fear makes them implacable, & very jealous."

16. Ibid., 91.

17. Hening, *Statutes*, 2:20–21.

18. Meyers, "From Refugees to Slave Traders," 93; Byrd's influence extended beyond his trade contacts. His economic success led to political opportunities, and he soon served as captain in the Henrico County Militia and as a member of the House of Burgesses. By 1680 he served on the Virginia Council and in 1688 purchased Westover Plantation from Theodorick and Richard Bland. The Westover property included twelve hundred acres and cost Byrd three hundred pounds sterling and ten thousand pounds of tobacco. The Westover property continued to be a site of significant Indian trading activity.

19. Byrd, *Secret Diary*, 3.

20. Hening, *Statutes*, 2:336; Washburn, *Governor and the Rebel*, 20–21.

21. Washburn, *Governor and the Rebel*, 20; Morgan, *American Slavery, American Freedom*, 260.

22. Morgan, *American Slavery, American Freedom*, 255; Berkeley, "Letter to Nathaniel Bacon, September 14, 1675," in Berkeley, *Papers*, 486–87.

23. Meyers, "From Refugees to Slave Traders," 92; Everett, "They shalbe slaves for their lives," 84–85.

24. Everett, "They shalbe slaves for their lives," 84–85. Governor Berkeley wrote to the secretary of the House of Burgesses, Thomas Ludwell, on April 1, stating, "Since that they kild two men at Mr. Birds house which I thinke were most foolishly lost more mischiefe I cannot heare they have done to us and to prevent more the Grand Assembly have ordered that five hundred men be immediately raysed to defend the heads of al the Rivers." "Governor Berkeley to Thomas Ludwell, April 1, 1676," in Berkeley, *Papers*, 507.

25. Morgan, *American Slavery, American Freedom*, 255; Coventry and Coventry, *Coventry Papers*, reel 64, vol. 77, frames 89, 101.

26. Morgan, *American Slavery, American Freedom*, 255; Coventry and Coventry, *Coventry Papers*, reel 64, vol. 77, frame 103.

27. Washburn, *Governor and the Rebel*, 35; Meyers, "From Refugees to Slave Traders," 87.

28. Ward and Davis, "Tribes and Traders," 137.

29. Everett, "They shalbe slaves for their lives," 88–89.

30. T. Snyder, *Brabbling Women*, 26.

31. Rice, *Tales from a Revolution*, 48–49.

32. "Letter to Thomas Ludwell, July 1, 1676," in Berkeley, *Papers*, 537.

33. Tyler, "Bacon's Rebellion"; Bacon's Rebellion Eggleston MSS: Being copies of State Papers now in the British Public Record Office, London, relating to the seventeenth century, Virginia State Library, "Mrs. Bird's Relation, who lived nigh Mr. Bacon in Virginia, and came from there July last for feare of the Indians," Eg 2395, Folio 550.

34. Andrews, *Narratives*, 25–27; Hening, *Statutes*, 2:346.

35. Rountree, *Powhatan Indians of Virginia*, 96; Clayton, "Another Account of Virginia," 434.

36. McCartney, "Cockacoeske, Queen of Pamunkey," 246–47; see also Schmidt, "Cockacoeske," 304–10.

37. McCartney, "Cockacoeske, Queen of Pamunkey," 247; Schmidt, *Divided Dominion*, 157. Schmidt points out that it is unlikely that Cockacoeske was speaking out of grief and that her motivations were more than likely shrewd and tactical.

38. Morgan, *American Slavery, American Freedom*, 266.

39. Andrews, *Narratives*, 25–27; Hening, *Statutes*, 2:346. It is likely no coincidence that Carolina would fight a very similar "civil war" in the 1680s over the control of Indian trade between the Lords Proprietors and the Goose Creek Men.

40. Andrews, *Narratives*, 138.

41. Ibid., 66–71, 129–36; Andrew Marvell to Henry Thompson, November 14, 1676, HM 21813, Huntingdon Library, Colonial Papers, 1/42, fol. 178.

42. Andrews, *Narratives*, 140; marginal note in original.

43. Berry, Moryson, and Jeffreys, "A True Narratives of the Rise, Progress, and Cessation of the Late Rebellion," Colonial Papers, 5/1371, fol. 393.

44. Andrews, *Narratives*, 140–41.

45. Ibid., 138.

46. Ibid., 66–71, 129–36; Andrew Marvell to Henry Thompson, November 14, 1676, HM 21813, Huntingdon Library, Colonial Papers, 1/42, fol. 178.

47. Westbury, "Women in Bacon's Rebellion," 40; Hening, *Statutes*, 2:385; Blackstone, *Commentaries on the Laws of England*, 4:28–29.

48. Spruill, *Women's Life and Work*, 320, 339.

49. Westbury, "Women in Bacon's Rebellion," 39; Andrews, *Narratives*, 111; Sarah Grendon to Herbert Jeffries, n.d., in Coventry and Coventry, *Coventry Papers*, reel 65, vol. 78, frames 5, 6.

50. K. Brown, *Good Wives, Nasty Wenches, and Anxious Patriarchs*, 176, referencing Colonial Papers, 1/39, fols. 180–81.

51. Tyler, "Heroines of Virginia," 41.

52. K. Brown, *Good Wives, Nasty Wenches, and Anxious Patriarchs*, 176, referencing Colonial Papers, 1/39, fols. 180–81; Oberg, *Samuel Wiseman's Book of Record*, 261.

53. Andrews, *Narratives*, 111; Sarah Grendon to Herbert Jeffries, n.d., in Coventry and Coventry, *Coventry Papers*, reel 65, vol. 78, frames 5, 6.

54. Oberg, *Samuel Wiseman's Book of Record*, 261.

55. Marambaud, "William Byrd I," 140, referencing Colonial Papers, 5/1371, fol. 340.

56. Tyler, "Personal Grievances."

57. McCartney, "Cockacoeske, Queen of Pamunkey," 250; Herbert Jeffreys, letter to Right Honorable, June 11, 1677, in Coventry and Coventry, *Coventry Papers*, reel 64, vol. 77, frames 64–65.

58. McCartney, "Cockacoeske, Queen of Pamunkey," 250.

59. The frontlet still survives but is no longer with the Pamunkey. It is housed at the Virginia Historical Society in Richmond. In May 2010, at Williamsburg, the Pamunkey received an exact replica commissioned by the Colonial Williamsburg Foundation. Ibid., 251–52; in her note on the subject McCartney writes, "From Berry and Moryson's letter requesting the presents we learn that she was 'of a meane or indifferent stature and somewhat plump of body' and that young John West, whom they called 'the Prince, her son and successor,' was a 'good, brave young man pretty full of stature and slender of body, a great war caption among the Indians and one that has been very active in the service of the English.'"

60. Ibid., 253–54; McIlwaine, *Executive Journals of the Council*, 1:4; Hening, *Statutes*, 2:275–77.

61. McIlwaine, *Executive Journals of the Council*, 1:4.

62. Hening, *Statutes*, 2:275–77.

63. McCartney, "Cockacoeske, Queen of Pamunkey," 255.

64. Thomas Ludwell, letter to Right Honorable, January 30, 1678, in Coventry and Coventry, *Coventry Papers*, reel 64, vol. 77, frames 202–3.

65. McCartney, "Cockacoeske, Queen of Pamunkey," 256; Queen of Pamunkey (Cockacoeske), The Agrievances of the Queen of Poemunkey and her Sonn Captain John West, June 5, 1678, in Colonial Papers, 1/42, fol. 177; Cockacoeske, letter to Colonel Francis Moryson, June 29, 1678, in Colonial Papers, 1/42, fol. 276.

66. McCartney, "Cockacoeske, Queen of Pamunkey," 259.

67. Marambaud, "William Byrd I," 141.

68. "Letter to Perry & Lane, March 29, 1685," in Byrd, *Correspondence*, 31; "Letter to Warham Horsmanden, March 1684/85," in ibid., 32; Tyler, "Personal Grievances."

69. "Letter to Warham Horsmanden, March 1684/85," in Byrd, *Correspondence*, 32; "Letter to Nordest Rand, March 31, 1685," in ibid., 35–36; "Letter to Robert Coe April 1, 1685," in ibid., 39; "Letter to Thomas Gower, June 8, 1685," in ibid., 42–43; T. Snyder, *Brabbling Women*, 126, referencing Lockridge, *On the Sources of Patriarchal Rage*, 1–27.

70. McCartney, "Cockacoeske, Queen of Pamunkey," 259–60, referencing McIlwaine, *Executive Journals of the Council*, 1:79; Francis Nicholson, letter to his Council, October 22, 1702, in Colonial Papers, 5/1312, part 1, fol. 318.

71. Hutner, *Colonial Women*, 96.

4 / In the Wake of War: Tributary Obligations

1. Billings, "Precis of the Treaty," in *Old Dominion*, 292–93.
2. Ibid., 283, 562.
3. Ibid., 341–50.
4. McIlwaine, *Journals of the House of Burgesses*, 69.
5. Surry County Orders; Haun, *Surry County*, 89.
6. Hening, *Statutes*, 2:440.
7. Ibid., 2:491.
8. Ibid., 2:562.
9. Palmer, *Calendar*, 1:19.
10. Hening, *Statutes*, 2:333, 251.
11. McIlwaine, *Executive Journals of the Council*, 3:140; McIlwaine, *Journals of the House of Burgesses*, 3:15–18.

12. Henrico County Miscellaneous Court Records; Weisiger, *Henrico County Virginia Deeds*, 18, 21, 33.

13. Henrico County Miscellaneous Court Records; Weisiger, *Henrico County Virginia Deeds*, 33. Bevill's will left an Indian girl (Dorothy) to her son John on his eighteenth birthday and the Indian Sarah, a slave, to her son Essex when he turned fourteen.

14. B. Stanard, "Will of Mrs. Mary Scarburgh," 222.

15. McIlwaine, *Executive Journals of the Council*, 1:262.

16. B. Stanard, "From Virginia Historical Society Papers of Governor Nicholson," 164.

17. Jennings, *New Worlds of Violence*, xvii–xix, 101, 112–113.

18. Lawson, *New Voyage*, 175.

19. Byrd, *Secret Diary*, 29; "Letter to Perry and Lane, February the 2d, 1684/85," in Byrd, *Correspondence*, 29.

20. Byrd, *Prose Works*, 219.

21. Lederer, "Discoveries," ed. Alvord and Bidgood, 169.

22. Hening, *Statutes*, 2:480.

23. McIlwaine, *Executive Journals of the Council*, 1:40; Byrd, *Secret Diary*, 4; Warren, *Worlds the Shawnees Made*, 89.

24. McIlwaine, *Executive Journals of the Council*, 1:153.

25. Hening, *Statutes*, 3:69.

26. "Letter to Perry and Lane, June 3, 1691," in Byrd, *Correspondence*, 153. Refers to "An Act for Free Trade with Indians," repealing laws restricting trade with Indians and prohibiting persons from "hunting remote from the plantations" without license.

27. "Letter to Perry and Lane, June 4, 1691," in Byrd, *Correspondence*, 154.

28. Harrison, "Western Explorations," 325–26.

29. For more on the college, see chapter 5; ibid., 332.

30. Ibid., 334–36.

31. Everett, "They shalbe slaves for their lives," 80; Colonial Papers, 1/44, no. 42, fol. 131.

32. Leder, *Livingston Indian Records*, 88–89.

33. "Letter to Francis Howard, Baron Howard of Effingham, June the 10th, 1689," in Byrd, *Correspondence*, 107.

34. "Letter to Arthur North, July the 23th, 1689," in ibid., 111.

35. "Letter to Perry & Lane, July the 21th, 1690," in ibid., 118; Byrd commented on these concerns in some personal letters as well: "Letter to Daniel Horsmanden, July the 25th, 1690," in ibid., 121; and "Letter to Nordest Rand, July the 25th 1690," in ibid., 122–23. To Rand, Byrd wrote, "Tho the greatest damage hath been here lately, was by Indians. I had one of my family kild & two carried away about a moneth since."

36. "Byrd to Unknown Addressee, May 10, 1686," in Byrd, *Secret Diary*, 59–61; "Byrd to Lord Effingham, June 10, 1689," in Ewan, *John Banister*, 91; McIlwaine, *Executive Journals*, 1:262. See chapter 4.

37. McIlwaine, *Executive Journals of the Council*, 1:104.

38. Byrd, *Secret Diary*, 121, 123. No mention of these events is included in a letter to his son William Byrd II, written on the same day.

39. McIlwaine, *Executive Journals of the Council*, 1:315.

40. Ibid., 1:333.
41. Ibid.
42. Traunter, "Travels of Richard Traunter," 2.
43. Ibid., 3.
44. Ibid., 5-6.
45. Ibid., 10-11.
46. Ibid., 18-20.
47. Ibid., 21-24.
48. Ibid., 28-30.
49. Kelton, *Epidemics and Enslavement*, xviii.
50. Traunter, "Travels of Richard Traunter," 4.
51. Ibid., 7-8.
52. Ibid., 11.
53. Everett, "They shalbe slaves for their lives," 92.
54. D. Brown, "Beyond the Blackwater," 1700:22, 1700:19.
55. Briceland, *Westward from Virginia*, 171.
56. Beverley, *History and Present State of Virginia*, 39.
57. Merrell, *Indians' New World*, 52. Robert Hix also had a slave named Bess, who was likely Appalachee. See D. Brown, "Beyond the Blackwater," 1700:22, 72. Her daughter Amy later sued for her freedom in Mecklenburg County.
58. McIlwaine, *Executive Journals of the Council*, 1:92-94. See also Parent, *Foul Means*, 23-24.
59. McIlwaine, *Executive Journals of the Council*, 1:122.
60. Ibid., 1:126.
61. Ibid., 1:280-81.
62. Ibid., 1:284.
63. Ibid., 1:337.
64. Ibid., 2:182.
65. Rountree, *Pocahontas's People*, 118-19. This is the same region where Colonel Fantleroy had land disputes with the Native inhabitants. According to Rountree, the concerns began as early as 1656, and by March 1658 "the Assembly had to assure the Rappahannocks of fifty acres for each bowman and order that their conflicts over land with Englishmen be settled." The Virginia Council sought to move the Rappahannock out of the region to create a buffer zone between English settlers and Iroquoian raiders. Ragan, "Scatter'd upon the English Seats," 228.
66. McIlwaine, *Executive Journals of the Council*, 1:284.
67. Ibid., 1:135.
68. Palmer, *Calendar*, 1:22.
69. Rountree, *Pocahontas's People*, 115.
70. McIlwaine, *Executive Journals of the Council*, 1:373.
71. Ibid., 2:94-95.
72. Rountree, *Pocahontas's People*, 105.
73. McIlwaine, *Executive Journals of the Council*, 1:439-40.
74. Ibid., 2:183-84. There is no mention of this case in the journals of the House of Burgesses.
75. A clear case of problems in the northern border of the colony can be found in the issues colonists had with the Piscataway. See Shefveland, "'Wholly Subjected'?" 132.

76. McIlwaine, *Executive Journals of the Council*, 1:13.
77. Ibid., 2:368–69.
78. Ibid., 2:383–86.
79. Ibid.
80. Ibid.
81. Ibid., 2:388–91.
82. McIlwaine, *Journals of the House Burgesses*, xxv.
83. Winfree, *Laws of Virginia*, 41–45.
84. McIlwaine, *Journals of the House Burgesses*, xxv.
85. Everett, "They shalbe slaves for their lives," 96–97.
86. Winfree, *Laws of Virginia*, 18; Hening, *Statutes*, 2:343.
87. McIlwaine, *Executive Journals of the Council*, 1:83–84.
88. Ibid., 2:315.
89. Winfree, *Laws of Virginia*, 41–45.
90. Ibid., 112.
91. Ibid., 152–53.
92. For a detailed discussion of the interviews, see Tyler, "Indians of Southern Virginia," 1–11. The interviews relay movements after Bacon's Rebellion and the names of participants in the Tuscarora War.
93. Byrd, *Correspondence*, 2:3.
94. McIlwaine, *Executive Journals of the Council*, 1:146–47.
95. Ibid., 1:157–58.
96. Ibid.
97. Ethridge, *Creek Country*, 228. Although Ethridge's work references the blood law of the Creeks for clan revenge, it is applicable here for the argument made by the Saponi and Nottoway as well as for the various examples throughout this chapter of reciprocal violence in reaction to white encroachment. For example, the Creek law of blood revenge is similar to the argument made by the Saponi and Nottoway. The Creek law had "mechanisms for mitigating some deaths and injuries, especially those that were accidental. The clan of the injured party could accept material compensation and let the matter rest." Ibid., 231.
98. McIlwaine, *Executive Journals of the Council*, 3:202–4.
99. Palmer, *Calendar*, 1:131.
100. Ibid.
101. Ibid.
102. McIlwaine, *Executive Journals of the Council*, 3:21.
103. Byrd, *Secret Diary*, 319.
104. Bushnell, "Account of Lamhatty," 568–569; Everett, "They shalbe slaves for their lives," 94–95; Ethridge, *From Chicaza to Chickasaw*, 152, 284n12. Controversy surrounds whether Lamhatty was kidnapped by the Tuscarora or by the Creek. See Waselkov, "Indian Maps"; and Bossy, "Indian Slavery."
105. Lawson, *New Voyage*, 208.
106. Lawson, *New Voyage*, 174.
107. Waselkov, "Lamhatty's Map," 26–27.

5 / The New Paradigm: Alexander Spotswood's Trade Policies

The epigraph is taken from Byrd, *Prose Works*, 246–48, 284. Byrd was critical of Alexander Spotswood's trade policies and educational goals.

1. Assistance that was promised by Spotswood but never received.
2. Merrell, *Indians' New World*, 52. Merrell describes this competition as not merely intercolonial, explaining that "if South Carolina was ever to establish what it termed a 'reputation' in these [Indian] villages, it would have to treat Virginians as it did Frenchmen or Spaniards and drive them out."
3. McIlwaine, *Executive Journals of the Council*, 3:177.
4. Ibid., 3:181–82.
5. Ibid., 3:198, 200.
6. Ibid., 3:204, 214.
7. Byrd, *Secret Diary*, 5; McIlwaine, *Executive Journals of the Council*, 3:207.
8. McIlwaine, *Executive Journals of the Council*, 2:217.
9. Byrd, *Secret Diary*, 131.
10. Ibid., 61–63; McIlwaine, *Executive Journals of the Council*, 2:207, 220.
11. Byrd, *Secret Diary*, 186.
12. McIlwaine, *Executive Journals of the Council*, 3:242. Spotswood acted as lieutenant governor under Governor George Douglas-Hamilton, First Earl of Orkney, who never visited Virginia.
13. The Virginians traded with the Tuscarora as early as the 1650s, since the Bland expedition successfully established trade contacts with the Tuscarora in their trading town of Katearas. By 1663 the Tuscarora threatened settlers and tributaries south of the James River but complaints from the Nottoway, Pamunkey, and Chickahominy escalated just prior to the outbreak of war between settlers in Carolina and the Tuscarora.
14. Robinson, *Early American Indian Documents*, 168–73; Tyler, "Indians of Southern Virginia," 337. North Carolina claimed that the northern boundary was the Nottoway River and the Virginians countered that it was the Wococon or Wicokocon Creek, fifteen miles south of the Nottoway River. The North Carolinian claim was proven correct in 1728 by William Byrd, William Dandridge, and Richard Fitzwilliams. See Byrd, "History of the Dividing Line."
15. McIlwaine, *Executive Journals of the Council*, 3:265.
16. Ibid.
17. Ibid., 3:287–88. See also McIlwaine, *Journals of the House of Burgesses*, 148.
18. "Letter to the Bishop of London, November 11th, 1711," in Spotswood, *Official Letters*, 1:126; McIlwaine, *Executive Journals of the Council*, 3:293–95. Agreeing to the peace were the towns of Raroucaithue, Kinquenarant, Taughousie, Chounanitz, Taughoutnith, Kinthaigh, Touhairoukha, Unaghnara (spoken for by Tuscarora delegates Chongkerarise, Rouiatthie, Rouiattat).
19. Byrd, *Secret Diary*, 417.
20. Ibid., 424–25. See also LaVere, *Tuscarora War*, 82–83.
21. Hatfield, *Atlantic Virginia*, 185.
22. Lawson, *New Voyage*, 41, 192, 194; Braund, *Deerskins and Duffels*, 89. Braund is referencing the Creek in the lower Southeast; however, traders in Virginia also took Native wives in exchange for trade relationships as part of Eastern Woodlands

trade customs. These relationships ran the gamut from casual encounters to lasting marriages.

23. McIlwaine, *Executive Journals of the Council*, 3:291–93; 301–3.
24. "Letter to Lord Dartmouth, May 8, 1712," in Spotswood, *Official Letters*, 1:146.
25. McIlwaine, *Executive Journals of the Council*, 3:313, 315–16.
26. Ibid., 3:324.
27. Palmer, *Calendar*, 1:158.
28. Dodson, *Alexander Spotswood*, 75.
29. McIlwaine, *Executive Journals of the Council*, 3:356–58; "Letter to ye Lords Comm'rs of Trade, Novem'r ye 16, 1713," in Spotswood, *Official Letters*, 2:42.
30. "Letter to ye Lords Comm'rs of Trade, Novem'r ye 16, 1713," in Spotswood, *Official Letters*, 2:42.
31. McIlwaine, *Executive Journals of the Council*, 3:356–58; "Letter to ye Lords Comm'rs of Trade, Novem'r ye 16, 1713," in Spotswood, *Official Letters*, 2:42; LaVere, *Tuscarora War*, 162–63; W. Stanard, "Examination of Indians," 17.
32. McIlwaine, *Executive Journals of the Council*, 3:362–66.
33. "Letter to the Lords Commis'rs of Trade, March 9th, 1713/14," in Spotswood, *Official Letters*, 2:57.
34. The Stukanox, Stuckanock, and Stegaraki are not listed elsewhere in the record except for in these agreements.
35. McIlwaine, *Executive Journals of the Council*, 3:367–68, 372–73. Spotswood wrote, "The Tuscaros, induced thereto (as they say), by the people of Carolina, have departed from their agreements with this Governm't, and gon[e] to settle once more upon that Province, I continue, all resolv'd, to settle out our Tributary Indians as a guard to ye Frontiers, and in order to supply that part, w'ch was to have been covered by the Tuscaruros, I have placed here a number of Prodestant Germans." "Letter to the L'ds Comm'rs of Trade July 21st 1714," in Spotswood, *Official Letters*, 2:70.
36. McIlwaine, *Executive Journals of the Council*, 2:188, 296, 310.
37. Ibid., 1:367–68, 372–73; "Letter to the L'ds Comm'rs of Trade, July 21st 1714," in Spotswood, *Official Letters*, 2:70; "Letter to the Earl of Dartmouth, May 15, 1713," in ibid., 2:18, "Letter to ye E'le of Dartmouth, June 10, 1713," in ibid., 2:25.
38. McIlwaine, *Executive Journals of the Council*, 3:352.
39. Ibid., 3:362–66.
40. Ibid., 3:366–67.
41. LaVere, *Tuscarora War*, 94–95. LaVere describes Blount as "wily" while discussing the ways Virginia attempted to manipulate the trade war.
42. McIlwaine, *Executive Journals of the Council*, 1:367–68, 372–73; "Letter to the L'ds Comm'rs of Trade, July 21st 1714," in Spotswood, *Official Letters*, 2:70; "Letter to the Earl of Dartmouth, May 15, 1713," in ibid., 2:18, "Letter to ye E'le of Dartmouth, June 10, 1713," in ibid., 2:25.
43. To save money, Spotswood disbanded most of the rangers in the colony except for twenty-four along the northern border and instead planned to utilize Fort Christanna as a buffer along the southwestern border. "Letter to ye Lords Commissioners of Trade, January 27, 1714/15," in Spotswood, *Official Letters*, 2:99, "Letter to the Commissioners of ye Customs, January 27, 1714/15," in ibid., 2:108. He also settled German protestants along the Rappahannock River as a buffer against the northern Indians.

44. "Letter to ye Lords Commissioners of Trade, January 27, 1714/15," in Spotswood, *Official Letters*, 2:99, 108; Billings, Selby, and Tate, *Colonial Virginia*, 179.

45. Dodson, *Alexander Spotswood*, 93–94.

46. "Letter to the Lords Comm'rs of Trade, May 9th 1716," in Spotswood, *Official Letters*, 2:144. See Greene, "Opposition to Lieutenant Governor Alexander Spotswood."

47. "Letter to the Lords Comm'rs of Trade, May 9th 1716," in Spotswood, *Official Letters*, 2:145–46.

48. Spotswood, *Official Letters*; Merrell, *Indians' New World*, 78. Merrell's take on the trade war between Carolina and Virginia still remains the most comprehensive study to date.

49. Hening, *Statutes*, 2:410.

50. "Letter to the Lords Commissioners for Trade and Plantations, April 5, 1717," in Spotswood, *Official Letters*, 2:227–28.

51. "Letter to the Lords Comm'rs of Trade, May 9th 1716," in ibid., 2:145–46.

52. Szasz, *Indian Education*, 64–65.

53. Hening, *Statutes*, 1:393–96.

54. Old Rappahannock County Orders; Sparacio, *Deed and Will Abstracts*, 1:10–11.

55. Hening, *Statutes*, 1:193.

56. Certainly one can argue that the sale of Indian children as slaves and servants did much to hamper Indian interest in providing hostage children.

57. McIlwaine, *Executive Journals of the Council*, 3:198.

58. Szasz, *Indian Education*, 68–69. In 1723 the college established a separate building, the Brafferton School, for Indian education.

59. Ibid., 68.

60. Blair cited in Robinson, "Indian Education and Missions," 161.

61. Hening, *Statutes*, 3:123.

62. McIlwaine, *Executive Journals of the Council*, 1:311.

63. Morpurgo Papers, College of William and Mary.

64. Jones, *Present State of Virginia*, 92. Even the English presented some concerns over the corruptible nature of the schoolmasters charged with Indian pupils. In a letter from Henry Compton, bishop of London, to Francis Nicholson dated January 5, 1698, Compton writes that "from ye example in Virginia," a school can be made "either unsafe or dangerous." Nicholson Papers, Colonial Williamsburg Foundation.

65. Brafferton Estate Collection, College of William and Mary. Individuals in peripheral tributary settlements gained some English skills, as is evident in the case of Robin, a Pamunkey shoemaker who requested to stay with the English. And there are many examples of adult tributaries who adopted some English habits while working as hunters and trackers who remained outside English settlements in a hybrid society based off the needs of the trade. Rountree, "Powhatans and the English," 198.

66. Beverley, *History and Present State of Virginia*, 231–32.

67. "To the Bishop of London, November 11, 1711," in Spotswood, *Official Letters*, 2:126–28.

68. Morpurgo Papers, College of William and Mary.

69. McIlwaine, *Executive Journals of the Council*, 3:287–88, 290–91.

70. The SPG was established in 1701 and by the time of Spotswood's appeal it was bolstered by a decree from King William III to send priests and schoolteachers to America.

71. "To the Bishop of London, November 11, 1711," in Spotswood, *Official Letters*, 2:126–28. Spotswood was constantly in a political tug-of-war with his Executive Council and the House of Burgesses.

72. "To the Bishop of London, May 8, 1712," in ibid., 1:156–57.

73. "To the Bishop of London, July 26, 1712," in ibid., 1:174–75.

74. "To the Archbishop of Canterbury, July 26, 1712," in ibid., 1:176–77.

75. Lawson, *New Voyage*, 243.

76. Hofstra, *Planting of New Virginia*, 56–60.

77. McIlwaine, *Executive Journals of the Council*, 3:188, 296, 310.

78. According to Hazzard and McCartney, the two treaties concluded with the tributaries and the Tuscarora that spring dealt primarily with trade and then Christianizing the Indians. "Spotswood felt that conducting trade on a just and equal footing, with a fair administration of justice, would have created a respect for English laws and government and a dependency upon the English to supply all trade goods." Hazzard and McCartney, *Fort Christanna*, 7.

79. McIlwaine, *Executive Journals of the Council*, 3:375–76; Winfree, *Laws of Virginia*, 104–13.

80. "To the Bishop of London, January 27, 1714," in Spotswood, *Official Letters*, 2:89.

81. Gamble, "Community of Convenience," 73.

82. McIlwaine, *Executive Journals of the Council*, 3:405–8; Fontaine, *Journal*, 93. The "Great Men" of local Indians, according to Fontaine, formed a council of twelve men who had the "power to act for the whole nation, and they will stand to every thing that thos twelve men agree to, as their own act."

83. McIlwaine, *Executive Journals of the Council*, 3:412, 440.

84. Dodson, *Alexander Spotswood*, 84.

85. Jones, *Present State of Virginia*, 15.

86. Goetz, *Baptism of Early Virginia*, 140–48.

87. "To the Bishop of London, January 27, 1714," in Spotswood, *Official Letters*, 2:91; Jones, *State of Virginia*, 70–71.

88. "To Ye Lords Commiss'rs of Trade, June ye 4th, 1715," in ibid., 2:113.

89. "To the Bishop of London, October 26th, 1715," in ibid., 2:138.

90. "To the L'ds Comm'rs of Trade, Feb'y 16th, 1716," in ibid., 2:141.

91. Fontaine toured the peripheral region of the Virginia colony on three separate trips covering nearly two hundred miles over the course of ten days. His parents in Dublin had sent him to Virginia to scope for good land for the family settlement. Alexander, "Indian Vocabulary," 303. The journal Fontaine kept was likely for his own personal viewing only, as it was not published until his great-grandniece, Ann Maury, included it in her 1853 book, *Memoirs of a Huguenot Family*.

92. Fontaine, *Journal*, 92.

93. Ibid., 94; Gamble, "Community of Convenience," 78–79; Lawson, *New Voyage*, 53–55.

94. Fontaine, *Journal*, 94; Byrd, *Secret Diary*, 424–25.

95. Fontaine, *Journal*, 97; Gamble, "Community of Convenience," 84. Gamble writes, "Despite living in the shadow of the colonial fort, the Saponis chose their town site and laid it out in their customary manner. They may have acceded to a new colonial relationship, but they also established some boundaries around their autonomy."

96. Fontaine, *Journal*, 98.
97. Ibid.
98. Ibid., 12. Robert Beverley quoted Philip Alexander, who wrote, "One may speculate as to how Fontaine secured the list. He may, of course, have talked with one or several Indians and spelled out the words phonetically as best he could." Beverley, *History and Present State of Virginia*. He likely learned them from Charles Griffin, the teacher.
99. Fontaine, *Journal*, 95.
100. Ibid., 98.
101. "To the Bishop of London, May 23d, 1716," in Spotswood, *Official Letters*, 2:159.
102. "To Mr. Popple, April 16th 1717," in ibid., 2:236; Rice, *Nature and History*, 187. Rice writes, "The 1717 attack on Ft. Christanna was an important turning point. It set off a sustained burst of north-south warfare, which in turn set off a burst of diplomatic activity that would eventually open the backcountry to colonial farming. . . . The attack on Ft. Christanna also inspired the first serious diplomatic initiative between Virginia and the Five Nations since the 1680s."
103. "To the Lords Commissioners for Trade and Plantations, Aug't 29th 1717," in Spotswood, *Official Letters*, 2:258.
104. It is relevant to consider Byrd's perspective not only because he was a contemporary of Spotswood and Fontaine but also because evidence clearly illustrates that Byrd considered himself to be a Christian man. For more on the religious beliefs of the emerging planter class in Virginia, see Winner, *Cheerful and Comfortable Faith*, 103–9. Byrd clearly had a model of what "appropriately pious prayer looked like, and he measured himself against that model." It is clear that he did not feel Native students met the standard. Additionally, one must question Byrd's involvement in the opposition to Spotswood and the assembly's open hostility to Spotswood's proselytization plans.
105. Byrd, *Prose Works*, 220–21.
106. Ibid., 115.
107. Billings, Selby, and Tate, *Colonial Virginia*, 180.
108. McIlwaine, *Journals of the House of Burgesses*, 155.
109. "Letter to the Lords Commissioners of Trade and Plantations, Jan'ry ye 16th, 1716/17," in Spotswood, *Official Letters*, 2:206, 230, 234.
110. "Letter to the Lords Commissioners for Trade and Plantations, April 5, 1717," in ibid., 2:227–28.
111. Greene, "Opposition to Lieutenant Governor Alexander Spotswood," 37.
112. "Feb'ry ye 27th 1718 To the Lords of Trade," in Spotswood, *Official Letters*, 2:263.
113. McIlwaine, *Executive Journals of the Council*, 3:478; McIlwaine, *Journals of the House of Burgesses*, 207.
114. Ibid.; Egloff and Woodward, *First People*, 50. Spotswood held council with the governors of New York, Pennsylvania, and Maryland, at which he suggested that the Iroquois might carry official passes and travel only west of the Blue Ridge Mountains while the Virginia Indians would stay in the east. For a history of Virginian-Iroquoian diplomacy and Spotswood's role, see Rhoades, *Long Knives and the Longhouse*.

6 / Peace at Albany: 1722

1. Warren, *Worlds the Shawnees Made*, 139–42.
2. Ibid., 150–51. For a detailed discussion of Maryland's role in this, see 143–45.

3. Ibid., 153.

4. Lakomäki, *Gathering Together*, 38.

5. Aquila, *Iroquois Restoration*, 46; see Venables, "Polishing the Silver Covenant Chain."

6. "Lords Commissioners of Trade and Plantations on February 7, 1715/16," in Spotswood, *Official Letters*, 2:193.

7. Ibid., 2:194–95.

8. Ibid., 2:205–06.

9. Ibid., 2:208.

10. "A Paper Containing the Resolves of ye Assembly of Virg'a, Sept'r Ye 2d, 1715, after w'ch was the following Letter directed to:—To the Lords Com'rs of Trade and Plantacons," in ibid., 2:219–20.

11. "May ye 30th, 1717. To Mr. Secretary Methuen," in ibid., 2:251–52.

12. McIlwaine, *Executive Journals of the Council*, 3:456; Dodson, *Alexander Spotswood*, 2:109–10.

13. "Aug't 27th, 1717. To Mr. Secretary Addison," in Spotswood, *Official Letters*, 2:256.

14. "Aug't 29th, 1717. To the Lords Commissioners for Trade and Plantations," in ibid., 2:257–59.

15. Billings, Selby, and Tate, *Colonial Virginia*, 195.

16. Aquila, *Iroquois Restoration*, 213.

17. "Feb'ry ye 27th, 1717 [1718]. To the Lords of Trade," in Spotswood, *Official Letters*, 2:261–62.

18. McIlwaine, *Journals of the House of Burgesses*, 6:189.

19. Ibid., 6:197.

20. Ibid., 6:199. It was also during this time that the House suggested the Catawba hostages be sent back, but the council argued that they were "apprehensive" of this move because it would look like "a Declaration that we could have no longer any Correspondence with those Indians the Consequences whereof might have been fatal" and they feared the danger the Seneca and Tuscarora posed to those Indians. This was visited more formally on May 28, when the council drafted a letter to Spotswood asking that the Saponi be treated like other tributaries, the Catawba children sent home, and the fort closed. Ibid., 6:199–201, 212–13.

21. McIlwaine, *Journals of the House of Burgesses*, 6:202.

22. McIlwaine, *Executive Journals of the Council*, 3:474.

23. Ibid., 3:478–79.

24. Ibid., 3:481.

25. Billings, Selby, and Tate, *Colonial Virginia*, 195.

26. McIlwaine, *Executive Journals of the Council*, 3:483.

27. "Aug't 14th, 1718. To the Board of Trade," in Spotswood, *Official Letters*, 2:289.

28. Ibid., 297. This indicates that Spotswood and the English likely never intended to keep the promises made in the 1722 treaty at Albany. In another letter, "Feb'ry ye 1st, 1719 [1720]," in ibid., 331, Spotswood repeats his concerns about French trading, this time with the Cherokee, writing that they were "the only Indians we ought to depend on to balla. the North'n Nation if they should attempt to be troublesome to these Plantacons."

29. "Aug't 14th, 1718. To the Board of Trade," in ibid., 302.

30. McIlwaine, *Executive Journals of the Council*, 3:498–99.

31. Ibid., 3:506–7.

32. Ibid., 3:507–10. At issue during this meeting as well was a murder allegation made by the Nottoway against the Saponi. At a later meeting, July 14, 1719, the Saponi alleged that a Catawba committed the murder, but the Nottoway said the scalp of their man was seen in the hands of a Saponi boy. The Saponi promised the council to bring them the accused boys "if any proofs shall appear agt them." The Nottoway complaint was revisited on September 4, 1719, when the governor asked the Nottoway to provide a list of English colonists who could prove the Nottoway complaint so that "Speedy Justice may be done for the Murder Complained of."

33. Ibid., 3:510.

34. Ibid., 3:511. Only Edmond Jennings, James Blair, Philip Ludwell, John Smith, and Mann Page were present.

35. Ibid., 3:514.

36. Ibid., 3:517–19.

37. Ibid., 3:520–21.

38. "Feb'ry ye 1st, 1719 [1720]," in Spotswood, *Official Letters*, 2:333. Note from the edited volume of letters that Schuyler "headed a successful expedition against the French north of Lake Champlain in 1691. In 1710, he took, at his own expense, five Indians chiefs to England for the purpose of exciting the government to vigorous measures against the French in Canada. In 1719, as the oldest member and President of the Council, the government of New York devolved on him."

39. McIlwaine, *Executive Journals of the Council*, 3:532.

40. McIlwaine, *Journals of the House of Burgesses*, 6:250.

41. McIlwaine, *Executive Journals of the Council*, 3:534.

42. McIlwaine, *Journals of the House of Burgesses*, 6:274, 286. The House revisited the matter briefly on November 30.

43. Ibid., 6:298–99.

44. Ibid., 6: 305, 311; topic briefly revisited December 21.

45. Ibid., 6:298–99, 305.

46. Bradford, "Particulars of an Indian Treaty," 4.

47. Aquila, *Iroquois Restoration*, 160.

48. Lakomäki, *Gathering Together*, 34–35.

49. Bradford, "Particulars of an Indian Treaty," 9. Another issue presented by the Iroquois in their meetings with Keith were their claims to Susquehanna lands. See Aquila, *Iroquois Restoration*, 161–62. The outcome of discussions with the Susquehanna and the Cayuga was that "the Pennsylvania government could no longer purchase land in the Susquehanna Valley without first obtaining consent from the Iroquois."

50. Bradford, "Particulars of an Indian Treaty," 5–6, 8–9.

51. Ibid., 10–11.

52. Lakomäki, *Gathering Together*, 39.

53. McIlwaine, *Executive Journals of the Council*, 3:549–50.

54. Pennsylvania Archives, *Minutes of the Provincial Council*, 3:206.

55. Ibid., 3:210.

56. Ibid., 3:211.

57. Ibid., 3:212.

58. McIlwaine, *Executive Journals of the Council*, 3:552–54. This would later prove to be an area of debate. Settlers moved quickly and persistently west of the mountains

and when the Iroquois later complained, the colonists claimed the agreement was only that the Iroquois could not come east, not that settlers could not move west.

59. Ibid., 3:554–55. The record stops here.

60. Ibid., 4:1.

61. Ibid., 4:2. The charges for the accommodation of these goods were laid before the board on November 3. Problems with western and southern trade arose with the South Carolina Act of Trade from November 1721. On June 13 Spotswood sought the opinion of the council, which agreed unanimously that that the South Carolinian act was "highly injurious" to the Virginian Indian trade, "destructive of the good correspondence between the English and the Western Indians." Their main argument was that rather than regulating the trade, the South Carolinians were imposing difficulties on the Virginians that would destroy the trade through taxes. They also argued that South Carolinians were misrepresenting the Virginians and that the Virginians were seeking peace with the Five Nations and Cherokee, while "it is demonstrable that the Schemes of the Carolina Assembly for continuing a War between those Indians, are founded upon the private Interest of their Traders." Ibid., 4:17–18.

62. McIlwaine, *Journals of the House of Burgesses*, 6:319.

63. Ibid., 6:323.

64. Ibid., 6:347.

65. McIlwaine, *Executive Journals of the Council*, 4:8–9.

66. Ibid., 4:13.

67. Ibid., 4:15.

68. Ibid., 4:22.

69. O'Callaghan, "Great Treaty of 1722," 673.

70. McIlwaine, *Executive Journals of the Council*, 4:24.

71. Lakomäki, *Gathering Together*, 40.

72. See D. Brown, "Beyond the Blackwater," 1720:9.

73. Billings, Selby, and Tate, *Colonial Virginia*, 196–97; Dodson, *Alexander Spotswood*, 274.

74. Egloff and Woodward, *First People*, 50.

75. Byrd, "History of the Dividing Line," 311.

76. Hazzard and McCartney, *Fort Christanna*, 34.

Conclusion

1. Spotswood, *Official Letters*, 2:235; George Chicken quoted from his journal in Crane, *Southern Frontier*, 154–57, 204–5.

2. Merrell, *Indians' New World*, 60. Merrell's chapter "The Triumph of Trade" charts this shift in Carolina.

Bibliography

Unpublished Sources

Accomack County Court Records. Microfilm. Accomack County Reel 79. Library of Virginia, Richmond.

Bradford, Andrew. "Particulars of an Indian Treaty between Sir William Keith & The Deputies of the Five Nations, 1721." Mss 970.5 P26. American Philosophical Society, Philadelphia.

Brafferton Estate Collection. Special Collections Research Center, Earl Gregg Swem Library, College of William and Mary.

Brown, Douglas Summers, ed. "Beyond the Blackwater, 1963–1993." Mss. 34568. Library of Virginia, Richmond.

Charles City County. *Order Book.* Microfilm. Charles City County Reel 13. Library of Virginia, Richmond.

Colonial Papers. General Series, 1574–1757 (CO1). United Kingdom National Archives, Kew, England.

Henrico County Miscellaneous Court Records, 1650–1807. Microfilm. Henrico County Reel 1. Library of Virginia, Richmond.

Morpurgo, Jack Eric. Papers. Special Collections Research Center, Earl Gregg Swem Library, College of William and Mary.

Nicholson, Francis. Papers. Addition 1, manuscript MS 86.10. John D. Rockefeller Library, Colonial Williamsburg Foundation.

Northampton County. *Orders, Wills, Deeds, Etc.* Microfilm. Northampton County Reels 1–3. Library of Virginia, Richmond.

Northumberland County. *Order Book.* Microfilm. Northumberland County Reel 47. Library of Virginia, Richmond.

Old Rappahannock County Orders, 1683–86. Microfilm. Old Rappahannock County Reel 13. Library of Virginia, Richmond.

Surry County Orders, 1671–91. Microfilm. Surry County Reel 28. Library of Virginia, Richmond.
Traunter, Richard. "The Travels of Richard Traunter on the Main Continent of America from Appomattox River in Virginia to Charles Town in South Carolina. In two Journals; performed in the Years 1698 and 1699." Mss5:9 T6945:1. Virginia Historical Society, Richmond.

Published Sources

Alexander, Edward P. "An Indian Vocabulary from Fort Christanna, 1716." *Virginia Magazine of History and Biography* 79, no. 3 (July 1971): 303–13.
Alvord, Clarence W., and Lee Bidgood, eds. *The First Explorations of the Trans-Alleghany Region by Virginians, 1650–1674*. Cleveland: Arthur H. Clark, 1912.
Ames, Susie M., ed. *County Court Records of Accomack-Northampton, Virginia, 1640–1645*. Charlottesville: University Press of Virginia, 1973.
Andrews, Charles M., ed. *Narratives of the Insurrections, 1675–1690*. New York: Charles Scribner's Sons, 1915.
Aquila, Richard. *The Iroquois Restoration: Iroquois Diplomacy on the Colonial Frontier, 1701–1754*. Lincoln: University of Nebraska Press, 1997.
Benson, Evelyn. *The Story of the Susquehannocks*. Philadelphia: Society for Pennsylvania Archaeology, 1958.
Berkeley, William. *The Papers of Sir William Berkeley, 1605–1677*. Edited by Warren M. Billings and Maria Kimberley. Richmond: Library of Virginia, 2007.
Berry, John, Francis Moryson, and Herbert Jeffreys. "A True Narrative of the Rise, Progress and Cessation of the Late Rebellion in Virginia, Most Humbly and Impartially Recorded by His Majesties Commissioners, Appointed Io inquire into the Affairs of the Said Colony." In *Narratives of the Insurrections, 1675 to 1690*, edited by Charles Andrews, 129–36. New York: Charles Scribner's Sons, 1915.
Beverley, Robert. *The History and Present State of Virginia: A Selection*. Edited by David Freeman Hawke. 1705; reprint, New York: Bobbs-Merrill, 1971.
Billings, Warren. *A Little Parliament: The Virginia General Assembly in the Seventeenth Century*. Richmond: Library of Virginia, 2004.
———, ed. *The Old Dominion in the Seventeenth Century: A Documentary History of Virginia, 1606–1689*. Williamsburg, VA: Institute of Early American History and Culture / Chapel Hill: University of North Carolina Press, 2007.
———. *Sir William Berkeley and the Forging of Colonial Virginia*. Baton Rouge: Louisiana State University Press, 2004.
———. "Some Acts Not in Hening's Statutes: The Acts of Assembly, April 1652, November 1652, and July 1653." *Virginia Magazine of History and Biography* 83, no. 1 (1975): 22–26.
Billings, Warren M., John E. Selby, and Thad W. Tate. *Colonial Virginia: A History*. White Plains, NY: KTO Press, 1986.

Binford, Lewis R. "An Ethnohistory of the Nottoway, Meherrin and Weanock Indians of Southeastern Virginia." *Ethnohistory* 14, no. 3-4 (Summer-Autumn, 1967): 103-218.
Blackstone, Sir William. *Commentaries on the Laws of England in Four Books.* Chicago: Callaghan, 1899.
Bland, Edward. "Discovery of New Brittaine, 1650." In *Narratives of Early Carolina 1650-1708*, edited by Alexander S. Salley, 1-20. New York: Charles Scribner's Sons, 1911.
Bossy, Denise. "Indian Slavery in Southeastern Indian and British Societies, 1670-1730." In *Indian Slavery in Colonial America*, edited by Alan Gallay, 207-50. Lincoln: University of Nebraska Press, 2009.
Bowne, Eric. *The Westo Indians: Slave Traders of the Early Colonial South.* Tuscaloosa: University of Alabama Press, 2005.
Boyce, Douglas W. "Iroquoian Tribes of the Virginia-North Carolina Coastal Plain." In *Handbook of North American Indians*, vol. 15, *Northeast*, edited by Bruce Trigger, 282-89. Washington, D.C.: Smithsonian Institution, 1978.
Braund, Kathryn E. Holland. *Deerskins and Duffels: The Creek Indian Trade with Anglo-America, 1685-1815.* Lincoln: University of Nebraska Press, 1996.
Briceland, Alan Vance. "Batts and Fallam Explore the Backbone of the Continent." In *Appalachian Frontiers: Settlement, Society, and Development in the Preindustrial Era*, edited by Robert D. Mitchell, 23-36. Lexington: University Press of Kentucky, 1991.
———. *Westward from Virginia: The Exploration of the Virginia-Carolina Frontier, 1650-1710.* Charlottesville: University Press of Virginia, 1987.
Brooks, James. *Captives and Cousins: Slavery, Kinship, and Community in the Southwest Borderlands.* Chapel Hill: University of North Carolina Press, 2002.
Brooks, James F., and Bonnie Martin, eds. *Linking the History of Slavery: North America and Its Borderlands.* Santa Fe, NM: School for Advanced Research Press, 2015.
Brown, Douglas Summers, ed. *Sketches of Greensville County Virginia, 1650-2000.* 1968; reprint, Emporia, VA: Riparian Woman's Club, 2000.
Brown, Kathleen M. *Good Wives, Nasty Wenches, and Anxious Patriarchs: Gender, Race, and Power in Colonial Virginia.* Chapel Hill: University of North Carolina Press, 1996.
Bruce, Phillip Alexander. *Economic History of Virginia in the Seventeenth Century.* New York: MacMillan, 1907.
———. *History of Virginia.* New York: American Historical Society, 1924.
Bushnell, David, ed. "The Account of Lamhatty." *American Anthropologist* 10 (1908): 568-74.
Byrd, William. *The Correspondence of the Three William Byrds of Westover, Virginia, 1684-1776.* Edited by Marion Tinling. Charlottesville: University Press of Virginia, 1977.

———. "History of the Dividing Line." In *The Writing of "Colonel William Byrd of Westover in Virginia ESQr,"* edited by John Spencer Bassett. New York: Doubleday, Page, 1901.

———. "Letters of the Byrd Family." Edited by William G. Stanard. *Virginia Magazine of History and Biography* 35 (July 1927): 221–45.

———. *The Prose Works of William Byrd of Westover: Narratives of a Colonial Virginian.* Edited by Louis B. Wright. Boston: Harvard University Press, 1966.

———. *The Secret Diary of William Byrd of Westover, 1709–1712.* Edited by Louis B. Wright and Marion Tinling. Richmond, VA: Dietz Press, 1941.

Clayton, John. "The Aborigines of the Country: Letter to Dr. Nehemiah Grew." In *The Reverend John Clayton*, edited by Edmund Berkeley and Dorothy S. Berkeley. 1687; reprint, Charlottesville: University Press of Virginia, 1965.

———. "Another Account of Virginia." Edited by Edmund Berkeley and Dorothy S. Berkeley. *Virginia Magazine of History and Biography* 76, no. 4 (October 1968): 415–36.

Colley, Linda. *Captives: Britain, Empire, and the World, 1600–1850.* New York: Anchor Books, 2002.

Coombs, John C. "Building 'the Machine': The Development of Slavery and Slave Society in Early Colonial Virginia." PhD diss., Department of History, College of William and Mary, 2003.

Coventry, Henry, and William Coventry. *The Coventry Papers.* East Ardsley, West Yorkshire, England: Microform Academic Publishers, 1985.

Crane, Verner W. *The Southern Frontier, 1670–1732.* 1929; reprint, Ann Arbor: University of Michigan Press, 1959.

Craven, Wesley Frank. "Indian Policy in Early Virginia." *William and Mary Quarterly*, 3rd ser., 1, no. 1 (January 1944): 65–82.

Custalow, Linwood, and Angela L. Daniel. *The True Story of Pocahontas: The Other Side of History, from the Sacred History of the Mattaponi Reservation People.* Golden, CO: Fulcrum, 2007.

Davis, R. P. Stephen, Jr., Patrick Livingood, H. Trawick Ward, and Vincas Steponatis. *Excavating Occaneechi Town: Archaeology of an Eighteenth-Century Indian Village in North Carolina.* Chapel Hill: University of North Carolina Press, 1998. CD-ROM.

Dodson, Leonidas. *Alexander Spotswood, Governor of Colonial Virginia, 1710–1722.* Philadelphia: University of Pennsylvania Press, 1932.

Egloff, Keith, and Deborah Woodward. *First People: The Early Indians of Virginia.* Richmond: Virginia Department of Historic Resources, 1992.

Ethridge, Robbie. *Creek Country: The Creek Indians and Their World.* Chapel Hill: University of North Carolina Press, 2003.

———. *From Chicaza to Chickasaw: The European Invasion and the Transformation of the Mississippian World, 1540–1715.* Chapel Hill: University of North Carolina Press, 2010.

Ethridge, Robbie, and Sheri Shuck-Hall, eds. *Mapping the Mississippian Shatter Zone: The Colonial Indian Slave Trade and Regional Instability in the American South.* Lincoln: University of Nebraska Press, 2009.

Everett, C. S. "They shalbe slaves for their lives." In *Indian Slavery in Colonial America*, edited by Alan Gallay, 67–108. Lincoln: University of Nebraska Press, 2009.

Ewan, Joseph, ed. *John Banister and His Natural History of Virginia, 1678–1692.* Urbana: University of Illinois Press, 1970.

Feest, Christian. "Virginia Algonquians." In *Handbook of North American Indians*, vol. 15, *Northeast*, edited by Bruce Trigger, 253–70. Washington, D.C.: Smithsonian Institution, 1978.

Fenstermaker, Gerald B. *History of the Conestoga Indians: Lancaster County, Pennsylvania.* Archaeological Research Booklet 12. Lancaster, PA: Gerald B. Fenstermaker, 1978.

Fleet, Beverly, ed. *Virginia Colonial Abstracts: Charles City County Court Orders, 1658–1661; 1661–1664; 1664–1665; and Fragments, 1650–1696.* Richmond, VA: self-published, 1941.

Fontaine, John. *The Journal of John Fontaine, an Irish Huguenot Son in Spain and Virginia, 1710–1719.* Edited by Edward Porter Alexander. Williamsburg, VA: Colonial Williamsburg Foundation, 1972.

Gallay, Alan. *The Indian Slave Trade.* New Haven, CT: Yale University Press, 2002.

Gamble, Stephanie. "A Community of Convenience: The Saponi Nation, Governor Spotswood, and the Experiment at Fort Christanna, 1670–1740." *Native South* 6 (2013): 70–109.

Games, Alison. "Beyond the Atlantic: English Globetrotters and Transoceanic Connections." *William and Mary Quarterly*, 3rd ser., 63, no. 4 (October 2006): 675–92.

Gleach, Frederic. *Powhatan's World and Colonial Virginia: A Conflict of Cultures.* Lincoln: University of Nebraska Press, 1997.

Goetz, Rebecca Anne. *The Baptism of Early Virginia: How Christianity Created Race.* Baltimore: Johns Hopkins University Press, 2012.

Greene, Jack P. "The Opposition to Lieutenant Governor Alexander Spotswood, 1718." *Virginia Magazine of History and Biography* 70, no. 1, pt. 1 (January 1962): 35–42.

Guasco, Michael. *Slaves and Englishmen: Human Bondage in the Early Modern Atlantic World.* Philadelphia: University of Pennsylvania Press, 2014.

Hahn, Steven. *Invention of the Creek Nation: 1670–1763.* Lincoln: University of Nebraska Press, 2004.

Hantman, Jeffrey L. "Monacan Archaeology of the Virginia Interior, A.D. 1400–1700." In *Societies in Eclipse: Archaeology of the Eastern Woodlands Indians, A.D. 1400–1700*, edited by David S. Brose, C. Wesley Cowan, and Robert C. Mainfort Jr., 107–23. Washington, DC: Smithsonian Institution Press, 2001.

Harrison, Fairfax. "Western Explorations in Virginia between Lederer and Spotswood." *Virginia Magazine of History and Biography* 30, no. 4 (October 1922): 323–40.
Hatfield, April Lee. *Atlantic Virginia: Intercolonial Relations in the Seventeenth Century.* Philadelphia: University of Pennsylvania Press, 2004.
———. "Spanish Colonization Literature, Powhatan Geographies, and English Perceptions of Tsenacommacah/Virginia." *Journal of Southern History* 69, no. 2 (May 2003): 245–82.
Haun, Weynette Parks, ed. *Surry County, Virginia Court Records, 1652–1691.* Durham, NC: self-published, 1986–90.
Hazzard, David K., and Martha W. McCartney. *Fort Christanna: Archaeological Reconnaissance Survey.* Williamsburg: Virginia Research Center for Archaeology, 1979.
Hening, William Waller. *The Statutes at Large: Being a Collection of All the Laws of Virginia.* Richmond, VA: Samuel Pleasants, 1810–23.
Hofstra, Warren R. *The Planting of New Virginia: Settlement and Landscape in the Shenandoah Valley.* Baltimore: Johns Hopkins University Press, 2004.
Hutner, Heidi. *Colonial Women: Race and Culture in Stuart Drama.* New York: Oxford University Press, 2001.
Jennings, Matthew. *New Worlds of Violence: Cultures and Conquests in the Early American Southeast.* Knoxville: University of Tennessee Press, 2011.
Jones, Rev. Hugh. *The Present State of Virginia, 1724.* New York: reprinted for Joseph Sabin, 1865.
Juricek, John T. "The Westo Indians." *Ethnohistory* 11, no. 2 (1964): 134–73.
Kelton, Paul. *Epidemics and Enslavement: Biological Catastrophe in the Native Southeast, 1492–1715.* Lincoln: University of Nebraska Press, 2007.
Kukla, Jon. *Speakers and Clerks of the Virginia House of Burgesses, 1643–1776.* Richmond: Virginia State Library, 1981.
Kupperman, Karen Ordahl. *The Jamestown Project.* Cambridge, MA: Harvard University Press, 2007.
Lakomäki, Sami. *Gathering Together: The Shawnee People through Diaspora and Nationhood, 1600–1870.* New Haven, CT: Yale University Press, 2014.
LaVere, David. *The Tuscarora War: Indians, Settlers, and the Fight for the Carolina Colonies.* Chapel Hill: University of North Carolina Press, 2013.
Lawson, John, ed. *A New Voyage to Carolina, 1709.* Chapel Hill: University of North Carolina Press, 1967.
Leder, Lawrence H., ed. *Livingston Indian Records, 1666–1723.* Gettysburg: Pennsylvania Historical Association, 1956.
Lederer, John. "The Discoveries of John Lederer." In *The First Explorations of the Trans-Alleghany Region by Virginians, 1650–1674*, edited by Clarence W. Alvord and Lee Bidgood, 131–72. Cleveland: Arthur H. Clark, 1912.

———. *The Discoveries of John Lederer: With Unpublished Letters by and about Lederer to Governor John Winthrop, Jr.* Edited by William P. Cumming. Charlottesville: University of Virginia Press, 1958.

Lee, Wayne E. "Peace Chiefs and Blood Revenge: Patterns of Restraint in Native American Warfare, 1500–1800." *Journal of Military History* 71 (July 2007): 701–41.

Locke, John. "The Journeys of Needham and Arthur." In *The First Explorations of the Trans-Alleghany Region by Virginians, 1650–1674*, edited by Clarence W. Alvord and Lee Bidgood, 209. Cleveland: Arthur H. Clark, 1912.

Marambaud, Pierre. "William Byrd I: A Young Virginia Planter in the 1670s." *Virginia Magazine of History and Biography* 81, no. 2 (April 1973): 131–50.

Mathew, Thomas. "The Beginning, Progress, and Conclusion of Bacon's Rebellion in Virginia, in the Years 1675 and 1676." Tracts and Other Papers Relating Principally to the Origin, Settlement, and Progress of the Colonies in North America. Thomas Jefferson Papers, 1606–1827, series 8: Virginia Records Manuscripts, 1606–1737. Library of Congress. https://www.loc.gov/item/mtjbib026582/.

McCartney, Martha. "Cockacoeske, Queen of Pamunkey: Diplomat and Suzeraine." In *Powhatan's Mantle: Indians of the Colonial Southeast*, edited by Gregory A. Waselkov, Peter H. Wood, and M. Thomas Hatley, 243–66. Lincoln: University of Nebraska Press, 1989.

McIlwaine, H. R., ed. *Executive Journals of the Council of Colonial Virginia*. Richmond: Virginia State Library, 1925.

———, ed. *Journals of the House of Burgesses*. Richmond: Virginia State Library, 1914.

———, ed. *Minutes of the Council and General Court of Colonial Virginia, 1622–1632, 1670–1676, with Notes and Excerpts from Original Council and General Court Records into 1683, Now Lost*. Richmond: Virginia State Library, 1924.

McKey, JoAnn Riley, ed. *Accomack County Virginia Court Order Abstracts, 1663–1676*. Bowie, MD: Heritage Books, 1996.

Merrell, James. *The Indians' New World: Catawbas and Their Neighbors from European Contact through the Era of Removal*. Chapel Hill: University of North Carolina Press, 1989.

Meyers, Maureen. "From Refugees to Slave Traders: The Transformation of the Westo." In *Mapping the Mississippian Shatter Zone: The Colonial Indian Slave Trade and Regional Instability in the American South*, edited by Robbie Ethridge and Sheri Shuck-Hall, 81–103. Lincoln: University of Nebraska Press, 2009.

Mirković, Miroslava. *The Later Roman Colonate and Freedom*. Transactions of the American Philosophical Society 87, pt. 2. Philadelphia: American Philosophical Society, 1997.

Morgan, Edmund. *American Slavery, American Freedom: The Ordeal of Colonial Virginia*. New York: W. W. Norton, 1974.

Morgan, Timothy Everett. "Turmoil in an Orderly Society: Colonial Virginia, 1607-1754: A History and Analysis." PhD diss., Department of History, College of William and Mary, 1977.

Morrison, A. J. "The Virginia Indian Trade to 1673." *William and Mary Quarterly*, 2nd ser., 1 (October 1921): 217-36.

Nicholls, Mark. "George Percy's 'trewe Relacyon': A Primary Source for the Jamestown Settlement." *Virginia Magazine of History and Biography* 113, no. 3 (2005): 212-75.

Oberg, Michael Leroy, ed. *Samuel Wiseman's Book of Record: The Official Account of Bacon's Rebellion in Virginia, 1676-1677*. Lanham, MD: Lexington Books, 2005.

O'Callaghan, E. B., ed. "The Great Treaty of 1722 between the Five Nations, the Mahicans, and the Colonies of New York, Virginia and Pennsylvania." In *Documents Relative to the Colonial History of the State of New York*. Albany: Weed, Parsons, 1855.

Palmer, William, ed. *Calendar of Virginia State Papers and Other Manuscripts, 1652-1781, Preserved in the Capital at Richmond*. Richmond: Commonwealth of Virginia, 1876.

Parent, Anthony S. *Foul Means: The Formation of a Slave Society in Virginia, 1660-1740*. Williamsburg, VA: Omohundro Institute of Early American History and Culture / Chapel Hill: University of North Carolina Press, 2003.

Pennsylvania Archives. *Minutes of the Provincial Council*. Philadelphia: Jo. Severns, 1852.

Piker, Joshua. *Okfuskee: A Creek Indian Town in Colonial America*. Cambridge, MA: Harvard University Press, 2004.

Powell, William S. "Carolana and the Incomparable Roanoke: Explorations and Attempted Settlements, 1620-1663." *North Carolina Historical Review* 51 (1974): 1-21. Available through the Colonial Records Project, North Carolina office of Archives and History, http://www.ncpublications.com/colonial/nchr/subjects/powell5.htm.

Ragan, Edward. "A Brief Survey of Anglo-Indian Interactions in Virginia during the Seventeenth Century." In *A Study of Virginia Indians and Jamestown: The First Century*, edited by Danielle Moretti-Langholtz. Williamsburg, VA: Colonial National Historical Park, National Park Service, 2005. https://www.nps.gov/parkhistory/online_books/jame1/moretti-langholtz/index.htm.

———. "'Scatter'd upon the English Seats': Indian Identity and Land Occupancy in the Rappahannock River Valley." In *Early Modern Virginia: Reconsidering the Old Dominion*, edited by Douglas Bradburn and John C. Coombs, 207-38. Charlottesville: University of Virginia Press, 2011.

Rhoades, Matthew Lawson. *Long Knives and the Longhouse: Anglo-Iroquois Politics and the Expansion of Colonial Virginia*. Lanham, MD: Fairleigh Dickinson University Press, 2011.

Rice, James D. *Nature and History in the Potomac Country: From Hunter-Gatherers to the Age of Jefferson*. Baltimore: Johns Hopkins University Press, 2009.

———. *Tales from a Revolution: Bacon's Rebellion and the Transformation of Early America*. Oxford: Oxford University Press, 2012.

Rights, Douglas. "The Trading Path to the Indians," *North Carolina Historical Review* 8 (1931): 403–26.

Robinson, W. Stitt, ed. *Early American Indian Documents: Treaties and Laws, 1607–1789*. Vol. 4, *Virginia Treaties, 1607–1722*. Frederick, MD: University Publications of America, 1983.

———. "Indian Education and Missions in Colonial Virginia." *Journal of Southern History* 18, no. 2 (May 1952), 152–68.

Rountree, Helen C. *Pocahontas's People: the Powhatan Indians of Virginia through Four Centuries*. Norman: University of Oklahoma Press, 1990.

———. *The Powhatan Indians of Virginia: Their Traditional Culture*. Norman: University of Oklahoma Press, 1989.

———. "The Powhatans and the English: A Case of Multiple Conflicting Agendas." In *Powhatan Foreign Relations 1500–1722*, edited by Helen C. Rountree, 173–205. Charlottesville: University Press of Virginia, 1993.

Rushforth, Brett. *Bonds of Alliance: Indigenous and Atlantic Slaveries in New France*. Williamsburg, VA: Omohundro Institute of Early American History and Culture / Chapel Hill: University of North Carolina Press, 2012.

Saunt, Claudio. *A New Order of Things: Property, Power, and the Transformation of the Creek Indians, 1733–1816*. Cambridge: Cambridge University Press, 1999.

Schmidt, Ethan A. "Cockacoeske, Weroansqua of the Pamunkeys, and Indian Resistance in Seventeenth-Century Virginia." *American Indian Quarterly* 38, no. 3 (Summer 2012): 288–317.

———. *The Divided Dominion: Social Conflict and Indian Hatred in Early Virginia*. Boulder: University of Colorado Press, 2015.

Scisco, Louis Dow. "Exploration in 1650 in Southern Virginia." *Tyler's Quarterly Historical and Genealogical Magazine* 7 (1926): 164–69.

Shefveland, Kristalyn M. "'Wholly Subjected'? Anglo-Indian Interaction in Colonial Virginia 1646–1718." PhD diss., Department of History, University of Mississippi, 2010.

Smith, John. "The General Historie of Virginia, New England, and the Summer Isles, 1624." In *The Complete Works of Captain John Smith (1580–1631)*, edited by Philip Barbour, 225–488. Chapel Hill: University of North Carolina Press, 1986.

Snyder, Christina. *Slavery in Indian Country: The Changing Face of Captivity in Early America*. Cambridge, MA: Harvard University Press, 2010.

Snyder, Terri L. *Brabbling Women: Disorderly Speech and the Law in Early Virginia*. Ithaca, NY: Cornell University Press, 2003.

Sparacio, Ruth, ed., *Deed & Will Abstracts of (Old) Rappahannock County, Virginia*. McLean, VA: Antient Press, 1989.

———, ed. *Order Book Abstracts of Northumberland County, Virginia 1652–1686*. McLean, VA: Antient Press, 1994–99.

Spotswood, Alexander. *The Official Letters of Alexander Spotswood, Lieutenant-Governor of the Colony of Virginia 1710–1722*. Edited by R. A. Brock. Richmond: Virginia Historical Society, 1882.

Spruill, Julia Cherry. *Women's Life and Work in the Southern Colonies*. New York: W. W. Norton, 1972.

Stanard, Bruce, ed. "Examination of Indians, 1713." *Virginia Magazine of History and Biography* 19 (1911): 272–75.

———, ed. "From Virginia Historical Society Papers of Governor Nicholson and the some of the Council, Letters Copied from Documents in the Archives of the State of New York." *Virginia Magazine of History and Biography* 7 (1897): 153–72.

———, ed. "The Indians of Southern Virginia." *Virginia Magazine of History and Biography* 7 (1900): 337–58.

———, ed. "Will of Mrs. Mary Scarburgh, 15 December 1691 of Accomack County." *Virginia Magazine of History and Biography* 11 (1903): 222–23.

Stanwood, Owen. "Captives and Slaves: Indian Labor, Cultural Conversion, and the Plantation Revolution in Virginia." *Virginia Magazine of History and Biography* 114, no. 4 (2006): 434–63.

Strachey, William. *The History of Travell into Virginia Britania (1612)*. Edited by Louis B. Wright and Virginia Freund. Hakluyt Society, 2nd ser., vol. 103. Cambridge: Hakluyt Society, 1953.

Swem, E. G. *Virginia Historical Index*. Roanoke, VA: Stone Printing and Manufacturing, 1934.

Szasz, Margaret Connell. *Indian Education in the American Colonies, 1607–1783*. Albuquerque: University of New Mexico Press, 1988.

Tyler, Lyon G., ed. "Bacon's Rebellion." *William and Mary Quarterly* 9, no. 1 (July 1900): 1–10.

———, ed. "Edward Hatcher Will." *William and Mary Quarterly*, 1st ser., 25 (1917).

———, ed. "Heroines of Virginia." *William and Mary Quarterly* 15, no. 1 (July 1906).

———, ed. "Indian Slaves." *William and Mary Quarterly*, 1st ser., 6 (1897–98); 1st ser., 8 (1899–1900).

———, ed. "The Indians of Southern Virginia, 1650–1711, Depositions in the Virginia and North Carolina Boundary Case." *Virginia Magazine of History and Biography* 7, no. 4 (April 1900); 8, no. 1 (July 1900).

———, ed. "Personal Grievances." *Virginia Magazine of History and Biography* 24 (1916): 370.

Van Zandt, Cynthia J. *Brothers among Nations: The Pursuit of Intercultural Alliances in Early America, 1580–1660*. New York: Oxford University Press, 2008.

Vaughan, Alden T., and Deborah A. Rosen, eds. *Early American Indian Documents: Treaties and Laws, 1607–1789*, vol. 15, *Virginia and Maryland Laws*. Bethesda, MD: University Publications of America, 1998.

Venables, Robert W. "Polishing the Silver Covenant Chain: A Brief History of Some of the Symbols and Metaphors in Haudenosaunee Treaty Negotiations." Last updated March 10, 2011. Onondaga Nation. http://www.onondaga nation.org/history/2010/polishing-the-silver-covenant-chain-a-brief-history-of-some-of-the-symbols-and-metaphors-in-haudenosaunee-treaty-negotiations/.

Voigt, Lisa. *Writing Captivity in the Early Modern Atlantic*. Williamsburg, VA: Omohundro Institute of Early American History and Culture / Chapel Hill: University of North Carolina Press, 2009.

Walczyk, Frank V. *Northampton County Virginia Orders, Deeds & Wills 1651–1654*. Coram, NY: Peter's Row, 1998.

Ward, H. Trawick, and R. P. Davis Jr. "Tribes and Traders on the North Carolina Piedmont, A.D. 1000–1710." In *Societies in Eclipse: Archaeology of the Eastern Woodlands Indians, A.D. 1400–1700*, edited by David S. Brose, C. Wesley Cowan, and Robert C. Mainfort Jr., 171–81. Washington, D.C.: Smithsonian Institution Press, 2001.

Warren, Stephen. *The Worlds the Shawnees Made: Migration and Violence in Early America*. Chapel Hill: University of North Carolina Press, 2014.

Waselkov, Gregory. "Indian Maps of the Colonial Southeast." In *Powhatan's Mantle: Indians of the Colonial Southeast*, edited by Gregory A. Waselkov, Peter H. Wood, and M. Thomas Hatley, 435–502. Lincoln: University of Nebraska Press, 1989.

Washburn, Wilcomb E. *The Governor and the Rebel: A History of Bacon's Rebellion in Virginia*. Chapel Hill: University of North Carolina Press, 1957.

———. "Seventeenth Century Indian Wars." In *Handbook of North American Indians*, vol. 15, *Northeast*, edited by Bruce Trigger, 89–100. Washington, D.C.: Smithsonian Institution, 1978.

———. "Lamhatty's Map: How Indians Viewed the South 300 Years Ago." *Southern Exposure* 16, no. 2 (1988): 23–29.

Weisiger, Benjamin, ed. *Henrico County Virginia Deeds, 1677–1705*. Athens, GA: Iberian, 1986.

Westbury, Susan. "Women in Bacon's Rebellion." In *Southern Women: Histories and Identities*, edited by Virginia Bernhard, Betty Brandon, Elizabeth Fox-Genovese, and Theda Perdue, 30–46. Columbia: University of Missouri Press, 1992.

Whittenburg, James P., and John M. Coski, eds. *Charles City County Virginia: An Official History: Four Centuries of the Southern Experience: Charles City County, Virginia from the Age of Discovery to the Modern Civil Rights Struggle*. Richmond, VA: Don Mills, 1989.

Wilson, Charles Reagan, ed. *The New Encyclopedia of Southern Culture*. Vol. 3, *History*. Chapel Hill: University of North Carolina Press, 2006.

Winfree, Waverly K., ed. *The Laws of Virginia: Being a Supplement to Hening's the Statutes at Large 1700–1750*. Richmond: Virginia State Library, 1971.

Winner, Lauren F. *A Cheerful and Comfortable Faith: Anglican Religious Practice in the Elite Households of Eighteenth-Century Virginia*. New Haven, CT: Yale University Press, 2010.

Wood, Abraham. "Letter from Abraham Wood to John Richards, August 22, 1674." In *The First Explorations of the Trans-Alleghany Region by Virginians, 1650–1674*, edited by Clarence W. Alvord and Lee Bidgood, 210–14. Cleveland: Arthur H. Clark, 1912.

Woodfin, Maude, ed. "Auditor Stegge's Accounts." *Virginia Magazine of History and Biography* 51 (1943): 355–65.

Woodward, Henry. "A Faithfull Relation of My Westoe Voiage, 1674." In *Narratives of Early Carolina 1650–1708*, edited by Alexander S. Salley, 125–34. New York: Charles Scribner and Sons, 1911.

Worth, John. *The Struggle for the Georgia Coast: An 18th-Century Spanish Retrospective on Guale and Mocama*. Athens: University of Georgia Press, 1995.

Wright, Louis B. *The First Gentlemen of Virginia: Intellectual Qualities of the Early Colonial Ruling Class*. San Marino, CA: Huntington Library, 1940.

———. "William Byrd I and the Slave Trade." *Huntington Quarterly* 8 (1945): 379–87.

Index

Accomack/Gingaskin, 17-18, 130
Anancock, 18
Anglo-Dutch Wars: ban on trade, 22, 30-33
Anglo-Powhatan Wars: 1609-1612, 13-14; 1622-1632, 14; 1644-1646, 14-16
Appomattox, 10, 17; as tributaries and guides: 26-27, 39-40; attack on English, 13; Bacon's attack on, 49-50; Haudenosaunee attack on, 66-68
Arrohattoc, 10, 14, 130
Arthur, Gabriel, 32, 41-42

Bacon, Nathaniel, 45-48; attack on Pamunkey, 53-54; ban from trade, 49; burning of Jamestown, 54;
migration to Virginia, 48
Bacon's Rebellion: attack on Occaneechee, 48, 50, 55; beginnings of, 48-50; Berkeley's response to, 48-52, 139; Indian slavery, 47-48, 50, 53, 61; legacy of, 49, 54; role of English women, 51, 54-56, 59

Battle of Bloody Run, 6, 30, 38, 46, 52, 137
Batts, Thomas, 40, 137
Bearskin (Saponi), 1-2, 129
Berkeley, William: death of, 59; encouragement of Indian trade and exploration, 16, 22, 26, 32, 38-39, 133; exile on Eastern Shore, 54; Indian policy, 3, 15, 50, 132; sale of Indians, 33, 36, 45, 53
Berry, John: King's commission, 56-57, 141
Beverley, Robert, *History and Present State of Virginia,* 15-16, 70-71, 78-79, 99, 132, 149
Blackwater Swamp, 71, 75, 79, 86, 91
Bland, Edward: 1650 expedition, 5, 23-28, 145; misunderstandings of Native names, 27; opinions on Native peoples, 26-28
blood revenge, 13, 77-78, 89, 105, 114 144
Blount, Tom, 87, 146
boundary line with North Carolina, 1, 76, 82, 94, 129, 145
Briggs, Henry, 28, 113

Byrd, William, I: African slave trade, 48, 63, 138; comments on Indian trade, 64-65, 67-68, 80-82; Falls Plantation, 46-47, 137; Indian slave Trade, 47-49; negotiations with Haudenosaunee, 66-67; Perry and Lane of London, 67; relationship with Sarah Stegge, 47, 51, 54, 58-59; wife, Mary Horsmanden, 51

Byrd, William, II: Indian Women, 84, 98; Nottoway Town, 83-84; Spotswood rivalry, 80, 88, 99-102, 123; Westover Plantation, 37, 48, 126, 137, 139

Canondodawe (Mohawk), 66
Carachkondie (Onondaga), 66
Carolina: establishment of, 21, 32, 41; exploration, 23, 50; Indian raids to, 43-44, 105; path to, 68-70, 101; rivalry with Virginia, 42, 47, 80-82, 120, 125
Catawba (Esaws): 47, 68, 95, 104, 150; allegations against, 151; attacked at Fort Christanna, 99-100, 108-109, 112, 123; attacks against, 105, 120, 122-123; migrations, 102, 107
Charles City County, 5, 28, 34, 36-37, 48, 51, 55, 101, 126, 130, 134, 136
Cherokee, 120-122, 133, 151-152
Chickahominy, 10, 12-18, 30, 74, 92, 122, 130, 145; disagreements with Cockacoeske, 58, 61
Chickasaw, 120-121
Chiskiack, 10, 13, 16, 130
Chounterounte (Nottoway), 26-27
Clayton, John, 47, 52, 137
coalescence, 3, 20, 31, 95, 134
Cockacoeske: Bacon's Rebellion, 53-54; death of, 59; leadership, 46, 51-52, 56-58,140; line of succession, 59, 138; son, John West, 52, 57-59, 141

College of William and Mary, Brafferton Indian School, 65, 71, 88-90, 92, 94-95, 102, 147
conversion of Native peoples: Alexander Spotswood, 80, 91-92, 95-96, 99; failure, 3, 100-101; Reverend Hugh Jones, 91, 96; Reverend James Blair, 89-90; Robert Boyle, 90-92; Society for the Propagation of the Gospel in Foreign Parts, 93
Culpeper, Thomas, 57

Doeg, 45, 48

Eastern Woodlands, 3, 8, 20, 44, 80, 84, 129, 131, 134, 145,
English Civil War, 55, 65, 132
Enoe Will, 68-71
Erie, 11, 28

Fallam, Robert, 5, 40, 137
Fleet, Henry, 15
Flood, John, 17, 129
Fontaine, John, 5, 97-99, 148-149
Fort Charles, 15
Fort Christanna: attacks on, 99, 107, 110, 112-114, 120, 149; closing of, 107, 109, 122-123, 125; debate about, 87-89, 94-96, 99, 100-101, 103, 106, 146, 148; Spotswood and Fontaine visit, 97-99
Fort Henry, 8, 17, 20, 22-23, 26, 28, 32, 39-40, 42-43, 50, 129,
Fort James, 15, 23,
Fort Royal (Ricahock Fort), 15, 17, 23, 33

Governor's Executive Council, 5, 20; Bacon's Rebellion, 51-52, 57-58, 139; Fort Christanna, 99-100, 139, 148, 150-152; land grievances, 71-78, 143; problems with Haudenosaunee, 67-68, 108-116, 118-123;

rivalry with Carolina, 81-87; trade, 46, 62, 65, 137
Griffin, Charles, 95-97, 100, 149

Harrison, Benjamin, 28, 77-78, 81
Harvey, John, 15
Haudenosaunee Iroquois: attacks on English settlements, 67, 87; attacks on Virginia natives, 66, 71, 86, 95, 99, 107, 109-110, 112-114, 120, 149; Cayuga, 66-67, 112, 123, 151; Mohawk, 66; mourning wars, 28, 31; negotiations with Virginia, 104, 108-109, 114-122; Oneida, 66-67; Onondaga, 66, 114; passes to travel, 120, 122; Seneca, 65-67, 87, 89, 100, 107-108, 110-114, 150; visit by Henry Coursey and 1677 Covenant Chain, 105
Henrico County, 5, 28, 36, 46-48, 51, 56, 58, 63, 101, 111-112, 130, 136-137, 139, 142
Hill, Edward, 30-31
Hix, Robert, 71, 81-82, 85, 109, 122, 143
hostage taking, 6, 8, 16, 34, 36, 46, 54, 66, 79, 85, 89-91, 95, 102, 129-130, 147, 150
Huron, 11

Indentured Servants: English, 23, 45, 49; importation of, 36, 41, 47, 62; Indians, 34, 36-38, 136
Indian John, 42-43
Indian slave trade, 3-4, 6, 20-23, 43-55, 63-64, 66-68, 70; captives, 36, 89-91, 147; Ligon family, 36, 136, 139; militarized polities, 8, 31-32, 34, 40; regulation of, 34-36, 47-48, 50, 53, 61-62; tributaries, 36; sales, 33-34, 36, 73-76,

Jackzetavon (Susquehannock), 39
James River Falls, 28, 40, 48, 50-51, 130, 134,

Jamestown, 9-10, 12-14, 20, 27, 49, 52, 54, 73, 89, 130, 137,
Jeffreys, Herbert, 57
Jones, Cadwallader, 65-66

Keith, William, 112, 115-116, 118
Kicoughtan, 10, 14, 130

Lamhatty (Towasa), 78-79, 144
land grievances, 8; Bacon's Rebellion, 52-53; colonist demand for land, 63; First Anglo-Powhatan War, 13-15, 132; merging tributaries, 86, 93, 123, 145, 151; Pamunkey Neck and Blackwater Swamp, 71-75, 91, Third Anglo-Powhatan War, 17-19, 49; Treaty of Middle Plantation, 60-61
Lawson, John, 64, 79, 84, 93
Lederer, John, 5, 36, 38-40, 64, 136
LeTort, James, 119
Lords Commissioners of Trade and Plantations, 57, 74, 85, 88, 96, 101, 105-108, 110, 115
Ludwell, Thomas, 45, 58

Mahican, 11
Mannahoac, 10, 12, 30
Marshall, Roger, 17, 23
Maryland, 26, 45, 48, 57, 73, 104-105, 108, 118, 121, 149; issues with Piscataway and George Mason, 67
Mattaponi, 10, 16, 18-19, 130-131
Meherrin, 10, 26-27, 98, 113-115, 122, 134; dispute with North Carolina, 74-76, 82-83, 85-87
mercantile plantation economy, 3-4, 21, 23, 31, 43-44, 60, 62, 129
Metoaka (Pocahontas), 12-13, 23, 132
migrations: colonists and traders, 47, 64, 67, 80; Indigenous, 4, 19, 26, 28, 30-31, 72, 75, 86, 88, 102, 104
Monacan, 10, 12, 15, 19, 30, 47
Moneton, 43

Moraughtacund, 10, 131
Moryson, Francis: King's Commission, 56-57, 141
mourning wars, 30-31, 67, 104, 107, 129

Nahyssan, 95
Nansemond, 10, 14-15, 17-19, 45, 57, 61, 74-75, 81-82, 86, 92, 101, 115, 122, 130
Nansiatico, 18, 50, 54, 72-76
Native trackers, 1, 16, 38-39, 127, 129, 147
Necotowance, 4, 8, 16-19, 30, 138, see also Treaties of Peace
Needham, James, 41-42
Neutral, 11
New York, 63, 76, 87, 107-108, 113-115, 118, 120-122, 149
Newcombe, Henry, 26
nontributary (foreign) Indians, 2, 4, 6, 8; conversion of, 90-91, 94; Lamhatty, 78-79; trade, 17-18, 22, 30, 32-34, 39-40, 48-50, 64, 67, 88; Treaty of Middle Plantation, 60-62; Westo, 45-46, 137
Nottoway, 10, 57, 61, 72, 74-75, 82-83, 86, 92; argument with Saponi, 77-78, 144, 151; Great Men held hostage, 95; Haudenosaunee allegations of poisoning, 121; negotiations with Haudenosaunee and Tuscarora, 111-115, 145; role in trade, 26, 28, 85, 134

Occaneechee, 6, 26, 32, 34, 45, 55, 61, 68-70, 86, 95, 115, 136; Bacon's attack, 50; dominance of 39-43, 47-48
Opechancanough, 2-3, 6, 8, 13-17, 19, 33, 46, 58, 132, 138
Oyeocker, (Nottoway), 26-27

Pamunkey, 6, 10, 14-19, 30, 45-53, 56-59, 71-72, 92, 122
Paspahegh, 10, 13-14, 130

Pennant, Elias, 26
Pennsylvania, 102, 104-105, 108-109, 112, 115-120, 123, 149, 151
Piscataway, 11, 48, 73, 75, 130, 143
Pocahontas, see Metoaka
Potomac, 45
Powhatan chiefdom, Tsenacommacah, 6, 8-18, 22, 46, 57-58, 130, 138
Powhatan, see Wahunsonacock
Pyancha (Appomattox), 26-27

Quiyoughcohannock, 10, 130

Rappahannock, 10, 16, 18-19, 39, 50, 58, 143
Rolfe, John, 13, 131; son Thomas, 23

Saponi, 1-2, 20, 39-40, 61, 84-88, 129; argument with Nottoway, 77-78, 144, 151; at Fort Christanna, 94-99, 110, 113-115, 122-123, 148, 150
Sara, 95
shatter zone, 6, 8, 31, 64, 102, 134
Shawnee, 43, 78, 104-105, 118, 122
Smith, John, 9, 11-12
Spotswood, Alexander: conversion, 80, 91-92, 95-96, 99; criticism of, 80, 88, 99-102, 123; problems with Tuscarora, 87-88, 93-94; tributary and defense system, 82-86; 88-90; see also Fort Christanna and 177 Treaty with Haudenosaunee at Albany
Stegg, Sarah, 46-59
Stegg, Thomas, 3, 6, 28, 30, 36, 40-41, 45-47, 137
Strachey, William, 9, 11
Stuckanock, 61, 86, 115
Susquehannock, 6, 11, 39, 45, 48, 131; alliance with Maryland, 104; attack on Bacon, 49-50; expedition against, 52; trade with Dutch and Swedish colonists, 30

Taggohergos (Oneida), 66
Tidewater Wars, see Anglo-Powhatan Wars
Tomahitan, 32, 42-43
Totopotomoy, death of, 30, 38, 46, 52
trade: differences between tributaries and nontributary items, 64; guns, 30-34, 40-44, 46, 50, 53, 64, 66, 81, 88, 137; skins, 20, 22-23, 28, 31, 39-40, 42-48, 50, 55, 70-71, 79, 82, 89, 97-99, 120, 126
Traunter, Richard: Journal, 68-71; death of Robert Stephens, 68
Treaties of Peace: 1646 with Necotowance, 19-20, 22, 35, 46, 49, 89; 1677 Treaty of Middle Plantation, 4, 56, 59-61, 72, 109; 1677 Covenant Chain, 105; 1714 Treaty with Tuscarora, Nottoway, and Saponi, 86; 1722 Treaty with Haudenosaunee at Albany, 113-122; interests of the Conestoga, Ganowass, and Showanoe at Albany, 115
tribute, 27, 58, 92; English plans for Virginia, 4, 11-14; European feudalism, 9; Powhatan chiefdom, 6, 9-10, 12; rights of Native tributaries, 16, 72, 76, 83-84; Spanish model, 11; see individual Native tributary groups
Tuscarora, 26-28, 39, 61, 65, 76, 80, 134, 145, 148, 150; as potential tributaries, 83-86, 91; attacks on Eno, 68-69; attacks on Saponi, 77-78, 113; war with North Carolina, 81-82, 87-88, 93-95, 98, 100, 108, 110
Tutelo, 20, 40, 61, 77-78, 85-86, 95, 97, 102, 123

Violence, theories of, 3, 63, 134; rumors and threats of, 6, 34, 50, 60-61, 63, 72, 105, 110, 114, 144; sexual, 84
Virginia Assembly, 48, 50-56, 62, 64-65, 72, 74, 80, 88-89, 92, 102, 106, 109, 143, 149
Virginia Company, 3, 9, 11-12, 23
Virginia House of Burgesses, 15, 19, 33, 36, 48, 62, 65, 73, 95, 101 102, 107 109, 115, 122, 139,
Virginia Indian Company and Act for Better Regulation of the Trade (1714): see Fort Christanna

Wahunsonacock (Powhatan), 9-14, 132
Warraskoyak, 10, 130
weroance, 3, 6, 8-10, 12-13, 16-18, 26-27, 30, 33, 43, 46, 57, 85, 132, 138
Westo, 30-31
Weyanoke, 10, 14-15, 17, 19, 27, 33, 36, 57, 82
Wicomico, 16, 18, 72, 131
Williamsburg, 20, 74, 111, 113-115, 118, 121, 141, 147
Wood, Abraham, 5-6, 17, 22-43
Woodward, Henry, 32, 41, 137

Youghtanund, 10, 130

Early American Places

On Slavery's Border: Missouri's Small Slaveholding Households, 1815–1865
by Diane Mutti Burke

Sounding America: Identity and the Music Culture of the Lower Mississippi River Valley, 1800–1860
by Ann Ostendorf

The Year of the Lash: Free People of Color in Cuba and the Nineteenth-Century Atlantic World
by Michele Reid-Vazquez

Ordinary Lives in the Early Caribbean: Religion, Colonial Competition, and the Politics of Profit
by Kirsten Block

Creolization and Contraband: Curaçao in the Early Modern Atlantic World
by Linda M. Rupert

An Empire of Small Places: Mapping the Southeastern Anglo-Indian Trade, 1732–1795
by Robert Paulett

Everyday Life and the Construction of Difference in the Early English Caribbean
by Jenny Shaw

Natchez Country: Indians, Colonists, and the Landscapes of Race in French Louisiana
by George Edward Milne

Slavery, Childhood, and Abolition in Jamaica, 1788–1838
by Colleen A. Vasconcellos

Privateers of the Americas: Spanish American Privateering from the United States in the Early Republic
by David Head

Charleston and the Emergence of Middle-Class Culture in the Revolutionary Era
by Jennifer L. Goloboy

Anglo-Native Virginia: Trade, Conversion, and Indian Slavery in the Old Dominion, 1646–1722
by Kristalyn Marie Shefveland

Slavery on the Periphery: The Kansas-Missouri Border in the Antebellum and Civil War Eras
by Kristen Epps

In the Shadow of Dred Scott: *St. Louis Freedom Suits and the Legal Culture of Slavery in Antebellum America*
by Kelly M. Kennington

Brothers and Friends: Kinship in Early America
by Natalie R. Inman

George Washington's Washington: Visions for the National Capital in the Early American Republic
by Adam Costanzo

CPSIA information can be obtained
at www.ICGtesting.com
Printed in the USA
LVHW040225200820
663648LV00005B/522